ESSENTIALS of Shared Services

Bryan Bergeron

John Wiley & Sons, Inc.

This book is printed on acid-free paper. ♾

Published simultaneously in Canada.

For general information on our other products and services, or technical support, please contact our Customer Care Department within the United States at 800-762-2974, outside the United States at 317-572-3993 or fax 317-572-4002.

Wiley also publishes its books in a variety of electronic formats. Some content that appears in print may not be available in electronic books.

Library of Congress Cataloging-in-Publication Data:

Bergeron, Bryan P.
Essentials of shared services / Bryan Bergeron.
p. cm.
Includes index.
ISBN 0-471-25079-1 (PAPER : alk. paper)
1. Shared services (Management). I. Title.

HD62.13 .B474 2003
658.4'02--dc21 2002011300

Printed in the United States of America

10 9 8 7 6 5 4 3 2 1

Contents

Preface

Leading a successful enterprise takes courage, insight, intelligence, people skills, knowledge, wisdom, and the fortune of good timing. In the context of business, knowledge is the distillation of experience—personal, didactic, and referential—often in the form of proven business models that have been shown to provide the manager with a degree of control over the myriad of chaotic market forces. For example, representing opposite ends of the spectrum of business models are centralized versus decentralized models of control and resources, as well as in-house versus outsourced production and support services.

Virtually all of these models are time- and context-specific, in that they come in and out of favor, depending on the market conditions. Regardless of the current applicability, the more models at the manager's disposal, the more likely he or she will be able to maintain and enhance corporate value in a rapidly shifting environment. To this end, the goal of this book is to provide the reader with exposure to the techniques and technologies related to the shared services model—which describes a collaborative strategy in which selected business functions are concentrated into semi-autonomous business units with management structures that promote efficiency, value generation, and cost savings for the parent corporation, in a manner akin to companies competing in the open market.

Specifically, *Essentials of Shared Services* explores models of shared services that work—and those that don't—through the use of concrete examples. The book assumes an intelligent CEO-level reader, but one who may be unaware of the vernacular of the shared services model or how to recognize superior shared services efforts. The reader will come to appreciate the benefits of the shared services model, from cost savings that come about through lowering headcount to increasing corporate value that comes about through increased efficiency and effectiveness and economies of scale. To drive the issues home in an easily understood fashion, each chapter contains a vignette that illustrates key issues from practical corporate and shared business unit management perspectives.

After reading this book, the CEO will be able to converse comfortably with shared services professionals, understand what to look for when hiring a shared services staff, and understand the budgetary implications of using shared services. That is, the reader will come to appreciate the advantages and disadvantages of the shared services model from a variety of perspectives.

Reader Return on Investment

After reading the following chapters the reader will be able to:

- Understand shared services from historical, economic, technical, and management perspectives.
- Appreciate why the shared services model is particularly relevant to contracting economies.
- Understand how shared services compares, and in some cases complements other business models, including those based on outsourcing, centralized, and decentralized management structures.
- Understand the significance of shared services on the company's bottom line, both long- and short-term.
- Understand the relationship of shared services to re-engineering, downsizing, total quality management, and, in the information technology field, traditional systems integration efforts.

- Understand how shared services professionals work and think, including why it is so difficult for staff transitioned to a shared services model to shift mindset from production efficiency to service.
- Have a set of specific recommendations that can be used to establish and manage a shared services effort.
- Understand the technologies that can be used to implement shared services.
- Appreciate best practices—what works, why it works, and how to evaluate a successful shared services effort in the company.

Organization of This Book

This book is organized into modular topics related to shared services. It is divided into the following chapters:

Chapter 1: Overview. The first chapter of this book provides an overview of the key concepts, terminology, and the historical context of shared services.

Chapter 2: The Corporation. Taking the perspective of the corporate senior management, this chapter explores the implications of embracing shared services as a means of enhancing corporate value. Topics range from strategic partnerships and alliances to changes in corporate culture, timing, range of control, and risk exposure.

Chapter 3: Shared Business Unit. The chapter takes the perspective of senior management in the shared business unit. Topics include customer relationship management (CRM), inside sales and marketing, customer loyalty, touch points, reporting structures, addressing legal issues, and how to establish career security for management and employees.

Chapter 4: Process. The chapter explores shared services from a process perspective. Topics include the generic transformation process from an internal operation to a shared services business unit as well as the translation of existing processes to more efficient ones in the shared services unit.

Chapter 5: Technology. This chapter explores the many technologies available for shared services, especially those that have value in supporting the transformation process early in the life of the shared services unit.

Chapter 6: Evaluation. This chapter looks at how the various approaches to shared services can be evaluated. Topics include benchmarking, including standards, tools, and processes, the service level agreement, as well as employee and customer satisfaction.

Chapter 7: Economics. The chapter explores the economic aspects of shared services, from the evolving value chain, likely return on investment, and pricing models, to investment in people, processes, and technology, to legal issues and accounting practices.

Chapter 8: Getting There. The final chapter explores the practical aspects of a shared services implementation. Topics include predictors of success, working with vendors, how to enable corporate culture change, the significance of the request for proposal, and risk management.

Further Reading. This section lists some of the more relevant works in the area of shared services, at a level appropriate to a CEO or upper-level manager.

Glossary. This glossary contains words defined throughout the text, as well the most common terms a reader will encounter in the shared services literature.

How to Use This Book

For those new to shared services, the best way to tackle the subject is to simply read through each chapter in order; however, because each chapter is written as a stand-alone module, readers interested in, for example, the economics of shared services can go directly to Chapter 7, "Economics."

Throughout the book, "In the Real World" sections provide real-world examples of how shared services is being used to improve the bottom line and increase quality of service. Similarly, a "Tips & Techniques" section in each chapter offers concrete steps that the reader can take to benefit from a shared services initiative. Key terms are highlighted and defined in context throughout the book, as well as in the Glossary. In addition, readers who want to delve deeper into the business, technical, or corporate culture aspects of the shared services model are encouraged to consult the list of books and publications listed in the Further Reading section.

Acknowledgments

I would like to thank my enduring editorial associate, Miriam Goodman, for her assistance in creating this work. In addition, special thanks are in order for my editor at John Wiley & Sons, Sheck Cho, for his insight and encouragement.

CHAPTER 1

Overview

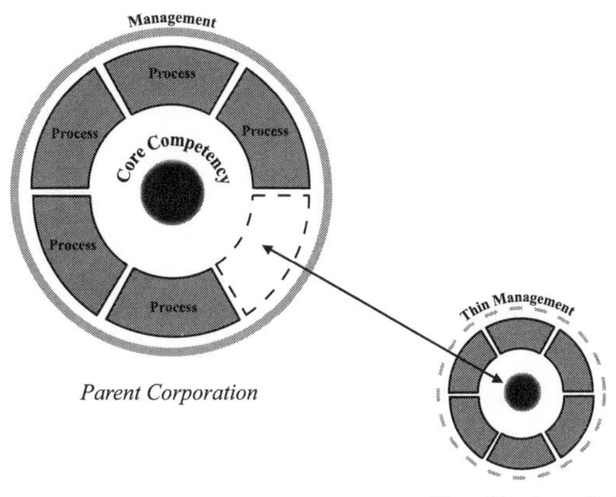

In the current global economic environment, which is characterized by downsizing, mergers, acquisitions, and uncertainty, managers are grasping for ways to simultaneously improve the bottom line while increasing competitiveness. Many managers are doubly challenged when their company's product and service portfolio is ill matched to the economic environment. Once overvalued services for the dot-com economy, from Web design to site hosting, are no longer in great demand, for example. With the realization that revenue has to be won through providing real value to customers and not simply creating an innovative business plan, many managers have been forced to analyze their business practices and, where appropriate, apply business models that hold more than the promise of a better bottom line.

Many companies with mature product lines have moved to an outsourcing model under the supposition that an outside vendor can provide products and services faster and less expensively—at least in the short term. Similarly, to extract as much profit as possible from the value chain, some companies are centralizing functions and services, a strategy in which common functions are combined into a central department or division that has a monopoly over one or more services. In contrast, other companies are relying on the merits of a decentralized business model, which provides individual divisions and departments with the flexibility they need to meet rapidly changing market demands.

Clearly, there is no one-size-fits-all, risk-free business model. The most appropriate model for a specific corporation is a function of the business, of what competing companies are doing in the market, and their success or failure. It is a function of how companies in any industry, following a different business model, are doing financially. For example, with the recent demise of several high-profile darlings of Wall Street, business models based on the reengineering movement have cycled out of favor among the top business consultants despite unprecedented popularity (or at least press) through the 1990s. Similarly, although there are several potential advantages to outsourcing, specific implementations often fail to produce the time and money savings that managers expect. However, there are many pockets of successful activity that are the result of local economic conditions and the expertise of individual managers.

Thriving in the new economic environment doesn't mean turning the clock back and ignoring all but the most conservative business practices. For example, as a result of the constant market pressure on companies to increase their competitiveness, many managers have no choice but to explore business models outside of the more traditional centralized, decentralized, outsourced, and insourced models.

Perhaps the most prominent of the alternative business models is shared services. The shared services model, which is a hybridization of traditional business models with a few interesting twists, can provide value to the corporation while addressing many of the limitations and constraints associated with using the more traditional business models in today's customer value-centric business environment.

Now, let's start the exploration of shared services with a definition, a review of what the shared services model promises, and a story to illustrate the concepts.

A Definition

Defining a business model is necessarily problematic, in part because every business operation is unique. Every industry imposes particular market limitations and requirements, senior management has its own biases and views of how things should be done, and the constantly changing economic environment demands that models be flexible enough to accommodate these pressures. Given these caveats, a definition of shared services that captures the intent and ideals of the model is this:

> Shared services is a collaborative strategy in which a subset of existing business functions are concentrated into a new, semi-autonomous business unit that has a management structure designed to promote efficiency, value generation, cost savings, and improved service for the internal customers of the parent corporation, like a business competing in the open market.

The shared services model is fundamentally about optimizing people, capital, time, and other corporate resources. In this regard, the shared services model describes a *collaborative strategy* or transitional process between a parent corporation and a business unit. The *business unit* is a well-circumscribed area of production or services, which can range from back office activities such as accounting, billing, customer support, to secretarial services, telecommunications, programming, training, and health care. The unit is created specifically to provide services to all or part of the parent corporation. The historical, monetary, and legal connection between the parent corporation and the shared business unit provides an advantage to the unit, such as an optimal location, potential of current or future funding, insurance against massive failure, and convenient access to the parent corporation's senior management.

Since a new, shared business unit handles a subset of the parent corporation's existing activities, typically, the activities or processes selected for inclusion in the shared business unit are non-strategic and outside of the core competency of the parent corporation. However, in theory, a shared business unit can handle any business function successfully, as long as there are adequate management and specific performance criteria.

In the shared services model, the selected production or services are *concentrated,* either geographically or through communications and process control. This is especially true where communications or computer services are concerned. For example, a corporation may move from a distributed operation in which batch copying and printing are performed in dozens of independently managed and funded copy centers to one shared copy center business unit. Similarly, a company's independently managed computer networks in each region of the country can be consolidated electronically into a single wide area network that encompasses information services across the country.

The shared business unit is *semi-autonomous* within a wide range of possible architectures in that the reporting structure necessarily breaks from the traditional corporate hierarchy. Even so, the parent corporation and the business unit are often linked in one or more ways. The parent company can be a stockholder in the business unit, or the management of the business unit can have stock in the parent corporation and vice versa. There can also be mutual cross-licensing arrangements between the parent corporation and the business unit. Most importantly, each shared business unit has its budget and bottom-line accountability.

Each shared business unit is created by consolidating the resources of an existing internal operation, supplemented by new resources as needed. In other words, although a business relationship along the lines of a shared services model could be created by simply acquiring an external business, shared services is about transforming and concentrating existing resources in a mutually beneficial way.

The unique aspects of the shared services *management structure* are related to the line of reporting, which reflects the heritage of the business unit. In addition, like an independent business, the shared business unit has a budget, administrative staff, and other business-related management. However, the director or CEO of the business unit enjoys a degree of autonomy from the corporate CEO and other senior managers. The degree of autonomy depends on the particular business, with the tradeoff being control versus pressure to optimize goods and services. That is, the more autonomy given the business unit, the greater the pressure on the unit to provide quality service at competitive prices. This pressure reflects user satisfaction with the goods and services produced by the business unit.

A direct product of the efficiency of the business unit is increased *efficiency, value generation,* and *cost savings* from the perspective of the parent corporation. That is, the goal of shared services is to improve the bottom line of the parent corporation, not to create a more efficient, internally streamlined shared business unit *per se.* As a result, an efficient business unit is a necessary but insufficient condition for a successful shared services implementation. This aim contrasts sharply with that of spinning off a separate subsidiary, where the first and overall game plan is to make the spinoff a profitable business.

The business units created under the shared services model are not run like monopolies, as they can be under the traditional centralized model. The traditional centralized business model often fosters an entitlement mentality among its employees, resulting in a "take it or leave it" attitude. Instead, the shared business unit is run more like an independent business.

The staff in the business unit has to compete for business, like a typical company in the *open market*. The nature of this competition defines the pressure on the business unit to evolve into an efficient, value-generating machine that benefits from economies of scale. In other words, the shared business unit is run like a customer-focused business based on current best practices, including the use of technology where appropriate, and provides goods and services that benefit from economies of scale.

Promises

The potential benefits of the shared services model are numerous and can potentially benefit every type of business. What can you expect from moving one or more of your business functions to a shared services model? From the parent corporation's perspective, shared services promises:

- *Reduced costs.* There is constant pressure from internal corporate clients to provide cost effective products and services.
- *Improved service.* The shared business unit's customer-oriented focus should result in better service to internal customers, than typical in-house services.
- *Fewer distractions from core competency activities.* With back office and other non-critical activities handled by shared services, the management of the parent company is free to focus the company on its core competencies.
- *A potential for creating an externally focused profit center.* At one end of the spectrum, a business unit following the shared services model can be operated as a nearly autonomous entity, with other paying outside clients.

From the perspective of the shared business unit, the shared services model promises:

- *Increased efficiencies.* Standardization of processes and applying technologies where appropriate can provide improved quality of services at comparable or lower prices. There is constant pressure on the business unit to increase efficiency and internal customer satisfaction. If the business unit evolves to the point that it has sufficient surplus capacity to sell services on the open market, then this pressure applies to external customers as well.

- *Decreased personnel requirements.* With the ability to concentrate and focus resources for particular purposes in a shared business unit, fewer employees are generally needed to provide the same results. In addition to downsizing or rightsizing, the shared services model often allows downscaling, in which new methodologies and efficiency improvements allow junior staff to take over tasks once controlled by more expensive senior staff.
- *Improved economies of scale.* Like a traditional centralized approach, shared services concentrates purchasing and other formerly dispersed business activities, resulting in greater buying power and greater concentration of specialized resources, such as specialists in certain aspects of accounting. This concentration allows for increased economies of scale, compared to the original corporate structure.

The shared services model is applicable in a variety of areas ranging from office administration, call answering and forwarding, catering, couriers, desktop publishing, mail handling and forwarding, photocopying and printing, to secretarial support. All are compatible with the shared services model. An expanded list is shown in Exhibit 1.1.

In order to illustrate the many corporate issues that shared services is intended to address, consider the following vignette.

Media Services

State General Hospital is a large, 350-bed teaching hospital with over 3,000 full-time employees distributed over ten departments. As a hospital affiliated with a medical school, its clinical faculty is active teaching

EXHIBIT 1.1

Opportunities for Shared Services

- Administration
  - Inventory
  - Mailroom
  - Printing
  - Records management
  - Supply
  - Training
- Customer Service
  - Computer customer support
  - Field service
  - Telephone customer support
- Finance
  - General accounting
  - Payroll processing
  - Purchasing
  - Taxes
  - Transaction processing
- Human Resources
  - Recruiting
  - Relocation
  - Staffing
  - Training
  - Workers' compensation
- Information Technology
  - Application development
  - End-user support
  - Maintenance
  - Training
- Real Estate & Physical Plant
  - Cafeteria services
  - Facilities information systems
  - Facilities maintenance
  - Security
- Sales and Marketing
  - Advertising
  - Direct mail
  - Field sales
  - Telemarketing

residents, holding conferences, and traveling throughout the country presenting their latest clinical research. The hospital's $800 million gross annual income comes from clinical operations, overhead payments from government-sponsored research, third-party payers, and government-sponsored residency training programs. Most individual researchers and about half of the clinicians have their own grants from federal, state, and private industry sources. Operational funding for the clinical departments is doled out annually, in an amount dictated by senior hospital management.

A board of directors and a senior management team run the

TIPS & TECHNIQUES

Understanding the Value of Shared Services

Before embarking on a shared services initiative, senior management should have a good idea of the potential value of shared services to their organization. In other words, what's wrong with the current model of conducting business? The four key questions to ask are:

1. How much money could be saved with a viable shared services system in place? That is, what are the potential cost reductions in ancillary processes?
2. How much could implementation of a shared services model improve the efficiency and effectiveness of the current business process?
3. How much will it cost to implement a shared services system, from consulting fees to investment in new management structures to employee training?
4. How long will it take for the shared services model to break even? In a rapidly changing economic environment, it may be more prudent to temporarily outsource some functions and wait for the environment to stabilize before embarking on a shared services initiative.

In evaluating the value of shared services to a company, it's important to first identify the problem areas and then devise ways of quantitatively measuring improvements.

hospital. In addition, a department chairperson who is responsible for clinical, teaching, research, and administrative functions within the department, manages each clinical and administrative department. Furthermore, individual clinicians may work full-time for the department or part-time for the department with the balance of their time spent in externally funded research. In other words, potential funding is available from a variety of sources, waiting for individual clinicians with entrepreneurial talents to capture it.

As a major teaching hospital, every clinician, researcher, and department head has to deal with making or acquiring videotapes of procedures, electronic slideshows for presentations to colleagues, audiotaping, and graphic illustrations for books, journals, and other publications. As a result, in the early 1990s, pockets of multimedia expertise sprouted like mushrooms throughout the hospital. Some researchers and clinicians spent their time creating PowerPoint presentations, and the more computer literate put video capture and editing hardware and software on the desktop PCs. Some departments had a secretary charged with the full-time task of creating electronic presentations, including graphics, for administrative and clinical staff.

As a result, there was massive duplication of effort within the hospital, and the quality of presentations varied from one group and one department to the next. What's more, secretaries and other support personnel were frequently distracted from their primary responsibilities to put together last-minute presentations for the clinical staff. The two best funded departments had the luxury of their own full-time media support staff, but they often found the artist underutilized at times, and overextended at others, depending on the load. In all, the hospital had the equivalent of about 30 FTEs (full time equivalent employees) involved in media creation and editing.

About five years ago, in an effort to control costs, the department chairpersons persuaded the hospital's senior management to create a centralized media services unit within the hospital. The hospital administration agreed and renovated an in-house pharmacy area, purchased a few high-end PCs, large monitors, slide and document scanners, a slide printer, and hired four full-time staff. Six of the staff were recruited from one of the departments with full-time media support staff, and three professional media specialists, a manager, and an administrator were hired from outside the hospital. The other full-time media staff in the hospital was let go.

When the central media services unit first came on line, some of the staff within departments that had previously used their local services switched to the hospital media services. Some of the researchers and a handful of the clinicians and administrators continued to make their own PowerPoint presentations and their own line drawings for publications because they didn't want to give up control or the ability to make last-minute changes in their presentations.

Within a few months, it became apparent to the other clinicians and researchers who had used the service that the central media services unit was far from what they expected. Jobs were late. In addition, the quality was only good, but not as good as some of the best that individuals within the hospital were capable of producing. Hospital administration was initially happy, however, because the move to a central service freed up over 15 FTEs to do clinical support work.

Part of the problem was that, as is typical of a centralized, monopolistic operation, the staff in the media center was unresponsive to suggestions from the clinical and research staff. The center offered a fixed set of services and was inflexible in scheduling and pricing. Within a year, most of the faculty was back to using their local department's media services, using their own PCs, or, for those without skills, using the Media Pro shop across the street from the hospital. The Media Pro shop, which offered a full range of services, including a two-hour stat slide making service, was the death knell for the hospital media center. The staff of the central media services unit was let go and the ideas of a centralized media services unit were soon forgotten.

Things changed with the installment of a new CEO a few years later. He examined the history of the media center concept (see Exhibit

EXHIBIT 1.2

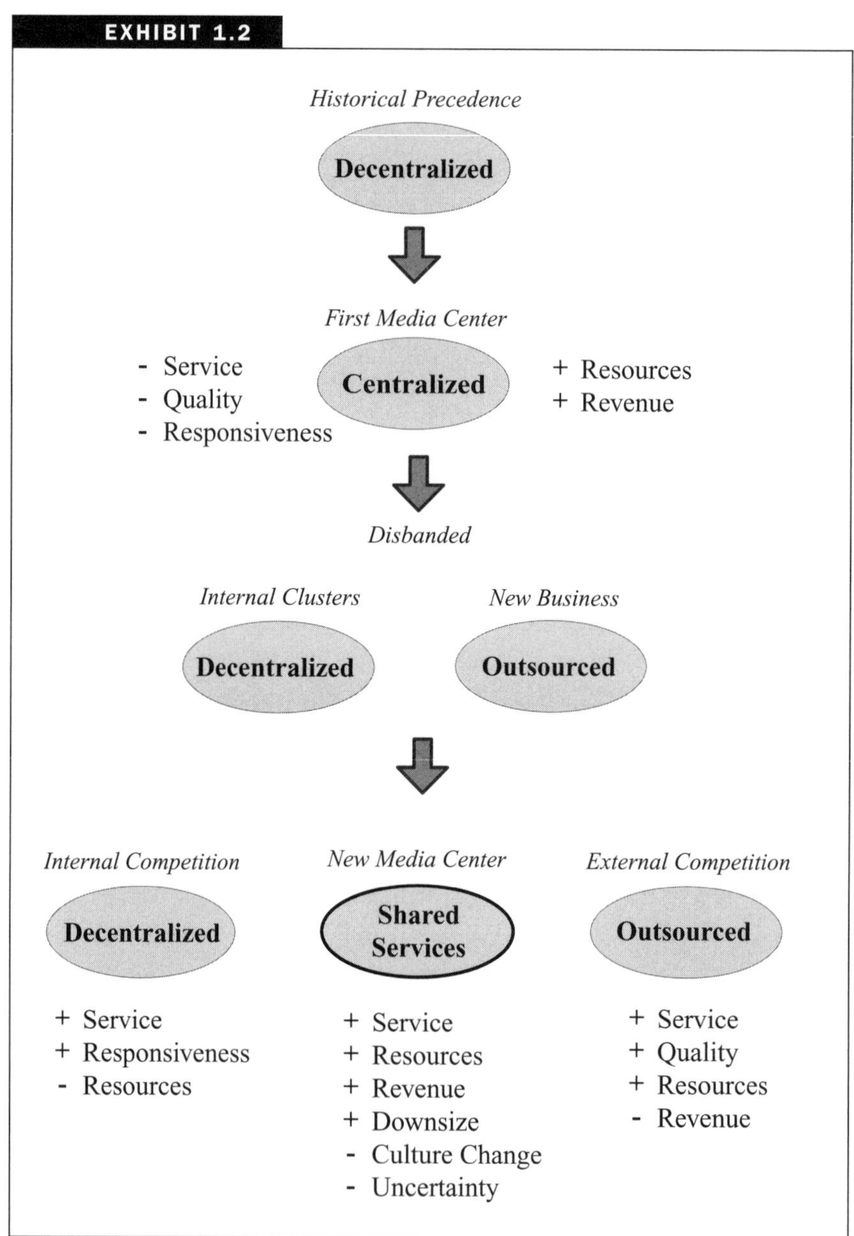

1.2) and explored the possibilities looking forward. For example, there was lost revenue due to business going to the vendor across the street in exchange for a high level of service and time savings. Outsourcing work to the external vendor did have the benefit of freeing internal hospital resources for more strategic purposes, however. In contrast, the clusters of media expertise distributed throughout the hospital, while revenue neutral, took time away from the core competency of the clinical support staff. They did, however, provide superior service and responsiveness to the staff's needs.

Given the failure of a traditional centralized approach, especially the poor, unresponsive service attributed to the first media center, the CEO considered the merits of a shared services model. If the new media center could provide competitive service, it could capture revenue from grants that would otherwise go to the external vendor across the street. Freeing up employees currently on the payroll now who developed presentations and other media would allow the work of these employees to be applied to the core functions in the hospital or, if the employees were let go, would result in cost savings. The necessary culture change and the uncertainty of the success of yet another media center were negative factors, but the CEO decided to establish the center and give it at least a year to prove or disprove the concept.

In order to avoid the mistakes of the past, the CEO hired a manager with experience running a commercial multimedia service for the shared business unit. Together with four hospital employees transferred from media service shops, the manager, who was given the responsibility of maintaining profitability and marketing the center's services, was given a budget and access to in-hospital services, including information services and the copy center, on a fee-for-service basis. The new manager was also free to rely on external vendors. With access to the hospital-wide e-mail system, the manager arranged for a notice to be sent to each hospital employee regarding the opening of the new media center, which included an aggressive pricing structure that was competitive with the service across the street. In addition, the manager offered to work on purchase orders referenced to grant work, even though it meant payment might not be forthcoming for three months. The manager also took advantage of access to the hospital bulletin boards in the cafeteria and other high traffic areas—places off limits to outside vendors.

Within six months of its creation, revenue for the shared business unit was significant and steady, but not yet to a level of profitability. In addition, there was still a significant number of hospital staff using the services of the Media Pro shop across the street. With a little investigation, the manager determined that most of this outsourcing activity was due to digital services, including digital video work, that the Media Pro shop offered. The media center was not equipped to work with the latest digital video, in part because it was initially thought that there wasn't enough demand in the hospital to provide a reasonable return on the investment.

The manager arranged a meeting with the hospital's CEO and presented a case for investing $140,000 in the latest digital video editing and production system, as well as $80,000 with overhead annually for one FTE to staff the system. The CEO said that before he would invest more of the hospital's capital in the media center, he wanted to see a more detailed analysis of breakeven and profitability. He also suggested that the manager consider different ways of competing with the Media Pro shop that wouldn't require an infusion of more capital. In other words, the manager was forced to use his own resources; the hospital wasn't going to hand him a blank check so that he could buy his way to profitability.

Key Concepts

The media services story, to be continued in later chapters, illustrates the following key concepts regarding shared services.

Shared Services Isn't Business As Usual

The story highlights the difference between shared services and more traditional business models, especially traditional decentralized, centralized, and outsourcing models. As illustrated in Exhibit 1.3, there are sig-

IN THE REAL WORLD

The Stats on Shared Services

Although the shared services model was formalized in the early 1990s as a means of saving costs while maintaining a degree of control over the product or service, the concept has been in practice for much longer. In the past decade, the model has been used by the big consulting firms—PricewaterhouseCoopers, Gunn Partners, McKenzie and Company, and London Perret Roche Group LLC. Most of the big-ticket consulting activity is in the large business arena, where large national and multinational companies are looking to shave millions of dollars per year off of their operating budgets.

About half of the Fortune 500 companies have established some form of shared services, primarily to support financial transactions, human resources, and information technologies. As with the application of any new business model, there have been both stellar successes and failures. Some businesses, such as American Express, are successful today primarily because of the shared services model. Similarly, since 1977, cost savings from Bristol-Meyers Squibb Company's Global Business Services unit has resulted in annual savings of $1.5 billion for the parent company. A two-year implementation effort, begun in 1995, consolidated similar financial transaction processing and manufacturing in over 85 locations, with the shared service unit allocating operating cost back to the individual business units. Representing the other end of the spectrum is Lucent Technologies, which, despite a highly visible shared services program, has consistently performed far below expectations of Wall Street.

nificant differences in revenue and reporting, employee reward systems, and management. The relative advantages and disadvantages of each model are a function of the structural organization.

EXHIBIT 1.3

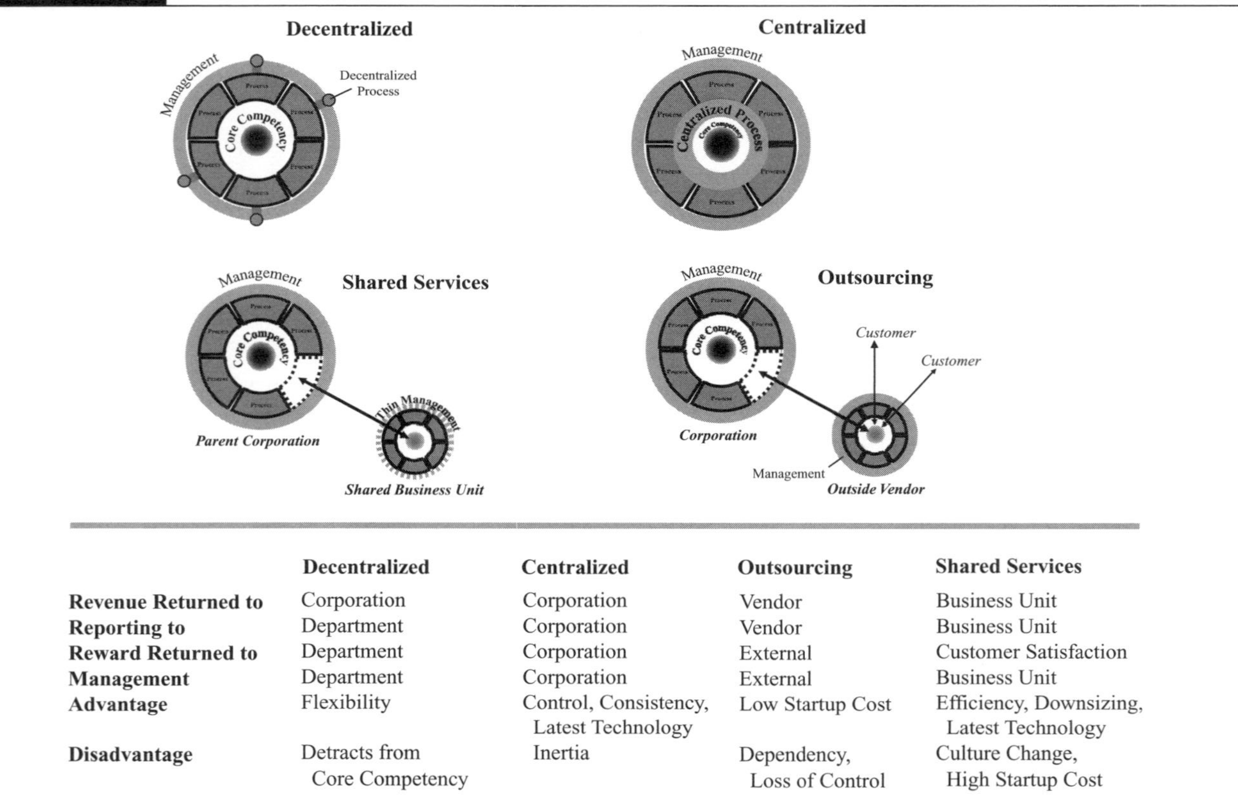

	Decentralized	Centralized	Outsourcing	Shared Services
Revenue Returned to	Corporation	Corporation	Vendor	Business Unit
Reporting to	Department	Corporation	Vendor	Business Unit
Reward Returned to	Department	Corporation	External	Customer Satisfaction
Management	Department	Corporation	External	Business Unit
Advantage	Flexibility	Control, Consistency, Latest Technology	Low Startup Cost	Efficiency, Downsizing, Latest Technology
Disadvantage	Detracts from Core Competency	Inertia	Dependency, Loss of Control	Culture Change, High Startup Cost

For example, the flow of revenue in the *decentralized* model is through the parent corporation. Because there is no central locus of control, reporting is typically through the local department or company division. Similarly, reward for employee performance is directed through the department or division. As illustrated in Exhibit 1.3, management is similarly local to the location of the decentralized activity, or else it is non-existent. For example, a researcher with external funding can equip her laboratory with high-end digital editing and rendering equipment capable of generating media for everyone associated with the laboratory, without having to ask anyone in the hospital to finance supplies or equipment. One of the obvious advantages to this approach, at least from the customer's perspective, is freedom from control and the flexibility to change tactics with little or no delay. The major disadvantage, from the perspective of the hospital, is that the activity detracts from the core competencies of the hospital, which are providing clinical services, teaching residents, and conducting research. In other words, the decentralized model provides a customer service orientation but at the cost of redundancy throughout the organization and poor integration.

In comparison, the *centralized model* offers a high degree of corporate-level control and economies of scale at the expense of customer service and responsiveness. Revenue, reporting, and employee reward are similarly funneled through the corporate management. Given the economies of scale, the centralized approach is more likely to result in a center of activity that can afford to maintain the latest technology and provide consistent results—but only if it can overcome the built-in inertia of a corporate-run entity.

In the information technology world, centralization is often referred to as Systems Integration, which involves merging of diverse hardware, software, and communications systems into a consolidated operating unit. The goals are to increase efficiency and add value to the organization by installing new hardware and software, restructuring applications, enhancing the underlying network infrastructure, and reconfiguring the system.

The *outsourcing model* assigns non-strategic business functions to an outside vendor who serves a number of other clients. Outsourcing is usually done to save costs, including avoiding hiring full-time employees for short-term projects, so as to free internal resources to work on core competency tasks. Outsourcing is especially attractive when the tasks to be performed require a high skill level but there is a low volume of demand—as in the case of the digital video editing within the hospital. The outsourcing model also has the benefit of a low startup cost.

The downside of outsourcing is a relative lack of control over the vendor's product or services, since the vendor handles revenue, reporting, employee reward and most management functions. This can be addressed somewhat by contractual arrangements. However, a tighter business relationship has the disadvantage of increased dependency on the vendor.

In the *shared services model,* illustrated at the bottom of Exhibit 1.3, primary management control, revenue, and reporting are in the hands of business unit management, with some degree of influence from the parent corporation. Revenue flow between the business unit and the parent corporation is usually predetermined by contractual agreements, where the business unit agrees to provide goods and services of specified quality and quantity in exchange for revenue. As in an independent business operation with profit sharing, employee reward is based on customer satisfaction.

Some of the advantages of the shared services model are increased efficiencies, the ability to lower head count in the parent corporation, and the critical mass of work to afford the latest in technology. The primary disadvantages are the required culture changes for employees in the business unit, high startup costs—sometimes on the order of starting a new business—and some duplication in administrative and managerial effort. For example, the shared business unit may need a separate accountant or accounting firm to maintain its book, depending on its size and level of business.

In addition to these major business models or approaches, there are several other business models that have similarities with the shared services model. For example, there is the *cooperative model,* which is designed to facilitate the joint acquisition of goods and services for the best available price through lower administrative costs, quantity purchasing discounts, and assured levels of business with vendors and suppliers. In the cooperative model, clients are also owners, and management control is in the hands of the owner/clients, as directed by their elected representatives. For example, an office supply cooperative is owned by the businesses that purchase office products through it. The cooperative model has been applied successfully to everything from health care and pharmacy to restaurant supply and day care.

Insourcing involves identifying internal resources with unused capacity and applying that capacity to other functions, such as making use of a receptionist's free time to do part-time cold calling for sales. Insourcing, which is most often employed when the workforce must be contracted because of economic constraints, is commonly used immediately after a failed outsourcing attempt. Because of the added demand on employees, insourcing is only practical as a temporary measure. A related model that aims to maximize use of internal resources is *shared resource management.* This involves a process of managing, scheduling, and monitoring of shared corporate resources other than personnel, such as real estate, vehicles, and equipment, with a goal of maximizing return on assets.

Co-sourcing is a combination of insourcing and outsourcing, where a third party provides resources as an extension of the company's resources. Co-sourcing is a means of outsourcing overflow of strategic processes without giving up control, especially during times of unexpected or seasonal demand. The process of determining which functions are best performed in-house and which are best outsourced is commonly referred to as right sourcing.

Corporate Culture Must Be Considered

Part of the attraction of the shared services model is the ability to achieve economies of scale through the merger of previously disparate centers of activity that are usually poorly coordinated. However, this merger typically has the effect of creating redundant staff that must be downsized, reassigned, or thrust into a different management structure. At a minimum, the employees spared downsizing have to become familiar with and embrace new concepts such as service level agreements and adjust their compensation expectations so that they are linked to customer satisfaction instead of seniority.

Another cultural shift is that the employees who are moved into a shared business unit may feel as though their roles have changed from a player in the larger corporation to a second-class citizen, now working for employees of the parent corporation. As a result of these cultural shifts, there is commonly employee resistance to a shared services implementation. This resistance can range from simple foot dragging to acts of sabotage. In some cases, the only practical option is to replace employees with those who can embrace concepts such as total quality management and appreciate the company's need to reengineer processes in order to make the company more competitive.

Technology Can Be Pivotal

Shared services, like a traditional centralized business model, concentrates resources so that the latest technology be purchased and shared, resulting in better quality services, time savings, and greater internal customer satisfaction. In addition, a central locus of control with a critical mass of customers often makes it possible to invest in technologies such as e-mail, databases of customer preferences, a Web page, and other components of a full-fledged customer relationship management system.

Competition Is Key

There must be real competition for the services, and not simply lip service demands, in order for the model to live up to its promises. Real competition for business from outside vendors is the pressure that keeps shared services competitive, forcing management and employees to keep up with best practices, and motivating employees to keep customers delighted, as opposed to simply satisfied. Unless the divisions and departments within the parent corporation at least have the real option of going through other sources, the shared services model devolves into a centralized model where business is carried on as usual.

Size Matters

There's a minimum company size and revenue stream, below which the shared services model doesn't make sense. However, this minimum size depends on the business focus of the parent corporation, the volume and unit cost of the product or service, and the relative cost of alternative models. Although the application of shared services is obvious with companies the size of American Express and Lucent Technologies, small companies can also benefit from the shared services model. A practical rule of thumb is that the shared services model is a viable option when the savings from reduction in staffing are greater than the added overhead of creating a management structure to run the shared business unit. That said, it's important to remember that shared services is much more than simply cutting a few $30,000 employees from the payroll.

Shared Services Is a Process

Implementing shared services is a dynamic, constantly evolving process of moving from a condition in which resources are dispersed or otherwise ill-focused to one in which there is constant pressure to improve to meet internal customer demands, based on cooperation and participation by management and employees. The relationship between the parent corporation and the shared business unit cannot be static.

Change Takes Time

Transforming an internal process into a shared business unit doesn't happen overnight. Furthermore, the larger and more diverse the corporation, the longer shared services takes to implement, and the more it costs. Realistic implementation times range from at least a year in simple domestic business scenarios involving one or two company locations to five years or more for a major international organization with dozens of locations. The pace of cultural change, not the availability of resources or technology, generally gates the limitation.

Expectations Must Be Managed

Implementing a shared services business model involves fundamental changes in how people interact, communicate, command, and get things done. Reporting lines, responsibilities, and management directives shift to meet the demands of the new model. However, since most people fear change, especially if it means disrupting a way of life that they've grown accustomed to, productivity can suffer unless everyone's expectations are proactively managed.

One way to manage expectations is to over-communicate plans and expectations, thereby alleviating fear of the unknown. Most people would prefer to deal with a known negative than to wait in fear; an imagined negative consequence is inevitably worse than reality. Avenues to improved communications include the company e-mails, memos, newsletters, meetings, quarterly reports from senior management, and testimonials from employees in other companies that survived the process.

Don't Forget the Lawyers

Given the likely resistance to the shared services model by some employees, the Human Resources and Legal Services divisions of the corporation are likely to be hard hit with new work, especially initially. For example, employees who willfully obstruct progress toward a shared services model must be dealt with. In addition, legally binding service level agreements must be developed to define the acceptable standards of performance of the shared business unit. It's especially critical to have a valid service level agreement in place in the event that middle managers and employees are downsized. The legal service level agreement survives, even if the original negotiating parties are no longer employed.

There is also potential for abuse and conflict of interest. For example, many of the first shared service-like operations in the medical industry were in fact elaborate kickback schemes in which clinicians created shared business units that they used to extract payment from the government and other third party payers.

Relationships Are Complex

It isn't sufficient to create a shared business unit, without advertising the new service to employees and other department managers. Business is about building relationships, and this takes time, effort, and attention to subtle details. Most businesses require several years to break even and reach profitability, in part because of the time required to build a relationship between the individuals involved in the business transactions. In advocating a shared services approach, it's critical to remember that business relationships are complex and success can't simply be mandated from above.

Reality Check

Although the shared services model has a lot to offer, like any other business model, it is by no means a panacea. As illustrated in Exhibit 1.4,

EXHIBIT 1.4

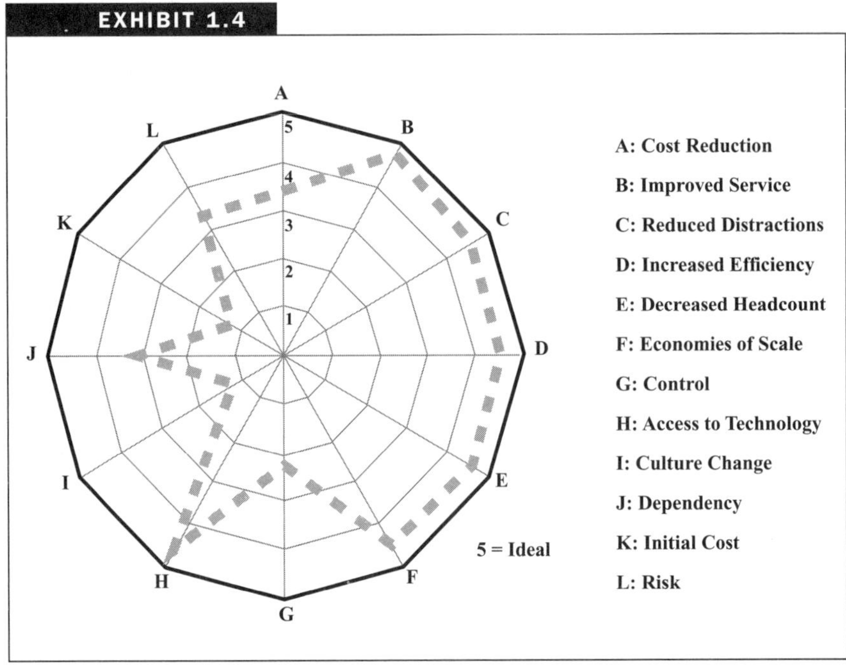

compared to the theoretical ideal, shared services has high marks in the areas of potential cost reduction, improved service, reduced distractions from core competency activities, increased efficiency, decreased headcount requirements, economies of scale, and access to technology. However, it has low marks in the areas of control, need for cultural change, and initial cost of implementation.

A more detailed summary of the major limitations of the shared services model includes:

- *Need to create a baseline.* In order to determine if the shared services model is working, it's necessary to establish a baseline, in terms of current costs, customer service, and efficiencies, as well as detailed specifications of what is currently done and what needs to be delivered. Although this seems obvious enough, few companies have this data readily available.
- *Inevitable corporate culture shock.* The loss of coworkers through downsizing, the new focus on customer service, and new

reward and reporting structures will take their toll on corporate culture, often resulting initially in a drop in efficiency.

- *Unavailability of in-house expertise.* Ideally, resources are simply and painlessly shifted around the organization. However, in reality, some expertise, such as shared business unit management, will have to be recruited from outside of the organization, either because it doesn't exist internally, or because the people involved refuse to relocate.
- *There is a minimum company size.* As noted earlier, the shared services model doesn't apply to mom and pop operations. The larger the company, the more distributed and diffuse the processes, and the more duplication of effort, the more likely the shared services model is applicable to the company.
- *Loss of control.* Moving to a shared services model means that management of the parent organization has to give up some control. Employees of the shared business unit must become customer focused as well as responsive to the business unit's needs.
- *Legal implications.* Detailed service level agreements and strong performance audits are required to keep the shared services model on track. In addition, these agreements must be in line with corporate, state, and federal laws.
- *Need for new accounting practices.* Chargeback practices that detail how the shared business unit is to be reimbursed for services rendered have to be established.
- *New training requirements.* Retained employees of the shared business unit will likely need training in the nuances of customer service and total quality management principles.
- *Increased communications overhead.* A shared business unit will necessarily be involved in internal sales and marketing, which requires resources focused on communicating with current and prospective customers.

- *Potential for developing an "us" vs "them" mentality.* Creating a separate business entity has the potential for creating a negative, adversarial relationship, even when the purpose of the shared business unit is to support the activities of the parent corporation. For example, employees may be sensitive to differences in compensation and working conditions. Employees of the shared business units may resent the uncertainty of their positions, while those of the parent organization may resent the bonus incentives established for shared business unit employees.
- *Increased overhead on the business unit management and administration.* There are additional business functions, such as customer service, that must be managed.
- *High startup costs.* Compared to outsourcing, establishing a shared services business unit can be expensive. The startup cost depends on the organization's relationship with the business unit, the length of its contract, and the scope of services provided.
- *Extended time to break-even.* Because creating a shared business unit is very much like starting a new business, it may take a year or more for the unit to break even and achieve break-even or profitability. In the meantime, the parent corporation should benefit from an increased level of service.

Whether or not shared services makes sense for a particular business application depends on the business, the corporate culture, the applicability of alternative business models, the economic health of the company, and the wants and needs of corporate senior management.

The following chapters examine these issues, as well as the impact of shared services from the perspectives of cost, effect on quality of service, impact on corporate culture, how to measure results, how to manage the shared business unit, as well as a variety of tactics and strategies that can be used to ensure success.

Summary

The shared services model is fundamentally about managing resources to improve the bottom line, improve internal service, and enhance the competitiveness of the parent organization. In many aspects, the shared services model is a hybrid approach that shares characteristics with more traditional models such as centralization (e.g., access to the latest technology, economies of scale, and downsizing), decentralization (e.g., customer focus and agility to better meet customer needs), and outsourcing (e.g., offloading of non-strategic activities).

The shared services model is not without its limitations, however. Unlike outsourcing, for example, which can be used with companies of any size, shared services can live up to its potential only when the parent corporation is above a minimum size. The size varies from one business to the next. In addition, achieving a successful shared services model implementation requires attentiveness to the corporate culture, the addition of the appropriate technologies to the mix, and investing the time and resources to manage employee expectations.

There are no secrets to success: Don't waste time looking for them. Success is the result of perfection, hard work, learning from failure, loyalty to those for whom you work, and persistence.

General Colin Powell

CHAPTER 2

The Corporation

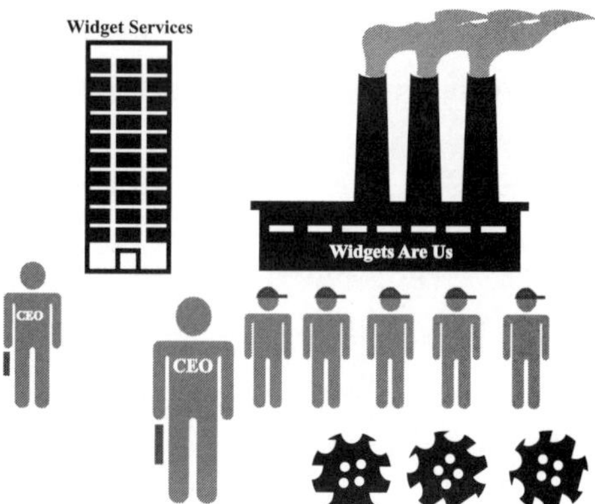

After reading this chapter you will be able to

- Appreciate the changes in corporate culture inherent in transitioning to a shared services model
- Understand the implications of embracing shared services to enhance corporate value for the shareholder and customer
- Understand the significance of strategic partnerships and alliances in the shared services model
- Recognize the exposure to risk associated with a shared services model
- Understand the knowledge management issues associated with deciding what intellectual capital to transfer to a shared business unit
- Appreciate the significance of proper timing in moving to a shared services model
- Understand the tradeoffs associated with controlling the shared business unit

A company's business model is so deeply embedded in its overall strategy, its approach to customers, its hiring and career development techniques, its relationship to investors, local, state, and federal governments, and its strategic partners that the model can't be separated from the organization. As such, a new business model—in effect a new scaffolding upon which existing business processes and corporate culture are hung—isn't something that can simply be thrust upon a company, regardless of how promising the model appears. However, just as the human body can be molded and reconstituted over the course of several months through a specific exercise routine, a corporation's existing business model can be completely transformed—given time and support for the transformation process.

Taking the perspective of the corporate senior management, this chapter explores the issues involved in implementing a shared services model. To illustrate some of these issues, let's continue with the vignette introduced in Chapter 1.

IN THE REAL WORLD

The 80-20 Rule

One of the major reasons for moving to a shared services model is to enable business divisions to do what they do best and consolidate and eliminate any activity that isn't considered a core competency. As such, 80 percent of employees at Dow Corning work with operations that have a direct bearing on their core business. Shared services, including human resources, public affairs, purchasing, and information systems, together with a few leveraged activities are handled by the remaining 20 percent of employees.

Telemedicine on the Rocks

State General Hospital is affiliated with a network of two other hospitals and about a dozen major satellite clinics throughout the region. Because it has the largest radiology department and the latest digital radiology equipment, State General Hospital handles the bulk of overflow and specialized radiology reading services for the satellite clinics through an ad-hoc fee for services agreement. Part-time, non-affiliated radiologists who cover the clinics on a fee per reading basis, the special cases, perform most day-to-day radiology reading services but special studies are digitized and sent over high-speed Internet connections to radiologists at State General Hospital. Radiologists in the hospital read the images on high-resolution computer monitors, and communicate their reports to the clinics electronically. In all, about 11 part-time independent radiologists support the outlying clinics (see Exhibit 2.1).

The senior management of State General Hospital creates a shared services telemedicine radiology unit to consolidate its satellite radiology

EXHIBIT 2.1

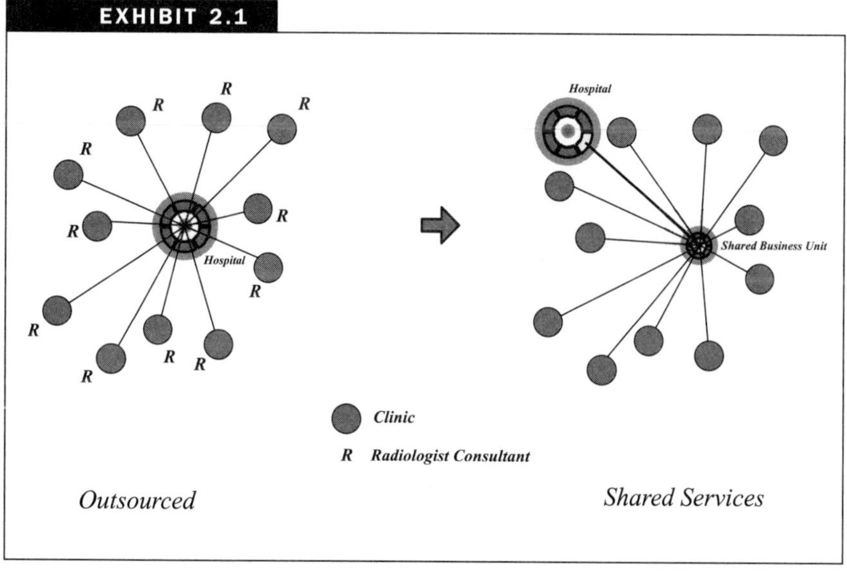

services, increase quality of service, better utilize staff radiologists, reduce or eliminate its reliance on independent radiology consultants, and capture additional business in small clinics throughout the state. In establishing the unit, senior management identifies key staff at the hospital to provide coverage in key specialty areas 24 hours a day, seven days a week. It also hires an interim manager for the unit. The manager, who is recruited from outside of the hospital, has experience running a small business, but is inexperienced in radiology. After arranging for staff to cover the telemedicine radiology unit and setting up the facility with the latest hardware and software, the manager began taking up business from the outlying clinics.

Since the new telemedicine unit is equipped with the latest digital reading and transcription services, a staff of six radiologists can perform the overflow as well as the work once performed by the consultants at the clinics, and at a much lower cost to the hospital. Within about three months of offering the service, the telemedicine unit had taken over not only the previous overflow, but all of the radiology reading services for the clinics. It turns out that the service was too successful, at least from the perspective of the downsized independent radiologists, many of whom had no other source of income. Most were semi-retired and supported the outlying clinics as a service to their community and to maintain their standard of living.

The downsized radiologists happened to be very influential on the state and national level in their specialty; many had been involved in training the radiologists now operating the telemedicine unit. Once the staff radiologists in the telemedicine unit were made aware of the plight of their former mentors, the efficiency of the unit, in terms of the number of cases read per hour, suddenly dropped. Soon, there was a backlog of unread studies in the clinics, and the radiology consultants had to be called in to help. Although they were under contract, the staff radiologist requested to be reassigned to some other service in the hospital. The close-knit radiology community shared their sentiments. As a result, the telemedicine shared services project closed after less than nine months of operation. Independent radiologist returned to the clinics, and the reading of overflow films continued as before, using radiologists on staff on an availability basis.

State General Hospital's experience with moving to a shared services model—which is based on an actual case from a Texas hospital in the early 1990s—illustrates several key issues:

- *Both internal and external customers are affected by a move to a shared services model of doing business.* While the telemedicine unit was in operation, images were interpreted and the reports

IN THE REAL WORLD

Downsizing Isn't Inevitable

When AlliedSignal moved to a shared services model, it was able to downsize 500 employees from a staff of 1,600. Similarly, Monsanto reduced its information services staff by 10 percent as a result of forming Monsanto IT Shared Services. However, implementing a shared services model needn't result in layoffs, especially when it's implemented at a time of increased demand for the services that would be provided by the shared business unit. When Amoco formed a shared business unit out of its information technology services, it reassigned the 1200 information services professionals who had been distributed into three business groups so that they then reported to a shared business unit with new management.

Implementing a shared services model typically results in decreased staffing requirements. However, this *can* be reflected in a decreased need for new hires instead of downsizing existing employees.

were filed electronically in only a few hours instead of in a day or more, as was the case with the previous ad hoc service.

- *Embracing a new business model involves a significant corporate cultural change.* Those downsized as well as the radiologists in the telemedicine unit resisted the downsizing of radiologists. Similarly, many unions negotiate downsizing policies that limit the rate, extent, and criteria for downsizing.
- *Strategic partnerships and alliances can be crucial for success.* The telemedicine unit manager neglected to form an alliance with a state or national radiology organization that could have primed the radiology community to accept the telemedicine unit.
- *There is risk inherent in any business model or process change.* The transition to a shared services model failed in favor of an outsourced model.
- *Timing a move to a new business model is crucial.* Senior management of State General Hospital rushed headlong into the conversion from an outsourced to a shared services model without first understanding the implications of the transition.
- *The degree of control exercised over the shared business unit has corporate-wide implications.* In establishing the charter of the telemedicine unit and directing it to take up the activities of the outlying clinics, senior management of State General Hospital set up the manager of the telemedicine unit for failure.
- *Identifying and installing leadership in the shared business unit has significant knowledge management ramifications.* The telemedicine unit manager had experience in telemedicine, but not in the nuances of radiology, and didn't appreciate the bond between radiologists.
- *Expectations must be managed at all levels in the organization.* By failing to create an acceptable vision of the long-term goals of the telemedicine unit, the telemedicine unit staff and the inde-

pendent radiologists were taken off guard. A better approach would have been to communicate with the radiology staff and consultants early on to set expectations. Even if the vision were rejected, it would have been better to discover the challenges before investing in the unit.

These issues are expanded and explored in the following section.

Customers

Customers are the lifeblood of every viable business operation. In the shared services model, customers are of three types: external-corporate, external–shared services business unit, and internal (see Exhibit 2.2).

As shown in the figure, external corporate customers are normally thought of as typical customers in that they interact with the corporate entity. External shared services business unit customers interact with the

EXHIBIT 2.2

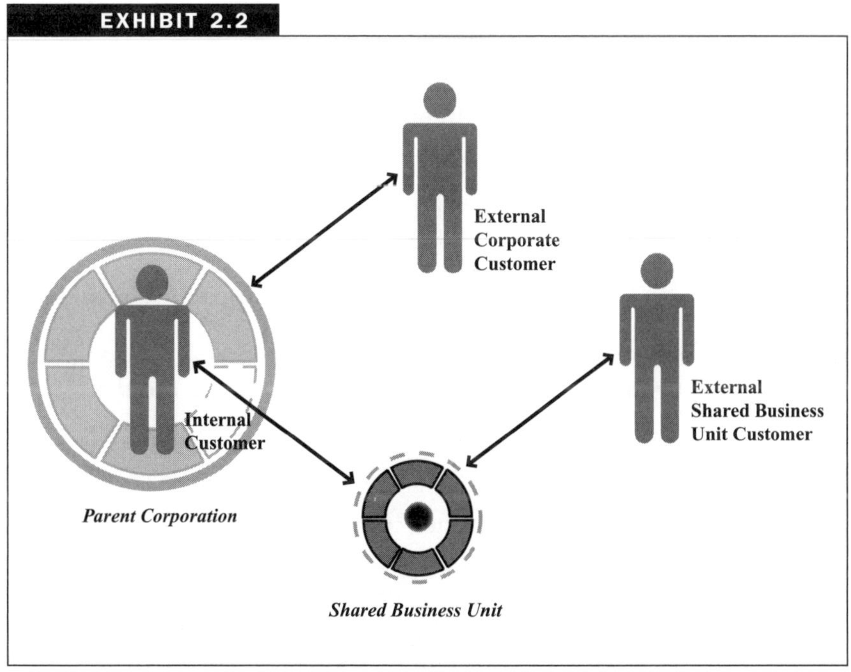

corporation indirectly, through the shared services business unit. In contrast, the internal customers are employees of the parent corporation.

All customers exchange money, promissory notes, purchase orders, or other value in exchange for goods and services. However, what makes a *willing* customer is a situation in which the company offers a product or service that provides the mix of quality, price, and on-time delivery that fulfills the expectations of the customer. As illustrated in Exhibit 2.3, most businesses operate within quality, price, and time constraints. The figure shows the tradeoffs associated with performing well in any of the categories. For example, a company that focuses on delivering quality service very quickly typically has to charge more for the service, compared to a company that provides a less timely service. Regardless of whether the customer is internal or external, there is a general issue of what the customer can reasonably expect from the business unit.

The quality-price-time constraint illustrates how a company must determine the axes on which it will compete, and what it will have to sacrifice. The challenge is amplified because these issues are just as important from the customer's perspective. At point "A" in Exhibit 2.3, for example, the customer's requirements are primarily in delivery time. Ideally, the shared business unit's operations support this quality. Later, customers may decide that product quality or service quality is the most important factor in their buy decision, as at point "B" in Exhibit 2.3. Again, the business unit will ideally respond to this requirement by modifying its production accordingly.

The quality-time-price requirements established by the three types of customers in the shared services model are reflected in different ways. For external corporate customers, the corporate management has to decide how to best meet customer needs in a timely and affordable manner. If the company is of significant size, then the inertia of the corporation may hinder response to the customer needs.

For external shared services unit customers, senior management of

EXHIBIT 2.3

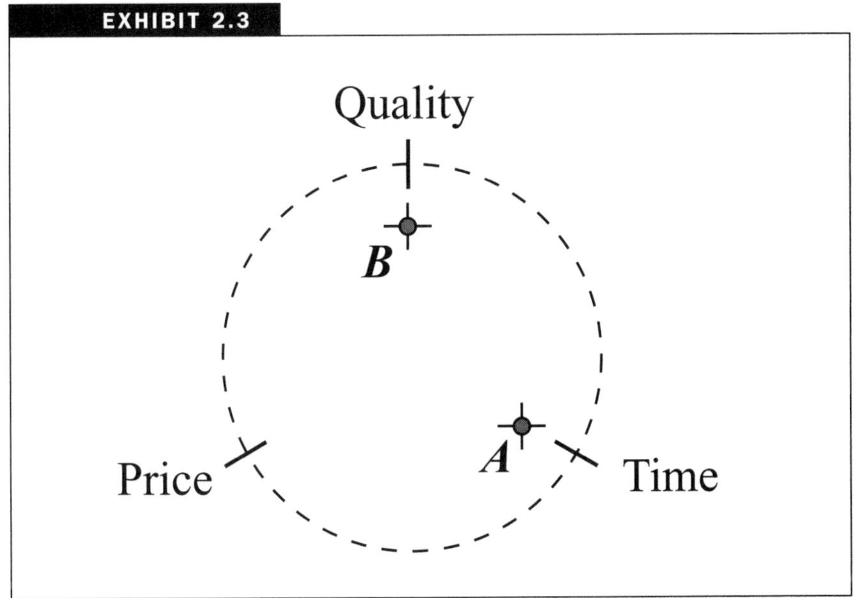

the shared services business unit has to determine how best to meet customer needs. Depending on the degree of control the parent corporation exercises over the shared business unit, the unit may be free to rapidly retool their internal processes to meet external customer demand or, at the other extreme, have to overcome the inertia of the parent corporation while operating at arm's length from corporate management.

Internal customers present the most complex situation and one that depends on the nature of the relationship. For example, if early on in the business unit's life, it can't meet expectations of internal customers who need delivery of services within 20 minutes (represented by "A" in Exhibit 2.3), for example, then the parent corporation may need to make an additional investment in new technology, more staff, or management support. It's also possible that the expectations of the parent corporation are unrealistic and these expectations may have to be redefined.

Assuming that the shared business unit can eventually meet the delivery time requirements of the internal customers, the issue that

TIPS & TECHNIQUES

Managing Internal Customer Expectations

In order to evaluate the potential value of using CRM techniques to satisfy the needs of internal customers, the key questions to ask during a transition to a shared services model of doing business include:

- What did the previous supplier of product or services—whether an outsourced vendor, central service, or decentralized service—do to manage customer expectations? Since customers are much more sensitive to *relative* changes in services than to absolute service levels, the previous service level sets the standard by which all subsequent service is measured.
- How have internal customer touch points changed from the customer's perspective? Is the shared business unit perceived as a different entity from the parent corporation or is its separation from the parent corporation invisible? In most cases, the latter is the ideal, and the touch points all project a sense of one homogeneous company. Providing this appearance can be a major challenge, however, especially if the shared business unit is relatively independent.
- Other than business volume, what metrics identify good internal customers? If the shared business service is mature and independent enough to operate as a freestanding unit, is profitability used as a metric to assess customer satisfaction? How does customer loyalty, as measured in quantity of repeat business, come into play? As in any business, business practices can profoundly affect success, even with a loyal customer following.

TIPS & TECHNIQUES CONTINUED

- What touch points tend to be the most frequented by good customers? How can the responsiveness of these touch points be improved?

Monitoring touch points, benchmarking customer service, and adapting to meet or exceed customer expectations in a mutually advantageous way are all core CRM activities.

inevitably surfaces later on is what to do when the requirements shift. For example, the parent corporation may eventually decide that quality (represented by "B" in Exhibit 2.3) is now the most important factor in their buy decision. To respond to this later change may require retooling, hiring new employees, or acquiring senior management with different management skills. How this later change is resolved depends on the independence of the business unit. For example, if the shared unit is at a stage where it reinvests profits for future investment, management can decide to make the investment to meet internal customer needs. Of course, skilled management should be able to foresee the need for a change to quality of service and plan for it.

Customer Relationship Management

Deciding when and if to modify business activity to meet customer demands falls under the rubric of customer relationship management, or CRM. As applied to external customers interacting with the parent corporation, CRM is generally understood to be a dynamic process of managing a customer-company relationship such that customers elect to continue mutually beneficial commercial exchanges and are dissuaded from participating in exchanges that are unprofitable to the company. That is, in profitable business operations, managing customer relations isn't simply saying yes to every demand.

From the company's perspective, there is a cost of an ongoing relationship with the customer, regardless of whether the relationship is profitable or not. There is the cost of doing business, which normally includes customer support. There is also lost opportunity cost, because corporate resources may be used on one group of customers at the expense of another group. The cost also involves the ongoing task of gathering and sorting data to determine what can and should be offered to the customer in exchange for repeat business.

In the context of the shared services model, the standard CRM definition has to be modified to reflect the customer-company relationships dealing with the shared business unit. For external customers dealing with a shared business unit, the most appropriate definition of CRM depends on the degree of autonomy given the business unit. At one extreme, where the business unit is virtually fully autonomous, the standard CRM definition holds. With a tightly managed shared services business unit, the standard definition should be changed to reflect the need of the customer-company relationship to benefit the parent corporation in some way. That is, the definition of CRM for a tightly controlled shared services business unit is:

> A dynamic process of managing a relationship between customer and shared business unit such that customers elect to continue mutually beneficial commercial exchanges that are profitable to the parent corporation and are dissuaded from participating in exchanges that are unprofitable to the business unit or parent corporation.

This distinction is especially important in the long-term shared business unit operation, where the shared business unit may approach an organization, independent of the parent corporation. At some point along the continuum of development of the shared business unit, it has a choice in determining which clients to serve and could decide not to shift operations from one that supports quality instead of delivery time.

This decision may make good business sense, especially if the other clients, who comprise most of the volume and profit, continue to demand minimum delivery time.

From the parent corporation's perspective, the ability to refuse work is critical, because it portends a potential hazard of granting the shared business unit full autonomy. It's in the parent corporation's best interest to have a shared business unit that will respond to its needs in favor of, for example, the competition's needs.

For internal corporate customers, the trajectory and end point of the shared services unit are nearly identical to those of external customers, with some important differences. A definition of CRM that applies to this class of customers includes a mix of services that suits the needs of the best, highest volume customers within the capabilities of the shared business unit. The definition of CRM appropriate for internal customers of a shared services business unit is:

> A dynamic process of managing a relationship between the internal customer and the shared business unit such that corporate customers elect to continue mutually beneficial exchanges that are advantageous to the shared business unit and are dissuaded from participating in exchanges that are unprofitable to the business unit.

The problem suggested by this definition of CRM is that corporate politics may come into play, especially favoritism. Another hitch is that simply following the wishes of internal customers can result in a structure in which high cost, low volume products or services are key to the parent corporation, even though the shared business unit is configured to provide high volume, lower quality products and services.

In the context of shared services, CRM is about the relationship between customer and companies, with each contributing to and receiving something from the relationship. Whereas customers expect value for their money, companies expect money and often a degree of loyalty in exchange for their goods and services. The challenges, from the corporate perspective, are to provide customers with value that meets their expectations and to gain the revenue from the relationship that the parent company expects, with minimal disruption to the internal processes of the parent company.

Touch Points

As illustrated in Exhibit 2.4, *external customers* interact with businesses through multiple touch points. In this example, customers interact directly with the parent corporation through the retail outlet, personal contact, and surface mail for some issues. External customers of the shared business unit interact indirectly through e-mail, the Web, fax, telephone, cell phone, and wireless devices for other issues. The most common touch points for a business include e-mail, fax, mail (flyers), media

EXHIBIT 2.4

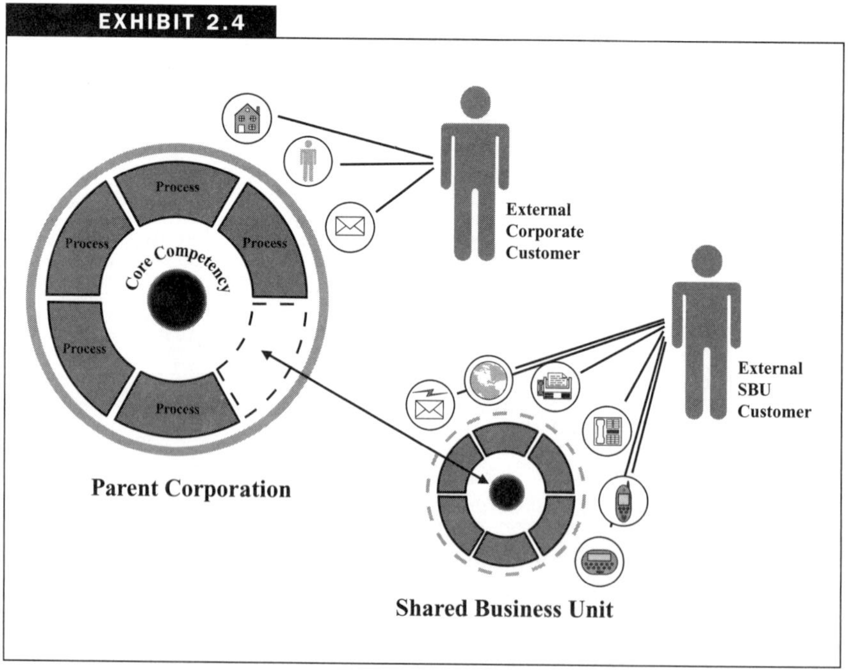

(through advertisements on TV and radio), personal contact (through retail outlet stores), over the telephone (voice messaging), on the Web, and through wireless, location-independent versions of e-mail, phone, fax, and Web access.

The key issue with touch points is that the message to the customer must be consistent. Every *touch point* is critical in providing service and potentially increasing customer satisfaction. In this regard, every customer interaction with the company through a touch point influences the customer's perception of the business, and whether the customer will return to do business in the future. Furthermore, customers expect the employees assigned to each touch point to recognize and remember them regardless of how they interact with the company. As such, those who interact with customers at a given touch point have to be able to access historical data about the customer. Such data includes every customer interaction with the business through every other touch point.

Customers expect a business to provide the same service through every touch point. If they interact with a business through the Web, for example, they expect to be able to verify the status of an order placed on the telephone or in person. It doesn't matter to the customer if the parent corporation headquarters handles the phone calls and e-mail is handled through a shared business unit that also provides Web services for the corporation.

When properly implemented, CRM extends beyond mere customer service. Sales and Marketing have a stake in a robust CRM system because it can lead to increased sales revenue from existing as well as new customers. Customer contact information, from e-mail addresses and cell phone numbers, provides sales professionals with qualified sales lists. For example, a customer who has already purchased a product from the company may be interested in a new model, an upgrade, routine maintenance, or an add-on product or service.

From a marketing perspective, CRM represents a vast source of customer feedback that can be used to tailor the marketing message to fit actual customer profiles. For example, if the best customers are teenagers who interact with the corporation through its Web site, then the marketing campaign can be adjusted to appeal to that age group.

Customer Loyalty

One of the corporation's major assets, and one that is developed through customer relationship management, is customer loyalty. In this regard, loyalty is an intangible asset that is difficult to quantify exactly. What can be quantified is customer behavior, and where customer loyalty is concerned, the closest factor that can be measured is customer behavior. The Loyalty Effect provides a model that can be used to predict customer behavior, based on factors that positively and negatively affect behaviors associated with loyalty, such as positive referrals, repeat business, and continuing a business relationship even when there are potentially superior competing products and services available.

Exhibit 2.5 shows the positive and negative contributors to behaviors consistent with loyalty. Positive factors include Value, Investment, Difficulty Locating Alternatives, and Emotional Bond. For example, the greater the perceived value of a company's goods or services, the greater the loyalty effect. Similarly, the more time, energy, or money invested in a relationship, the more likely the relationship will continue. In addition, the more unique or readily available a product or service is to a particular company, the more likely a customer will continue buying it from that company. Similarly, a personal, emotional bond with a company representative is often the most important factor in creating a loyal customer. With the exception of companies like Apple, Dell, or the Gap, people don't normally form bonds with companies, but with the people who represent the companies.

EXHIBIT 2.5

The Loyalty Effect

Contributors to Loyalty Behavior:

Difficulty Locating Alternatives The number of alternative businesses that offer comparable products and services at similar prices.

Emotional Bond Trust, and, to a lesser extent, accountability, respect, and other emotional issues. The emotional bond has a multiplicative effect on *Value* and *Investment.*

Investment A customer's total investment of time and energy, in their relationship with your business.

Value The perceived value that a consumer places on the product and services that your business offers.

Detractors from Loyalty Behavior:

Affordable Alternatives The number of alternative businesses that offer a comparable service or product in a comparable price range.

Frustration Level The customers' level of frustration with their relationship with the business.

The negative contributors to loyalty behavior are affordable alternatives and customer frustration. The more affordable alternatives that are available, the less loyal customers are to a particular brand or company. For example, on the Web, where alternatives are a click away, potential customers can locate viable alternatives in only a few seconds. Finally, nothing poisons an otherwise ideal business relationship faster than customer frustration.

The Loyalty Effect model shows how customer behavior can be influenced, depending on what elements in the model are stressed. For example, immediately attending to good customers when they call for support, responding promptly and appropriately to their written and e-mail messages, and, in the retail setting, attending to their needs in a courteous, professional manner will all contribute to continued business with the company.

Cultural Revolution

The merger of formerly separate centers of activity has the effect of creating redundant staff that must be downsized, reassigned, or thrust into a different management structure. Those employees who remain have to become familiar with and embrace new concepts such as service level agreements. Frequently, they must adjust their compensation expectations, and reassess their relative status within the corporation.

Perhaps the greatest fear of any manager or employee in the corporate environment is change from the familiar to the unknown. At the start of a shared services implementation, downsizing, compensation changes, relocation, modified management situations, and reassignment to a second-class citizen status are all factors that create trepidation and resistance to change at all levels in the corporation.

Instituting a shared services model is nothing short of a cultural revolution for those directly affected by either downsizing or reassignment. For other employees and management, the cultural changes, while less profound than those in the shared business unit, can be just as significant. For example, employees and managers of the parent corporation may be given permission to choose service from a commercial service provider and/or the shared business unit.

This flexibility brings with it added responsibility. For example, lower level managers who simply assumed service would be provided by in-house expertise are now pressured to evaluate quality, dependability, delivery time, and value to the corporation, in particular, the bottom line of the department or division. As a result, lower level managers who are charged with choosing a vendor may need to be trained to identify the product that provides the most value for the company. The cultural changes for employees in the shared business unit are discussed in the following chapter.

Strategic Partnerships and Alliances

The fate of the telemedicine center in this chapter's vignette illustrates the importance of strategic partnerships and alliances in implementing a shared services business unit. Because management of the telemedicine unit didn't presell the long-term concept of the shared business unit to staff radiologists and the radiology consultants who worked the clinics, the venture failed. An alliance with the American Board of Radiology or other official professional body, for example, together with a proposal to "study telemedicine," might have nullified individual resistance from the radiology consultants.

Obvious strategic partners and alliances to seek out for virtually every company are those with local, state, and federal governments. For example, federal law makes it illegal for doctors and lawyers to practice across state lines using computer and communications technology (telelaw and telemedicine, respectively) unless the individual practitioners are licensed in the state in which the patient resides. Changes in federal laws are necessary for these and other telepresence services to move into practical, everyday use.

Risky Business

Moving to a new business model involves significant risk to the parent corporation. As shown in Exhibit 2.6, the major risks to the corporation moving to a shared services model can be managerial, economic, legal, technical, or in marketing. In the managerial category, the chief risk is the disruption in services and the related subsequent fallout. For example, if the corporate culture is such that there is resistance to change from all levels in the corporation, there will be cost overruns and

EXHIBIT 2.6

Areas of Risk to the Corporation

Managerial

Overly disruptive transition	Diversion of resources
Time overruns	Grassroots rejection

Economic

General economic slowdown	Cost overruns
Unexpected drop in demand	Business unit failure
Internal customer rejection	Low return on investment
External customer rejection	

Legal

Customer privacy violations	Loss of intellectual property
Fraud	

Technical

Insufficient capacity	Lack of security
Poor responsiveness	Disruption of service
Poor scalability	

Marketing

Insufficient internal market

a diversion of resources associated with the transition. As a result, the entire transition project could fail.

Major risk to the corporation can also arise from external economic forces. The risk is from bad timing, that is, a weak economy, or economic downturn, or new competition, occurring just when the company has extended itself financially in order to save money later on. As in the telemedicine example, it's also possible that the shared business unit will fail.

There are multiple legal complications associated with creating and supporting a shared services model. For example, there is a significant potential for fraud in the form of illegal kickbacks from the shared business unit to the parent corporation in exchange for business. As illustrated by the Enron debacle, even the largest corporations are susceptible to creative accounting practices.

The major technological risk is disruption of service, especially when mission-critical functions are transferred to a shared business unit. For example, if a distributed information services system is shifted to a shared business unit, then any significant downtime can bring the parent corporation to its knees. Another technological risk is that a limited implementation of a solution that works for part of the corporation doesn't scale to the entire organization, either because of inherent limitations in the technology or because the technology is used inappropriately. Finally, the major risk to marketing and sales is simply the lack of a significant internal market. This turn of events can come about because of the introduction of a disruptive technology, such as personal printers and copiers, which redefine business process to the extent that the advantages of moving to a shared business model are negated.

Risk Management

Just as risk is an inescapable component of doing business, risk management is an important aspect of every CEO's responsibility. A prerequisite for effective risk management is recognizing signs of trouble before it gets out of control. The major factors that put businesses involved in a shared services implementation at risk are shown in Exhibit 2.7.

Managing risk includes acquiring an awareness of risk factors. Risk factors in the area of corporate management include a failure to recognize the corporation's core competencies. If senior management of the parent corporation is uncertain of the business they're in, there is a risk of moving the core competency of the business to a shared business unit and eventually losing control over a strategic competency. Sometimes a company's core competencies may not be intuitively obvious, even to management. For example, Domino's Pizza's core competency isn't

EXHIBIT 2.7

Corporate Risks Factors

Managerial

Failure to recognize core competencies	Failure to understand the business
Overly disruptive transition	Flawed organization structure
Inability to collaborate	Misalignment of vision and focus
Inappropriate business model	Poor implementation strategy
Ineffective leadership	Relationship management failure
Failure to enforce service level agreement	Ineffective/inaccurate reporting
	Planning incomplete

Economic

Incorrect pricing	Large lost opportunity costs
No critical mass of products or services	Lack of strategic partnerships
Non-supportive economic environment	Undue time pressure
Insufficient infrastructure investment	Unexpected costs
	Unexpected budget contraction

Legal

Poorly written contracts

Technical

Disruptive technologies introduced	Poor usability of technology
Overly complex implementation	Rapidly evolving standards

Marketing

Failure to market internally	Resistance to culture change
Heightened customer expectations	Shifting and increasing customer expectations

creating pizza pies. Although the highly successful chain creates a reasonable product, it isn't cheaper, tastier, or fresher than what most independent corner pizza shops can produce. Domino's real competency is its delivery service. Domino's is really a transportation company that happens to deliver pizzas.

Another risk factor in the area of management is applying the incorrect business model to correct a shortcoming of the company. Specifically, a shared services model may be inappropriate for a given corporation because of an inflexible culture, embedded resistance to change, and more attractive short-term models, such as outsourcing. Knowing when to walk away from a business model in favor of another is a challenge for senior management. An economic risk factor related to this decision is larger lost opportunity costs. Going down the wrong path in the face of impending failure at best results in huge sunken costs. At worst, there can be significant cost overruns and business unit failures.

Managing risk also includes the use of traditional business tools that can help senior management assess risk. These tools include:

- *Market Research.* Use focus groups, surveys, and related means to acquire information on the likely market for the product or service to be shifted to the new unit. A reasonable question to ask is: Is there likely to be sufficient long-term demand and volume to warrant the change? If so, what are the conditions for success? For example, corporate employees may be willing to give up local control of, say, copying, if the shared services copy center can return most jobs within the hour. However, if volume and capacity are such that most jobs will take three to five hours to complete, internal customer demand may be insufficient to support a shared services model.
- *Cash Flow Analysis.* Determine investment costs and how much cash will be generated each year in different scenarios.
- *Porter Five Forces Model.* Assess the competitiveness of a business based on analysis of the fundamental market forces that

are driving the industry: threat of substitutes, threat of new entrants, bargaining power of suppliers, bargaining power of buyers, and the intensity of rivalry among competitors.

- *Decision Tree Analysis.* Diagram a decision tree to organize the alternatives, risks, and uncertainty associated with a shared services implementation.

The results of these analyses have to be interpreted in light of senior management's instinctive view of the situation, including the unknowns. Managing in the face of uncertainty is simply a fact of life. Managing risk is doing the economically feasible to reduce the uncertainty to a point that decisions regarding risk reduction have some validity.

Failing Gracefully

Despite all of the steps taken to assure success, failures happen. As in the telemedicine example, unforeseen factors may crush what was once seen as a sure thing. Preparing to recover from a failure takes as much forethought as prevention. Preparing for a failure before it happens—akin to equipping an ocean liner with lifeboats—is usually handsomely rewarded. Having a backup plan in the event of a failed shared services initiative can be as simple as maintaining an established distributed model infrastructure in place until the shared services concept has proven itself over a period of acceptable performance.

Timing Is Everything

In moving to a shared services business model, change takes time and requires the coordinated timing of events. Signs that the timing is right for implementation of a shared services model include a general awareness of high internal cost of service, poor service quality, grassroots support for the change, and a corporation already faced with the need to downsize. However, even if the shared services business model seems viable, it may not be the most appropriate means of increasing corporate value at a particular point in the corporation's evolution.

Relevant questions to ask before making the move are:

- Is the current business model viable?
- Is the corporate culture ready for change?
- Is there a critical mass of internal customers?
- Is there general dissatisfaction with the way the corporation operates?
- What is the motivation to change now?
- What is the risk of changing now?
- What is the risk of not changing now?

For example, if the corporate culture isn't ready for change because of recent turmoil in the company or if there isn't yet a critical mass of potential internal customers, then it may be better to consider an outsourcing strategy and later, in six months or a year, reconsider a shared services model.

Control

The degree of control exercised by the parent corporation over the shared business unit defines many other aspects of the relationship between employees and management in the parent corporation and shared services business unit. The factors that require management control, and the degree of control they require are illustrated in Exhibit 2.8.

A shared business unit that is tightly controlled by the parent corporation may not benefit significantly from competition in the marketplace because the parent corporation will probably not abandon the unit. Senior management and employees of the shared business unit assume that the parent corporation is always in the position to back up the unit in times of dire need, and they act accordingly. If nothing else, senior management assumes that with control comes the financial

EXHIBIT 2.8

Effects of Corporate Control

Factor	Low Control	High Control
Shared Business Unit Benefit from Competition	High	Low
Parent Corp. Cultural Shift	High	Low
Parity	Variable	Low
Shared Business Unit Employee Security	Low	High
Corporate Management Resource Requirements	Low	High
Political Influence of Parent Corp. on Shared Business Unit	Low	High
Responsiveness of Shared Business Unit to Parent Corp.	Variable	High
Susceptibility of Shared Business Unit to Market Forces	High	Low

assistance or enough political clout to guarantee loans and other sources of capital.

The degree of control influences how internal customers interact and view the employees of the shared business unit. With tight control, which includes strict adherence to parent corporation policies, employees of the shared business unit may be perceived as internal slave labor. Similarly, employees of the shared business unit may feel like second-class citizens because they are in a subservient role to employees of the parent corporation.

A parallel in the civil sector of society would be the imposition of taxation without equal representation. Employees of a tightly controlled shared business unit have to abide by the rules and regulations of the parent corporation, but typically don't hold the same rights and privileges of corporate employees. For example, in the area of job security, employees of the shared business unit may feel that if they don't perform at 100 percent of their abilities, they'll be immediately downsized. For employees of the parent corporation spared the knife of the shared services model, it's business as usual.

The more autonomy given the shared business unit, including the choice of whether to accept business from the parent corporation, the more likely employees and management will feel and act as though they're operating at parity with internal customers. The ability to say no, even if it isn't exercised frequently, moves the employee of a shared business unit from a position of subservience to equality.

Knowledge Management

On one level, the shared services model is about reorganizing and redefining organizational behavior. More specifically, it's about manipulating the intellectual capital (knowledge assets) of the corporation; that is, whatever is of value to the organization in terms of human, structural, and customer capital (see Exhibit 2.9).

Human capital is the knowledge, skills, and competencies of the people in an organization. Human capital, which is owned by individuals that possess it, is the renewable component of intellectual capital. Structural capital is the process, structures, information systems, and patents that are independent of the people who created them. An efficient process for creating widgets is considered structural capital, for example. Customer capital is the value of an organization's relationships with its customers. Customer loyalty, usually defined by customer purchasing patterns, includes loyalty to a particular product or to any company product. Customer capital is partially owned by employees when the customer relationship is with the individual, and not the corporation.

Creating a shared services business unit involves moving human, structural, and, to a lesser degree, customer capital. For example, if the

EXHIBIT 2.9

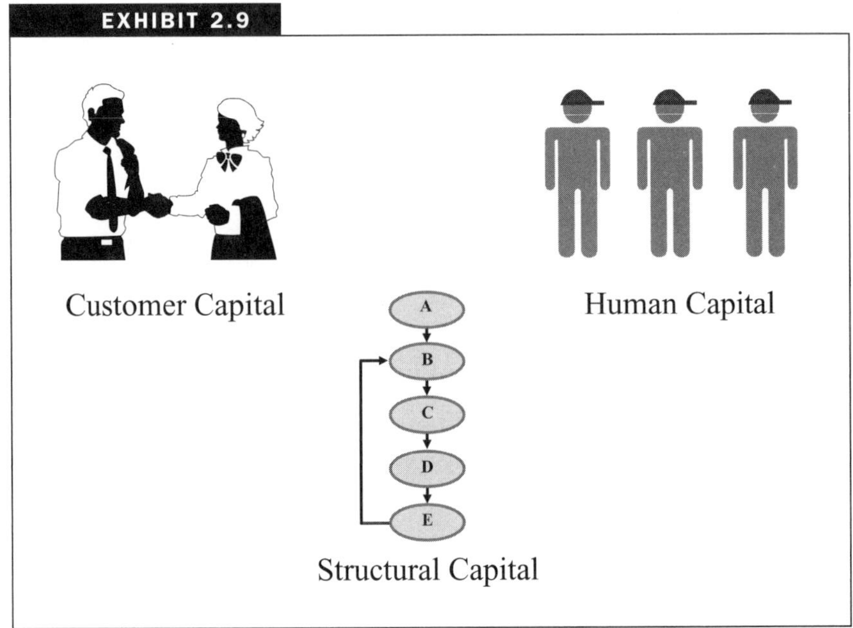

information technology functions of an organization are condensed into a separate shared services information technology center, then people (human capital), processes (structural capital), and potentially relationships with external customers (customer capital) are all affected. Knowledge management is relevant to this discussion because to compete successfully in today's economy, organizations have to treat the knowledge that contributes to their core competencies just as they would any other strategic, irreplaceable asset. Instituting a shared services model involves the preservation and packaging of corporate knowledge—information in the context in which it is used—and the selection of what knowledge stays with the parent corporation and what is distilled out to go with the shared business unit.

Every successful organization uses knowledge management to some degree, though not necessarily in a sophisticated, formalized way. Typical knowledge management practices include acquiring knowledge from customers, creating new revenues from existing knowledge, capturing an individual's tacit knowledge for reuse, and reviewing the predictors of a successful initiative. Abiding by knowledge management principles can help facilitate the adaptability of the shared services business models and processes, especially when implementation involves the consolidation of multinational centers. For example, as noted earlier, knowledge about core competencies should normally remain with the parent corporation.

In partitioning shared business unit activities from those of the parent corporation, determining what intellectual capital stays with the company and what goes with the new business unit is a typical knowledge management decision. For example, a key issue in managing the knowledge of the parent corporation is determining whether the leadership of the shared business unit should come from the parent organization or from outside the corporation. The advantage of identifying and growing leadership inside the parent organization is that the competency, vision, and goals of the management can be closely assessed and cultivated so that they are congruent with those of the parent corporation's senior management. The downside is that a manager spun off from the parent corporation to run the shared business unit also represents a potential loss in human capital that may be irreplaceable.

Summary

From the perspective of the parent corporation, moving to a shared services model entails a degree of risk. In transferring employees and management to a shared business unit, there's a chance of losing intellectual capital, especially as the degree of control over the shared business unit is lessened. There's a risk of losing customers because of a disruption of services caused by a problematic transition. There's also the risk of alienating large numbers of employees, and of the small business unit failing to meet expectations of improving the parent corporation's bottom line. Fortunately, there are numerous tools and techniques, traditional management tools and knowledge management techniques, to help senior management reduce these and other risks.

The next chapter examines these and other factors from the perspective of the shared business unit—it employees and its management.

People seldom improve when they have no other model but themselves to copy after.

Oliver Goldsmith

CHAPTER 3

Shared Business Unit

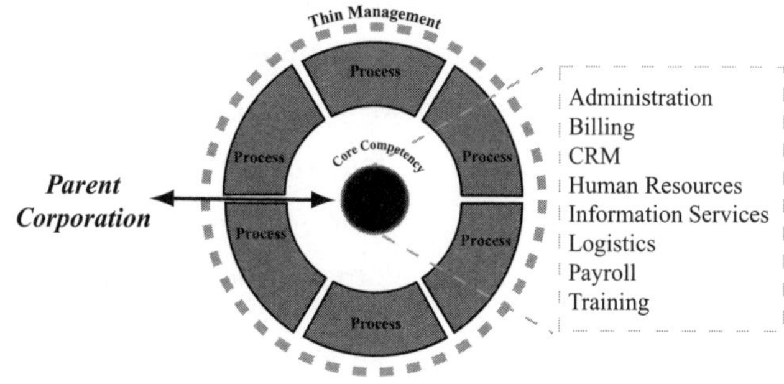

Shared Business Unit

After reading this chapter you will be able to

- Appreciate the unique challenges faced by the shared business unit's senior management
- Understand the significance of separating governance from the delivery of service in the shared business unit
- Understand the significance of chargeback and other billing practices in establishing the culture in the shared business unit
- Understand the evolution of a shared business unit from tightly held unit to a freestanding, competitive, market-driven company capable of competing in the open market
- Appreciate the challenges faced by human resources, in terms of maintaining employee morale, attracting and keeping good employees, and operating with uncertainty in the work environment
- Understand the range of possible customer relationships between the shared business unit and employees in the parent corporation

For most companies, so-called back-end functions such as billing, human resources, information services, payroll, and training, while necessary for operation, don't normally provide a competitive advantage. For a business in, say, the medical industry, most potential customers comparing two competing companies probably won't consider how payroll is handled—even if the information were publicized. What potential customers will consider, however, is the relative price of medical services, quality of the service, or the timeliness of service. In this regard, a payroll service that is inexpensive, efficient, and requires a minimum of oversight may allow the business to offer medical services at a slightly better price, at a better level of quality, or perhaps with more timely delivery, depending on how the resources recovered from extracting the inefficiencies in the payroll system are redistributed in the company.

The cost of back-end functions takes center stage when mergers and acquisitions create redundancies in personnel and operations. Bloated back-end functions are a target for downsizing and cost-cutting measures such as shared services. Similarly, when companies need to focus on growth through decreasing their time to market or increasing product or service quality, the ability to move back-end functions off-site and under separate management frees up physical space, management, and other resources. The new resources can result in a competitive advantage for the company.

This chapter explores the issues involved in implementing a shared services model from the perspective of the senior management of the shared business unit. To illustrate, let's continue to explore the events at State General Hospital.

Payroll Services

With pressure from Medicaid and other third-party payers, the senior management of State General Hospital decides to become part of the

HealthCare Partners network. The move legitimizes the hospital's prior ad-hoc affiliation with other teaching hospitals and satellite clinics in the area and promises cost cutting opportunities by combining redundant services.

One of the first moves by the senior management of HealthCare Partners, which includes the CEO from each of the member institutions, is to form a shared services payroll business unit that processes payroll for all member institutions (see Exhibit 3.1). The move should reduce employee count at each of the institutions to 15, down from over 50, save about 30 percent on each transaction, and free up office space. Nearly 10,000 employees are on the combined payroll of the HealthCare Partners system, 3,000 of whom are from State General Hospital.

To implement the shared payroll service, the senior management of the HealthCare Partners system names a transition team composed of an

EXHIBIT 3.1

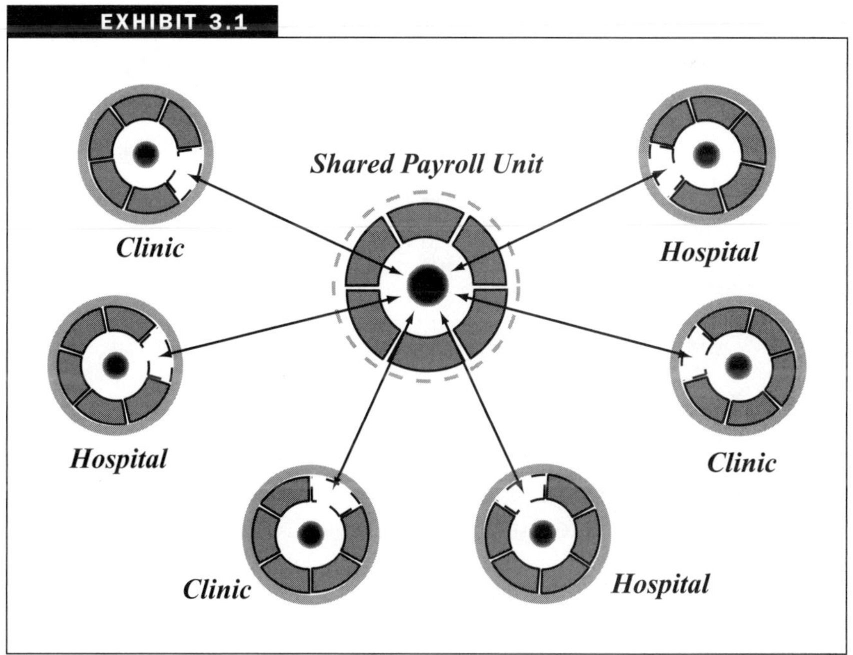

TIPS & TECHNIQUES

Getting to Know Your Employees

In evaluating your employees in terms of levels of stress, it helps to have a baseline with which their current behavior can be compared. Although there are a variety of psychological instruments and tests that can be applied to classify employees in terms of personality types, an easy approach is to simply categorize employees into one of four basic styles. In their book *People Styles at Work* (Amacom, 1996), Robert Bolton and Dorothy Grover Bolton classify employees as either analytical, amiable, driver, or expressive, based on their relative assertiveness and responsiveness (see exhibit).

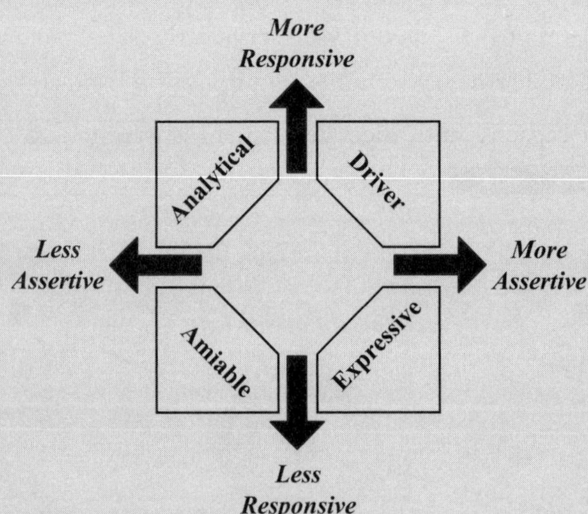

Using their classification scheme, analytical types score low on the assertiveness and responsiveness scale, whereas Expressives score high on both accounts. Drivers are more assertive and less responsive, while Amiables are less assertive but more responsive.

interim manager, a human resources (HR) director, and an outside consultant, and provides the team with a budget and a timeline for the transition. In order to prevent disruption of payroll services, it's decided that the shared payroll service will operate in parallel to existing payroll functions until the system is functioning adequately, and then, institution by institution, the service will cut over to the new system. The rolling transfer of payroll function is intended to be complete within the year, meaning that the downsizing of employees now covering the payroll function will occur over a period of about nine months.

The HR director's first step is to travel to each of the institutions affected and interview the employees associated with the payroll function. She describes the transition process, the timetable, and offers a few employees jobs in the new unit. The employees who will be downsized are offered assistance in transferring to another department in their institution or outplacement assistance. Employees are encouraged to work at their current capacity until their department is transitioned over to the unit; encouragement takes the form of a generous severance package.

Part of the reason for the transition time is to identify employees to transfer or downsize, to understand each institution's payroll process, and to work with information services at each institution to funnel payroll data electronically into the shared services payroll unit. A parallel information services initiative will combine the payroll systems, but that won't be finished in time for the payroll transition. In the interim period, a patchwork of interfaces to existing payroll systems will be used. An outside consultant manages this initiative.

The ancillary processes associated with the new payroll unit include customer service, marketing and sales, accounting, materials stocking, and information services, purchasing, orders, shipping, human resources, and management, which includes production planning and scheduling, as illustrated in Exhibit 3.2. That is, the shared business unit, implemented to allow the parent corporation to focus on its core competencies,

EXHIBIT 3.2

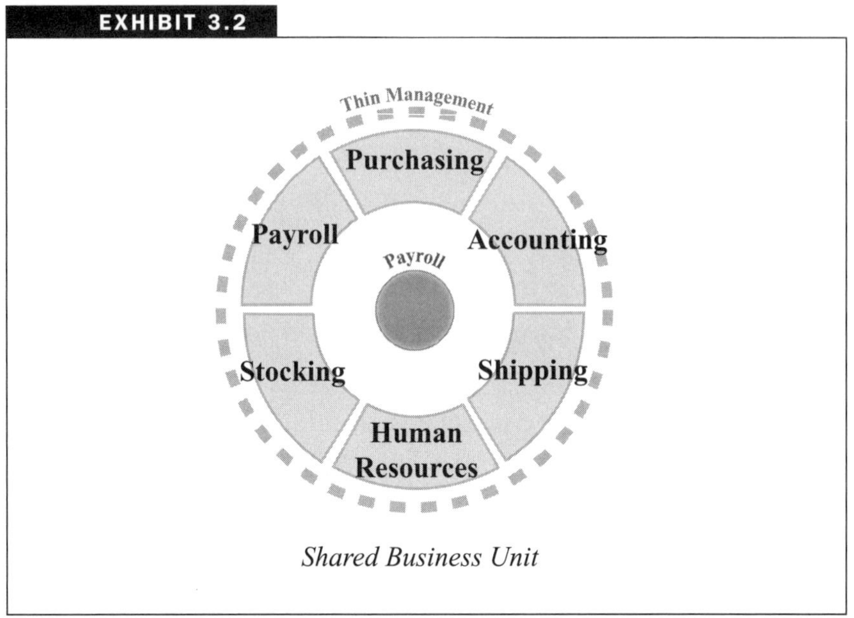

Shared Business Unit

is itself faced with the overhead of back-end processes that don't directly add to its competitiveness. Nonetheless, these functions, such as human resources, are vital to the continued operation of the unit. Since the unit's employees don't know some of these back-end functions, they are offered training over the Web to bring them up to speed.

From the perspective of senior management of HealthCare Partners, the payroll function is simply a back-end function that is overseen by the unit's manager. As long as checks are issued on time, accurately, and at or below target cost, senior management is content with the unit's management. Senior management can focus instead on the core business of the health-care system—improving patient care. However, from the unit manager's perspective, the operation is much more than a box on an organization chart. It's a complex system with a variety of functions supporting the core payroll function. As shown in Exhibit 3.3, from a process perspective, there are multiple steps that affect various employees and the institutions involved.

EXHIBIT 3.3

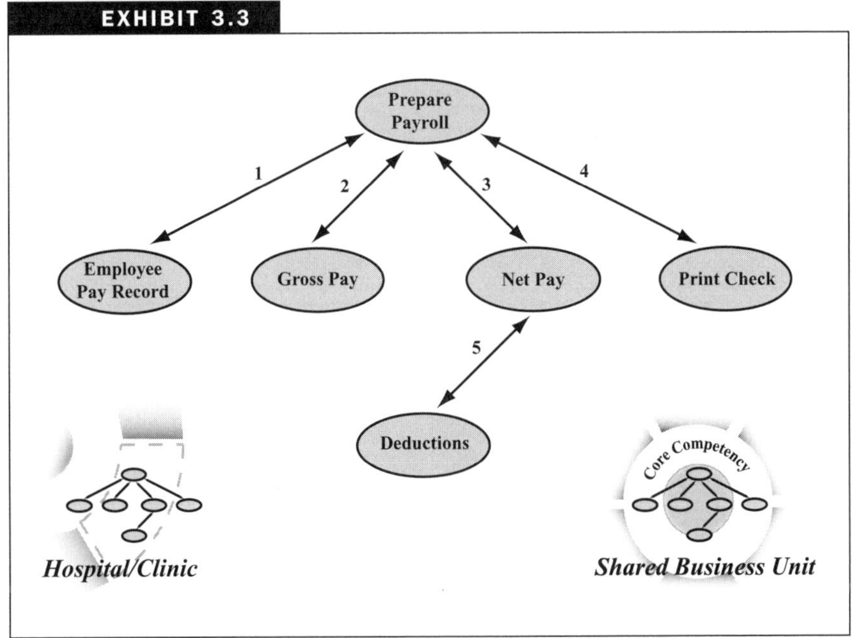

One of the manager's tasks is to streamline each step in this process so that the core competency of the unit—getting checks out to employees of HealthCare Partners—occurs on time and within the budgetary constraints established by senior management. The manager knows that these constraints are based on payroll processing rates available from a large commercial payroll service. The manager's job is to cut costs so that parity is reached with outside service prices. One of the manager's other responsibilities is internal marketing and sales. Since payroll isn't something normally considered at board meetings as long as it's functioning properly, his charge is to highlight the unit's performance, compared to industry standards of cost, error rate, and customer satisfaction, based on the number of complaints handled by his customer services representatives. The unit manager is also quick to offer new services tailored to each participating institution basis, including automatic deposit and a variety of payroll deductions.

From the perspective of employees of the new unit, there is a feeling of both uncertainty and excitement. Because the HR director is careful to offer positions only to those employees with high energy and an entrepreneurial spirit, morale is good, despite the long-term uncertainty of the unit's existence. Everyone in the unit is aware of the competition, and their need to compete successfully with the competition in order to stay in business. As such, they are encouraged to submit ideas on how to streamline operations, and employees are rewarded for ideas that are eventually adopted. Individuals now bear increased accountability for the unit's performance.

Part of the reason why the unit's employees feel like second-class citizens is related to their new relationship with the hospitals and clinics. In their prior jobs, they worked under the umbrella of a huge employer with hundreds or thousands of coworkers. Now, in the service unit, those same coworkers are customers, working within the same expectations for good service as they had before. Although some employees were spared downsizing, their transfer to the shared services unit is perceived as a demotion of sorts, especially when former coworkers-turned-customers demand service. On a positive note, the customer support personnel of the unit are pleased to be free of having to enforce the rules for payroll established by their former employers. Their challenge becomes providing the customer with the best service possible.

Two years into the shared service unit's existence, the criteria established by HealthCare Partners senior management in terms of revenue and quality of service are met. The consultant, who was relied on increasingly less since the system transitions fully after one year, moves on to another project within HealthCare Partners. Similarly, the transition manager is replaced with an operations-oriented manager and moved over to Information Services where his expertise is needed to help management with a much larger shared services implementation in progress.

The experiences of management, human resources, and the

employees of the shared services unit illustrate several key issues for shared services:

- *A successful shared services implementation demands a special breed of employee.* Employees who are content with maintaining the status quo or afraid of change won't survive in the shared business unit. More important, risk-averse employees without an entrepreneurial spirit won't contribute to the success of the unit.
- *Managing human resources is key.* The parallel functioning of existing payroll systems and the new unit was possible only because of the way the transition was handled. Both downsized and transferred employees were fully informed about the transition process, including the timeline. Furthermore, the morale and productivity of employees destined to be downsized was maintained by outplacement services and a generous severance package. Employees were given between three and nine months notice—more than enough time for them to secure other employment.
- *A shared services implementation doesn't occur in a vacuum.* There are interdependencies that must be addressed in transitioning to a new system. For example, existing lines of communications must be evaluated and modified if necessary so that the processes handled by the shared business unit can be supported. In this example, the former ties with Information Services in each institution had to be modified to support the shared payroll services until the system-wide information network could be developed.
- *Training transitioned employees is key to success.* Simply throwing employees into a new management structure and work environment without additional training is a recipe for disaster. In this example, employees of the unit had to be given training on back-end processes associated with the unit—processes such as billing and accounts payable that had been invisible to employees in the past because they were handled by another back-end service at their institution.

- *The quality and experience of the transition team largely define the odds of success.* The transition manager, consultant, and human resources specialist were obviously experienced in handling a transition process to a shared business unit with minimal disruption to existing services. When performed properly, the employees in the parent organization are unaware of the change.
- *The culture established for the shared business unit is a good predictor of success.* An environment in which innovation is rewarded, an entrepreneurial spirit is fostered, and where everyone knows what's expected of them promotes success, regardless of the endeavor.
- *Specific skills are required of the transitional manager.* Given that creating a shared business unit is like creating a startup operation, a transitional manager with an entrepreneurial bent, flexibility in approach, and with a good presence or charisma is key to success. In the example of HealthCare Partners, much of the transition manager's role is in marketing and selling the payroll unit's services to customers within the network.
- *A factor that distinguishes the shared services model from internal services is the separation of delivering service and management.* Employees of the payroll unit no longer had to contend with enforcing corporate policies, such as minimum payroll deduction amounts, but were free to focus on serving the customer as efficiently and effectively as possible.
- *Information technology provides much of the leverage for downsizing.* Part of the reason that so few employees are required in the HealthCare Partners payroll system is that most processes are controlled or enabled by computer technology.

These and related issues are expanded in the following section.

Implementation Phases

The creation of the shared services payroll system for HealthCare Partners illustrates the typical process of forming a shared business unit.

The five phases of business unit genesis, Identification, Mobilization, Consolidation, Extraction, and Encapsulation are depicted in Exhibit 3.4. The five phases are discussed in relation to the HealthCare Partners example, below.

Phase I: Identification

In this, the first phase of implementation, the parent company identifies the back-end processes to be moved to the shared business unit. For example, the payroll processing in each of the hospitals and clinics in the HealthCare Partners system was identified as the back-end process to move to the shared business unit. Identifying back-end services to move should take into account the timing of other events in the organization, such as a reorganization following a merger. It should also take into account the functions that will provide the most visible and likely "win" for a shared business model, and supply traction for following shared

EXHIBIT 3.4

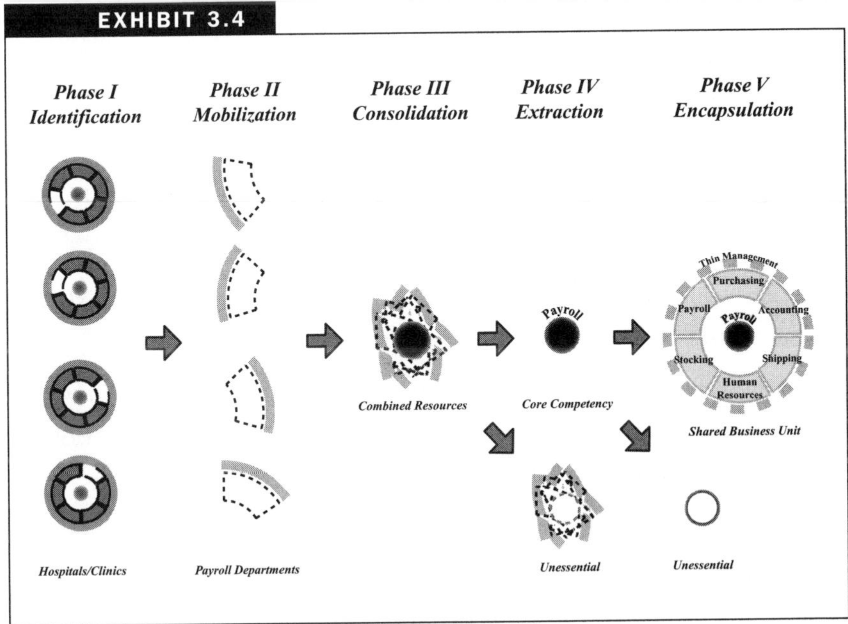

services implementations. The risks associated with moving a particular service to a shared services model must also be considered.

Of course, for the manager charged with running the business unit, there may be no choice in the matter. However, if the manager identified as the shared services expert can select from several projects to champion, the risks of failure should be weighed against any prospect of gain. For example, if the move to a shared services payroll system fails, it's likely that most employees in the organization will be aware of the failure, and the manager may lose his job. However, if the accounts payable process is disabled for a month or two, at worst a few vendors may be upset over late payments.

Phase II: Mobilization

In the mobilization phase, the processes are moved out of the disparate centers of activity within the parent corporation. The mobilization phase is selective in that some resources are earmarked for the new shared business unit, while the parent corporation will absorb or discard others. In the HealthCare Partners example, the HR director was faced with the challenge of identifying potential future employees of the shared business unit. Those employees who did not represent the future core competency of the shared payroll system were slated for downsizing.

Phase III: Consolidation

In the consolidation phase, the resources identified as part of the shared business unit are combined with an eye to further streamlining operations and identifying unnecessary employees, management, and process support. The distinction between mobilization and consolidation is often a soft one, as in the case of HealthCare Partners, when the move to a shared business unit isn't sudden and all encompassing, but rather occurs over several months and is instituted on a department-by-department or institution-by-institution basis.

Phase IV: Extraction

In the Extraction phase, the resources and processes that will form the core competency of the shared business unit are put in place and extraneous resources, that is, redundant employees, are downsized. Downsizing is limited in scope and typically involves a reduction in force. Employees and managers who don't fit the new culture are let go or transferred.

Phase V: Encapsulation

In this phase, the resources supporting the core competency of the shared business unit are encapsulated in back-end functions. For example, the employees of the business unit are given standard back-office functions, such as human resource, payroll, stocking, accounting, and purchasing support—business processes that were formerly provided by the individual institutions in the network. During encapsulation, the management structure crystallizes into a tight, organized unit

Throughout this process, there are multiple instances of downsizing as it becomes clear which resources are needed to provide the core competency of the shared business unit. This places considerable responsibility on the HR director, who must attend to bolstering the morale of those employees who stay, while culling unnecessary resources from the employee pool.

Customer Focus

As noted in Chapter 2, a shared business unit can cater to both internal and external customers, where internal customers are employees of the parent corporation and external customers are from the open market. As shown in Exhibit 3.5, external customers can interact with the shared business units through a variety of touch points. However, this situation represents the end-point in the maturation of the shared

EXHIBIT 3.5

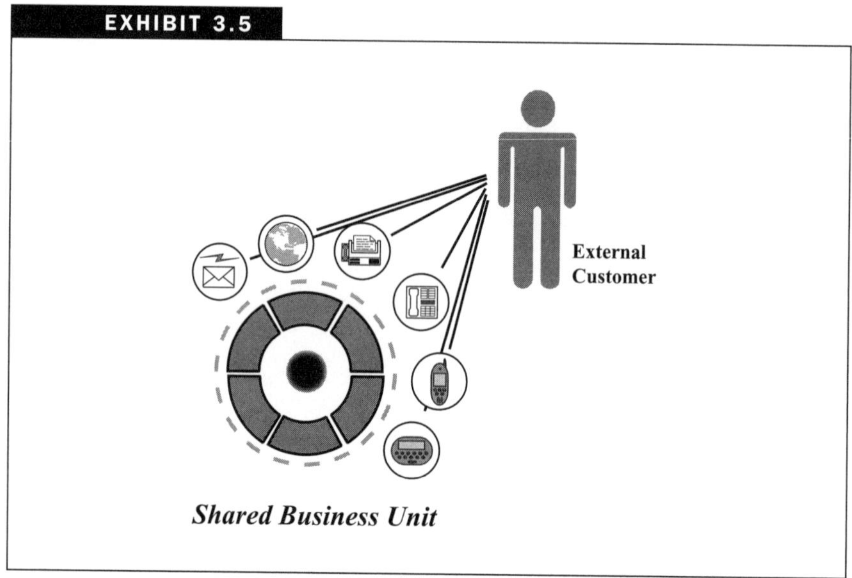

business unit. The customer of a newly created shared business unit, and even one that has been in existence for several years, is much more likely to be internal, with interactions like those shown in Exhibit 3.6.

The interactions with external customers through the shared business unit are virtually identical to those that existed through the parent corporation. The main difference is in the management of the customer relationship. The interactions between external customers and the shared business unit have to be beneficial to the parent corporation, regardless of whether they are advantageous to the shared business unit. For example, the shared business unit may be forced to provide a service outside of its core competency, simply to appease the parent corporation.

However, when internal customers interact with the shared business unit, the focus is mutually beneficial exchanges between the customers and the business unit, with little or no regard to the parent corporation. This shift in focus is central to the maturation of the shared business unit to a semiautonomous entity capable of eventually taking on external customers in the open market.

EXHIBIT 3.6

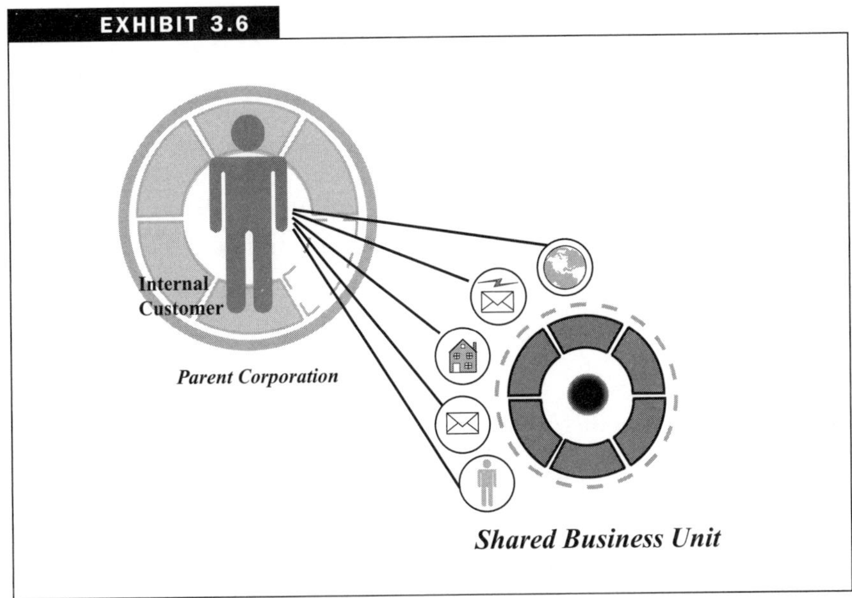

In a tightly held, newly created shared business unit, management may have no choice but to provide the services dictated by the parent corporation, even if the relationship results in a poor use of internal resources. For example, customers may demand personal, custom service, when the shared business unit is understaffed to provide anything but a standard service package. In addition, from the perspective of the shared business unit, there is a cost of an ongoing relationship with internal customers, regardless of whether the relationship is profitable or not. For example, there is the cost of doing business, which may include ancillary services such as internal customer support. The shared business payroll service in the example earlier may have to invest one or two employees in providing customer support for all of the employees in the HealthCare Partners network, even though its main competency is handling payroll.

Shifting employees to customer support, in addition to distracting management and employees of the payroll unit from payroll functions, also incurs a lost opportunity cost associated with supporting ancillary functions. The cost of doing business also involves the ongoing task of gathering and sorting data on internal customers to determine what can and should be offered to groups of internal customers in exchange for repeat business. However, despite these costs, the shared business unit may be compelled to serve employees of the parent corporation, especially early on in the life of the shared business unit.

Treating all internal customers as valued customers has the advantage of simplicity. Unlike businesses that must compete on the open market, there is no need to create customer profiles and track customer activity over time to discover which customers are profitable and which ones are not, or which types of service provide the greatest profit margins. The disadvantage is that the shared business unit may be dissipating its resources on activities that don't add to long-term viability as an autonomous business.

With maturity and looser control by the parent corporation, management of the shared business unit may be able to engage in CRM activities that improve its profitable activities. Achieving a profitable or at least mutually beneficial relationship with the parent corporation involves gaining a better understanding of the internal customer.

360-Degree View of the Internal Customer

Acquiring a better understanding of the internal customer for better managing the customer relationship requires an investment in data collection and management. Data from all customer interactions are collected, verified, and then analyzed to obtain a better view of the customer. The first and most important thing to know about customers is whether they are a current or potential source of revenue (in excess of expenses), or whether the customer is a loss for the shared business unit.

If a customer is expected to remain unprofitable for the duration of the relationship, then the business unit lacks motivation to continue the relationship past its contractual obligations, and has no need to gather more customer information. For example, management of the shared payroll unit may determine that processing payroll for the smaller clinics in the HealthCare Partners network is unprofitable, in part because of the cost of customer support. As a result, in the long-term, management of the shared payroll unit has to focus on the profitable hospital employees if the unit is to become an autonomous business that can compete in the open market.

Information that should be gathered to provide a complete, 360-degree view of the customer (see Exhibit 3.7) includes:

- *Needs.* Corporate employees look to the shared business unit to satisfy their needs. In the context of the shared business unit, needs are defined as the services addressed by the core competencies of the unit, such as payroll or billing services. Customer needs should be readily quantifiable, because the parent corporation largely defines them. For example, the number of employees in the parent corporation defines the number of checks that must be processed every two weeks for payroll.
- *Wants.* In contrast to absolute needs, wants are services that are desired though not essential. Customers of the payroll unit

EXHIBIT 3.7

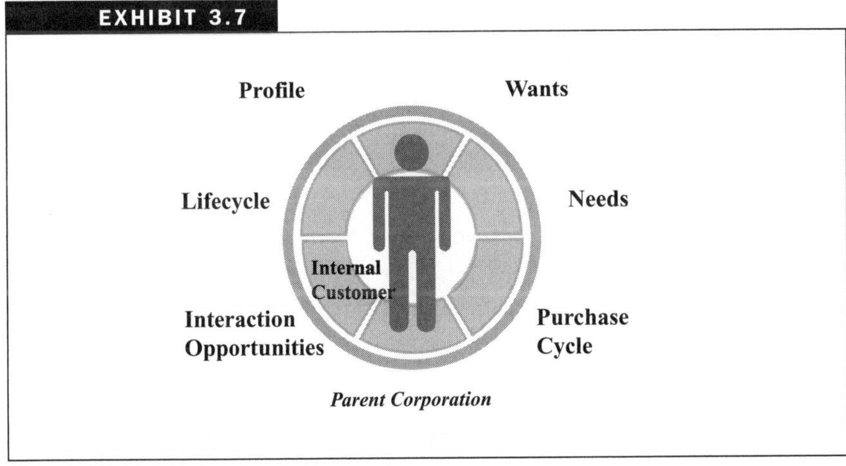

may want personal, immediate customer service regarding their payroll account. It's important for the shared business unit to be able to accurately predict customer wants so that it can decide which ones to address and which ones to ignore. Customer desires represent opportunities for added services that can be provided at an extra margin later in the evolution of the business unit. For example, one of the hospitals in the HealthCare Partners network may want additional payroll services such as faster turn-around or more frequent checks for consultants, temporary workers, and other employees, and be willing to pay a premium for them.

- *Purchase Cycle.* One of the criteria in evaluating the value customers present for future business is the customer purchase cycle, the time between a customer's repeat purchase of services. The frequency and likelihood of additional purchases as well as the nature of those purchases depend on both the customer and the product. For some services, such as payroll, the purchase cycle is fixed. However, other services, such as training, can be cyclical and topic-dependent. For example, in the HealthCare Partners network, new employees may be required to go through a biohazard safety training program as part of employee orientation. The demand for this training or orientation is a function of employee turnover, which is influenced by the external economy, the time of year, and other, unknown factors.
- *Interaction Opportunities.* Every customer interaction represents an opportunity to gather customer information and increase the odds of future business. However, there is also a cost for each customer interaction, especially if it's through customer service or some other high-cost interaction. In evaluating the value of a particular customer or class of customers, management of the shared business should be able to quantify the costs and benefits of all customer interactions.
- *Lifecycle.* The customer lifecycle includes the typical career

IN THE REAL WORLD

Not All Spin-offs Are Created Equal

One way companies grow and achieve greater market share is to spin off a subsidiary that offers a core competency to the open market. For example, Apple Computer spun off the Claris Software and Palm Inc., maker of the popular handheld personal digital assistant (PDA), spun off its software division into a separate subsidiary.

Forming a separate company in this way provides a legal mechanism for transferring patents, code, employees, and other assets to the new company in exchange for stock in the new venture. Financial independence for the subsidiary can be attained through an initial public offering or by taking on an outside investor. In either case, as a separate company, services are billed and paid for just as they are with any other supplier-customer relationship.

The practice of spinning off companies contrasts with the shared service model, where the parent organization intentionally maintains control of the shared unit for several years, only releasing it after a relatively long gestational period.

events of classes of customers. By accurately predicting the lifecycle of its customers, management can proactively offer appropriate products and services to its customers to extend its relationship with them. For example, customers of computer training services can be expected to progress through different needs as their careers advance. Employees may require basic computer skills training when they first join the parent corporation, progressing to more sophisticated software applications, including spreadsheets, databases, and statistical analysis or graphics applications as they grow within the organization and take on different roles.

- *Profile.* In order for management to allocate its resources most effectively, it's in the shared service unit's best interest to know as much relevant information about the customer as possible. A shared business unit that offers specific training in, say, the use of computers for word processing, can expect a much greater demand from secretaries than professional staff, who may be more interested in, for example, training in statistical analysis and graphing tools.

Segmentation

The rationale for going through the trouble and expense of gathering data to create customer profiles is to segment customers into homogenous groups of similar behavior. As shown in Exhibit 3.8, marketers traditionally group customers into geographic, demographic, behavioral, and psychographic segments.

EXHIBIT 3.8

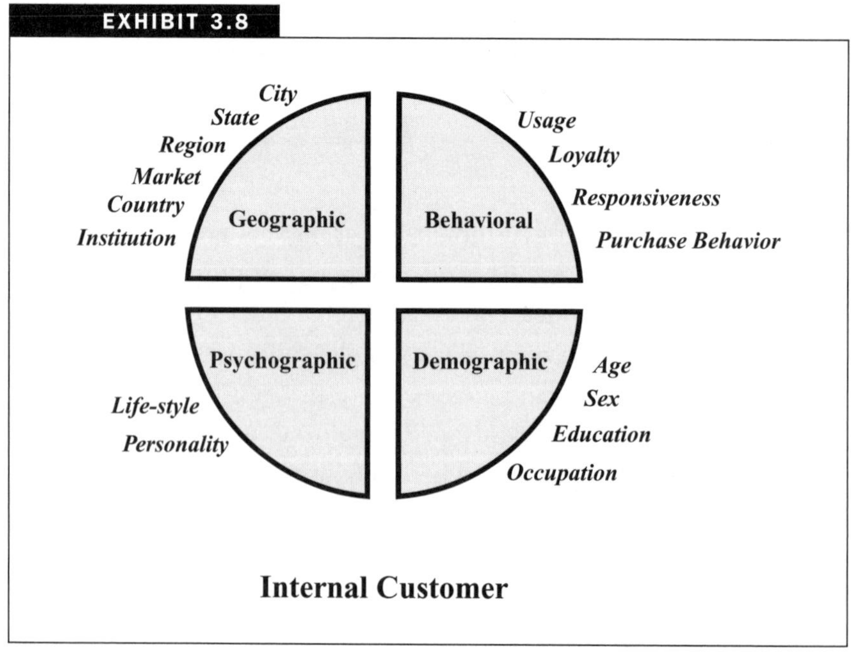

Geographic segmentation groups customers by political borders, such as city, state, region, or country, as well as by institution or economic market. From the perspective of the shared business unit of a multinational corporation, with dozens of offices located around the world, it may be critical to segment customers by country in order to market and deliver its services efficiently. For example, a shared business unit that provides human resource support to offices in the United States, Australia, China, Japan, and Germany will likely encounter widely varying costs, regulation overhead, and legal representation requirements in each market. If the shared unit is located in the United States, then there is also the transportation cost issue, in that human resource-related affairs have to be handled in person in China and will be much more resource intensive than similar tasks in the United States.

Demographic segmentation divides customers based on characteristics such as age, sex, education, and occupation. In the workplace, where law forbids discrimination or special treatment by age or sex, education and occupation are more relevant predictors of customer behavior. For example, in the HealthCare Partners network, clinicians are likely to have markedly different computer training requirements than administrative support staff. A shared services training unit might offer clinicians training in accessing and completing the network's online medical record, for example, an application that would be off-limits to nonclinical employees.

Behavioral segmentation groups customers based on observable behaviors such as service usage, loyalty to the service unit, responsiveness to promotions, and purchase behavior. As noted in Chapter 2, customers who exhibit loyalty behaviors are more likely to continue to do business with the unit in the future.

Psychographic segmentation is the softest of the four segmentation strategies, in that it is based on qualitative measures such as lifestyle and personality. Lifestyle measures include activities, interests, and opinions, whereas personality measures include risk-aversion, status-seeking behavior, and degree of gregariousness. Psychographic segmentation can be valuable in identifying customers who will likely respond to particular marketing strategies.

Segmentation is especially useful in allocating limited resources outside of the core competency of the unit, such as customer service representative time, and to identify customers who may be willing to pay extra for service to fulfill their wants. Segmentation is also useful in creating marketing campaigns targeted at a specific subset of internal customers. Once customers within the parent organization have been segmented, management should be able to more easily decide how to allocate resources maximum unit revenue or profitability.

The advantage of marketing to the internal customers of the parent corporation is that they are a finite, well-defined market. With sufficient historical or current connections with senior management and other members of the corporation, the manager of the shared business unit should be able to definitively create a 360-degree view of the customer. In addition, the touch points with customers are limited in number, but those that are available typically extend deep into the parent corporation. For example, although TV, radio, and perhaps the phone are off-limits as touch points because of inappropriateness or disruptiveness, e-mail and personal contact may provide rich avenues to communications and relationship development. The availability of other touch points depends on the corporate culture and the physical proximity of the shared business unit to the parent corporation.

Damage Control

Inevitably, some customers will be disappointed with the service provided by the shared business unit. If the customers are profitable or otherwise benefit the shared business unit, then management should take measures such that the disappointed or even disgruntled customers return despite their bad experience. Damage control typically entails:

- *Service-recovery training.* Not only should employees who interact with customers receive training in which problems are the most common and how to handle them, but how to enlist the customer's support in finding solutions to their problems.
- *Defining recovery standards.* Formal and informal standards of recovery from mistakes should be established. Recovery standards established before problems arise save time and minimize the disruption of normal business activity.
- *Establishing a complaint system.* Policies and procedures for complaint resolution should be established to minimize disruption and maximize responsiveness to customers.
- *Providing organized support for employees.* Procedures should be established so that others can support employees who interact directly with customers in the shared business unit. For example, if a customer poses a technical question, there should be a point person in the technical side of operations who can be available to assist the customer.
- *Organizational standards on quality.* Given that one reason for moving to a shared services model is to provide enhanced levels of service, standards on service quality should be established so that everyone in the service unit is aware of what is expected of them. Ad-hoc standards lead to inefficiencies and rewarding customers who make the most noise instead of those with the greatest need.

Damage control is most effective when it's defined a priori and not a reflexive response to an acute failure to deliver service to a customer. A manager with a thorough understanding of shared business unit operations and the range of possible failures is in the best position to define damage control scenarios that minimize disruption and expense on the unit's side while addressing the customer's needs.

At the Core: Strategic Services

Typical back-end processes that don't directly add to the competitiveness of the parent corporation, such as human resources and payroll, become the core competency of the shared business unit. In general, the value of these back-end processes is defined in terms of cost, assuming that delivery is timely and within some reasonable range of service. Otherwise, one billing service is difficult to differentiate from another, and lack of differentiation means ease of substitution.

However, a parent corporation may also rely on a shared services model to handle strategic services that are specialized and more difficult to replace with the generic services of a third party. The strategic services that can be supplied by shared business units generally fall into one of five categories:

1. *Market Intelligence.* Provide trend and market analysis, survey results, and information on what the competition is up to.
2. *Marketing.* Create advertising campaigns, slogans, corporate logos, messages, and manage promotions.
3. *Sales Support.* Create catalogs, performing customer needs analysis, and ordering.
4. *Customer Support.* Provide CRM expertise and support.
5. *Technology.* Provide networking, database, and software support, and information-based processes that can streamline internal and external operations.

Shared business units charged with supplying these and other strategic services have the greatest likelihood of progressing to an autonomous, profit-driven company that can compete in the open market.

Human Resources Challenge

The human resources manager on the shared services implementation team is faced with a potentially daunting array of challenges (see Exhibit 3.9). Given that one of the major responsibilities of the human resources

EXHIBIT 3.9

Human Resources Challenges

Attracting new staff
Corporate approach inappropriate
Employees must be trained
Employees need to master new interactive styles
Must do the dirty work of downsizing
Original employee pool may be too small
Potential for employee burnout
Retaining good employees
Understanding shared services

manager is deciding which employees to downsize, transfer or keep, the job is definitely not for the thin-skinned manager. In addition, the employees transferred into the shared business unit are typically in a state of disarray.

The employee culture within a shared business unit is typified by increased stress, owing to factors such as the drastic culture change, uncertainty about their future with the company, and lowered self-esteem (see Exhibit 3.10). The employees of the business unit are under pressure to produce more, with higher accountability, and in a new reporting structure under new management. As in the case of HealthCare Partners, the shared business unit is home to employees from several institutions, most of whom have never worked together before. Considering that the employees in the parent corporation may look down on the business unit employees as dedicated servants of sorts, it's understandable that many shared business unit employees feel like second-class citizens. Add to this diminished self-esteem at work, the personal disruption for employees who have to relocate their families to

EXHIBIT 3.10

Employee Stressors

Culture Change
Greater Management Expectations
Greater Uncertainty
Higher Accountability
Lowered Self-Esteem
Pressure for Innovation and Efficiency
New Management Style
New Reporting Structure
Personal Lifestyle Disruption

another state or country, and it's obvious that the human resources manager is going to have a challenge on his or her hands.

One characteristic of the shared business unit is that there is constant pressure to provide a higher quality service at competitive prices. However, the focus on efficiency is counter to that of innovation. Innovation requires flexibility and time for strategic analysis. If the time crunch and focus on efficiency extends from ground-level employees to management, then the business unit may not be able to sustain itself in the long run as an autonomous entity, but will be tied to the parent corporation, which will do the thinking and planning for the unit. However, from the perspective of the shared business unit, there has to be time for local, internal innovation. There are also issues of safety concerns and poor quality service when efficiency is the primary driving force.

In the early transition periods where the culture is undergoing transformation and employees are finding a new place for themselves in the organization, there is significant potential for employee burnout. For the typical employee transferred from large corporate setting to a smaller, lean, shared business unit, the relative changes in the working environment can be profound. The most obvious change is that there are fewer people doing more work, and doing it faster, often in tighter quarters, with less support, and with higher quality requirements than before.

Given the potential for employee burnout, it's important for management to both minimize stress and recognize signs of undue stress. For example, people under stress typically respond to stressful situations by exaggerating their basic coping style. An employee who is normally socially engaging may lash out and verbally attack management or coworkers when under stress. Similarly, employees who are normally authoritative become autocratic, while those who are normally supportive and cooperative simply acquiesce. The quiet and less emotional employees may avoid participation altogether and eschew emotional involvement with other employees or management.

At extreme levels of stress, employees may show behaviors that are opposite of what they normally exhibit. For example, someone who is normally socially engaging may turn quiet. At very high levels of stress, employees may "flip" into other behaviors as well. For example, employees and managers once considered friends could suddenly become bitter enemies.

One way to minimize the chances of employee burnout is to eliminate uncertainty in the work environment. To this end, employee performance expectations should be specific, achievable, time-bound, measurable, and results-oriented. Even if the environment is constantly shifting below their feet, most employees will take solace in knowing exactly what is expected of them and that the expectations are realistic and achievable.

Money Matters

In the progression of a shared business unit from a tightly controlled entity to an autonomous profit-oriented business, one of the major distinctions is how money or the exchange of value is handled. As in the case of an internal, centralized service model, the first stage of billing is typically to assign the cost of the shared services unit to overhead cost, where the service provided by the shared services is unmanaged and hidden (see Exhibit 3.11). The next stage is to base transactions on a negotiated fee, where the value of the service provided by the shared services unit is negotiated by management of the business unit and the parent company. This method is typically followed by the practice of assigning a fee based on allocation of services. Last is the fee-for-service stage, when a standard fee is paid by the parent corporation, in the form of cash, charge card, or check for services rendered by the shared business unit.

Both allocation and negotiated fee practices are chargeback mechanisms. Chargeback is a transitional system of internal charging for services that provides a visible means of exchanging value for value. The use

EXHIBIT 3.11

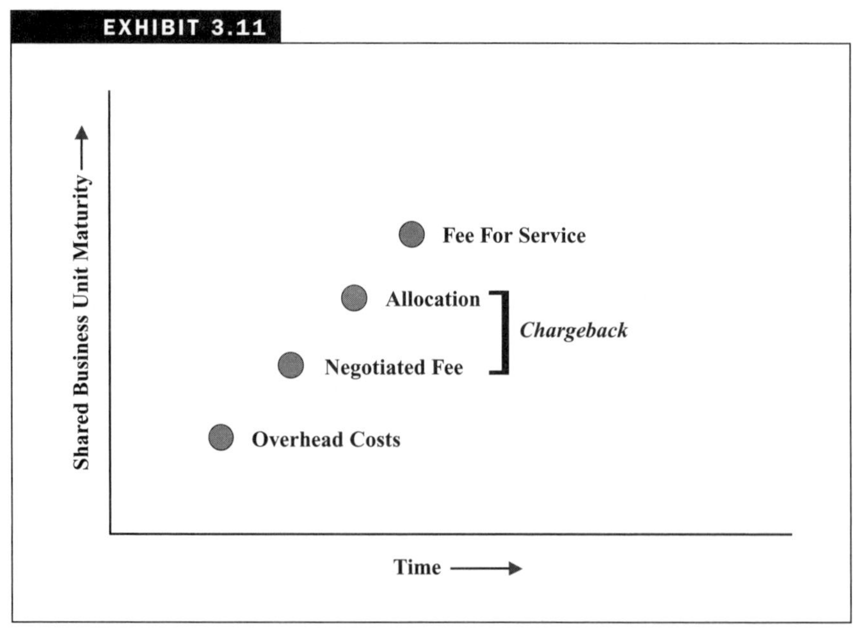

of chargeback is important in that it gets the culture of both the parent corporation and the shared service unit thinking about the exchange of value between the two organizations. Using a transitional chargeback period makes it easier for the parent corporation and the shared business unit to move to fee for service billing later.

Governance

The major distinctions between a back-office service that is simply consolidated and centralized and a shared business unit are that the delivery of service and governance are delivered together in a typical centralized business model. In contrast, the focus of the business unit is strictly on the delivery service, with no policing by or governance of parent corporation employees involved.

That is, there is no enforcement of corporate policy by the shared business unit. As in outsourcing, the shared business unit is in the business of providing service, not of enforcing corporate policy rules. The shared business unit has its own internal policy, which shared services employees follow. In contrast, employees working with back-end functions in the parent corporation deliver both governance and service.

Summary

Globalization, competitive markets, and mergers and acquisitions are the primary stimuli for moving back-end processes into a shared services business unit. Foremost is the effect of the transition on employees of the shared business unit. The stress of a new culture and heightened expectations can lead to burnout, poor quality service, and potential safety issues. The new emphasis on customer satisfaction shifts the focus from governance and service to a pure service provider environment and the wants and needs of the customer.

The next chapter continues this line of reasoning by exploring the processes that can be used by management and staff to work efficiently while providing a quality service in a non-harried work environment.

All is flux, nothing stands still.

Heracleitus

CHAPTER 4

Process

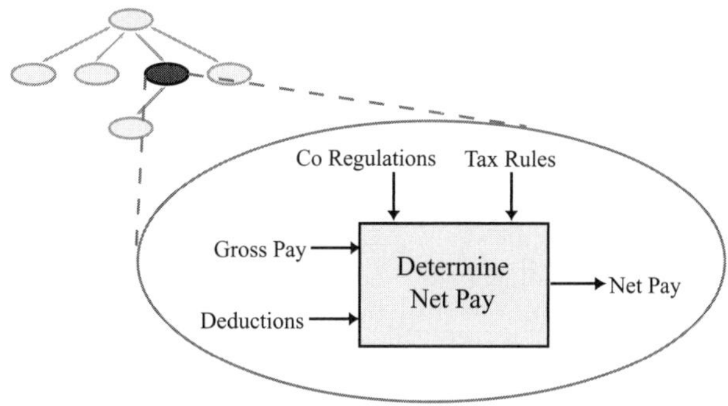

After reading this chapter you will be able to

- Understand the generic processes involved in transforming an internal business operation to a shared services business unit
- Understand the challenge of translating an original process in the parent corporation to a more efficient process in the shared business unit
- Understand the characteristics of the shared business unit at each stage in the transformation process
- Understand the issues related to providing the shared business unit with back-end services
- Appreciate the synergies possible between back-end and core processes in the shared business unit
- Appreciate the quantitative methods available for reducing uncertainty and risk in evolving a shared business unit to a mature business operation.

The chapter explores shared services from the perspective of a consultant saddled with the task of facilitating the transformation process from internal operation to shared business unit. The vignette offered here parallels the one in Chapter 2, but instead of seeing the world through the eyes of management, it assumes the perspective of the shared services consultant.

Payroll Services through a Consultant's Eyes

During the shared services implementation processes, while the HR director and the payroll unit manager were focused on employee and management issues, respectively, the shared services consultant was examining the payroll system for HealthCare Partners from a process optimization perspective. For example, he traveled with the HR director to each of the institutions in the network and interviewed employees. However, whereas the HR director's goal was to decide who should be let go and who should be given an offer to work with the new unit, he was concerned with documenting the current payroll process in each institution. He was primarily concerned with capturing current best practices in each hospital and clinic in the HealthCare Partners network and in answering the following questions:

- How much slack or unused production capacity is in the current system?
- Where are the current inefficiencies?
- Are they due to people, processes, or both?
- What are the current bottlenecks?
- How can they be eliminated?
- What are the critical paths for delivering service on time and within specifications?
- In the event that one or more of these pathways fail, are there backup procedures in place?

- If so, have these backup procedures ever been tested?
- What technologies are used at each point in the process?
- Are the technologies up to industry standards?
- What are the similarities and differences in the processes used to accomplish the given tasks at each institution in the network?
- Are the different processes compatible between one institution and the next?
- How do the processes used in each of the institutions compare with industry-wide best practices?

In addition to mapping out the process of the core payroll functions, the consultant explored the processes associated with back-end services, including customer service, marketing and sales, accounting, materials stocking, and information services, purchasing, orders, shipping, human resources, and management in each hospital and clinic. Armed with this data, and through working with the managers of the payroll unit and of Information Services, the consultant mapped out a timetable for converting the current distributed payroll system over to a single, shared services business unit. Much of the plan was contingent on the progress of Information Services. The manager of Information Services planned a two-phase implementation, with the first phase consisting of temporary interfaces between incompatible payroll systems and the shared business unit. Once this system was up and functioning, Information Services would begin work on an integrated payroll system that would be homogeneous across every member of the HealthCare Partners network.

In planning the implementation of the shared payroll service, the consultant considered the existing processes at a much finer level of granularity than did either the transition manager or the HR director. While the transition manager was concerned with streamlining to provide on-time and on-budget service, the consultant held down expenses, trying to extract the last bit of efficiency out of the available resources. Together with input from the HR director, the two formulated a process that was practical, efficient, and made maximum use of the employees and facilities.

Both the consultant and transition manger knew that the optimum process at the start of implementation wouldn't be sufficient later, when HealthCare Partners senior management loosened its grip on the shared services payroll unit. By mapping out these and other expected changes associated with the maturation process, the consultant, manager, and HR director created a process roadmap to help guide the management of the shared business unit several years into the future.

The consultant's activities during the conversion of the disparate payroll service centers in the HealthCare Partners network to a shared services payroll illustrates several key issues related to a shared services implementation:

- *Moving to a shared services model lends itself to process improvement.* The translation of one or more processes into a single, uniform process is an opportunity not only to downsize employees, but to improve efficiencies and cut costs by working smarter, not harder.
- *The internal processes of the typical shared business unit are in a state of constant disequilibrium.* In the shared services payroll unit, for example, change is counterbalanced by the inertia of established processes inherited from the individual institutions comprising the parent corporation.
- *The coordination of critical functions like payroll must go smoothly in a shared business unit, and its supporting computer system must be deployed smoothly, and with few glitches.* Less critical functions like cafeteria services demand less diligence and coordination between other service providers.
- *The level of granularity used in analyzing processes in the parent organization defines the degree to which the process can be made more efficient in the shared business unit.* However, defining every

operation in exhaustive detail takes additional time—a commodity that's increasingly rare in the conversion of a distributed model of doing business to a shared services model. A practical compromise solution is to use a level of detail commensurate with the implementation timeline and budget.

- *The transitions of the business model and employees are interdependent.* Ultimately, employees must enact the process defined by management. A process that looks perfect on paper may be unusable in reality because of unreasonable demands placed on employees.

These issues are expanded in the following section.

A Matter of Timing

A shared services unit is a unique business entity from several perspectives. For example, the shared business unit's lifecycle is much more involved than that of a typical company because the maturity of the shared services unit corresponds to the start of a traditional, freestanding business. In this regard, the genesis and maturation of a shared business unit into an independent, profit-oriented entity can be viewed as one potential outcome. The relatively slow rate of maturation is a distinguishing feature of the shared services model. It may take many years for a tightly held shared business unit to reach adolescence, where it may either mature to a for-profit entity or remain an adolescent forever.

As shown in Exhibit 4.1, the maturation of a shared business unit is reflected by several factors that change characteristically over time. For example, the human resources challenge at the birth of a shared business unit is that of downsizing unnecessary employees. Only later in maturity does the human resources challenge shift to ensuring employee satisfaction.

The composition of management tends to follow a pattern of maturation too. Initially, the manager is likely to be a corporate transplant who is later replaced by a professional transitional manager. Only after the shared business unit reaches maturity does a CEO typically run it.

EXHIBIT 4.1

Maturation of the Shared Business Unit

Changing Factor	At Birth	At Adolescence	At Maturity
Billing	Overhead	Chargeback	Fee for Service
Competition	None	Possible	External Market
Culture	Some Governance	Mixed	Independent
Customer Base	Internal	Internal	Internal and External
Focus	Cost Savings	Quality	Profit
Governance	Combine with Service	Separate from Service	Separate from Service
Human Resources Challenge	Downsizing	Downsizing	Employee Satisfaction
Management	Corporate Transplant	Transitional	CEO
Pricing	Dictated Price	Reasonable Price	Market Price
Revenue Sink	Corporation	Mixed	Business Unit
Risk of Failure	Low	Moderate	High
Service	Mandatory	Optional	Self-Directed
Source of Internal Policy	Corporate	Mixed	Business Unit
Supplier Status	Exclusive	Open	Open

Established companies typically compete on quality, time, or cost. In contrast, the focus of a shared services business typically shifts from cost to quality to profit as it matures. At birth, the parent corporation is primarily concerned with saving money, and the focus of the shared business unit is necessarily on cost saving measures, dictated prices, downsizing, and process reengineering. Later, during adolescence, one of the other promises of the shared services model—increased service—comes into focus, and quality becomes the mantra of employees and management. With this change of focus comes a moderate increase in the risk of failure and a move from an overhead method of billing to value-based chargeback.

With all of the changes associated with the maturation process, it might seem that staying in a state of arrested development would be the most economical and least disruptive to the business unit's operation. However, there is considerable pressure on the business unit to progress from birth through adolescence and on to maturity. These pressures, listed in Exhibit 4.2, include the shared business unit management's desire for autonomy and self-direction, the ability to grow the business into a leaner operation capable of competing with other businesses on the open market, and the potential for profitability. There may also be pressure from the parent corporation's senior management for the unit to achieve profitability or at least partial autonomy so that the drain on corporate resources is minimized.

Transformation

From a high level abstraction, the birth of a shared business unit—the transformation of an internal business operation into an external, shared business unit—can be viewed as a five-phase process involving

EXHIBIT 4.2

Pressures for Maturation

Competition with other businesses
Desire for autonomy and self-direction
Leaner operation
Pressure from parent corporation senior management
Potential for profitability

Identification, Mobilization, Consolidation, Extraction, and Encapsulation, as introduced in Chapter 3. Although this abstraction of the transformation process is useful as a management tool for determining, for example, reporting hierarchy, it lacks the detail necessary for identifying inefficiencies and contingencies in the process. Fortunately, over the past several decades, a number of process analysis tools and techniques have been developed to display business processes from a variety of perspectives, with the goal of identifying potential problems.

One such technique is process mapping, also known as structured analysis and design. Process mapping is one of several graphical techniques used in the field of process re-engineering. A feature of process mapping is that it can document detailed decision-making information, and provide a view of the transformation process to any level of detail.

As shown in Exhibit 4.3, process mapping can be used illustrate activity (top) or data (bottom), depending on the requirements. In illus-

EXHIBIT 4.3

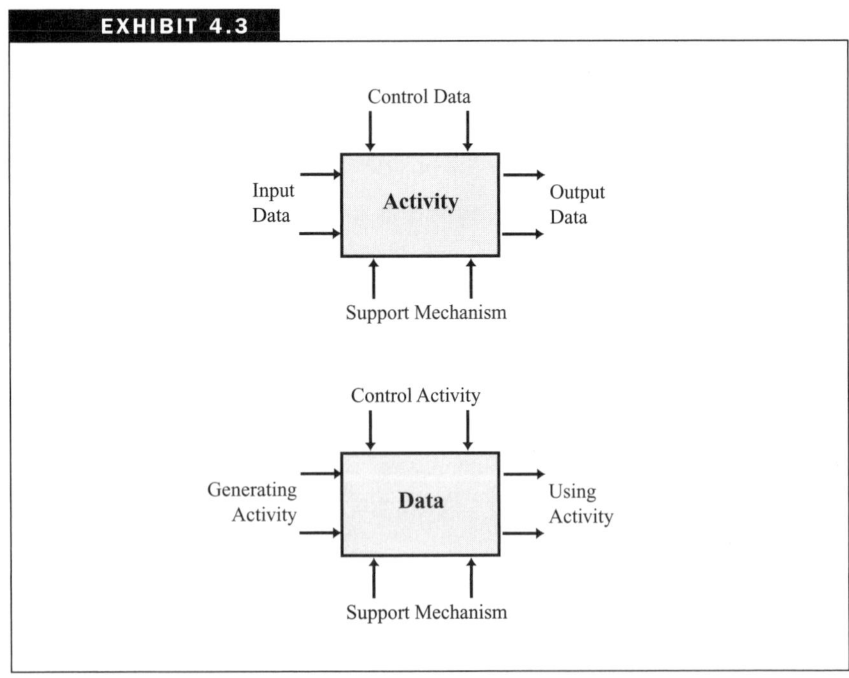

trating activity, the boxes correspond to activities and the arrows correspond to data. Conversely, when process mapping is used to illustrate the flow of data, the boxes correspond to data and the arrows correspond to activities related to the data. In this way, a process map provides a separate representation of data, activities, and their relationships.

Using process mapping, consider the five phases of the shared services transformation process, as illustrated in Exhibits 4.4 to 4.8.

Recall that Phase I, the Identification phase, involves identifying potential resources to be moved, establishing evaluation procedures, identifying employees for downsizing, interviewing employees and management to determine current processes, quantifying output for baseline measurements, and defining associated resource requirements. The process map of the identification process, shown in Exhibit 4.4, illustrates the interdependence activities related to employee retention and

EXHIBIT 4.4

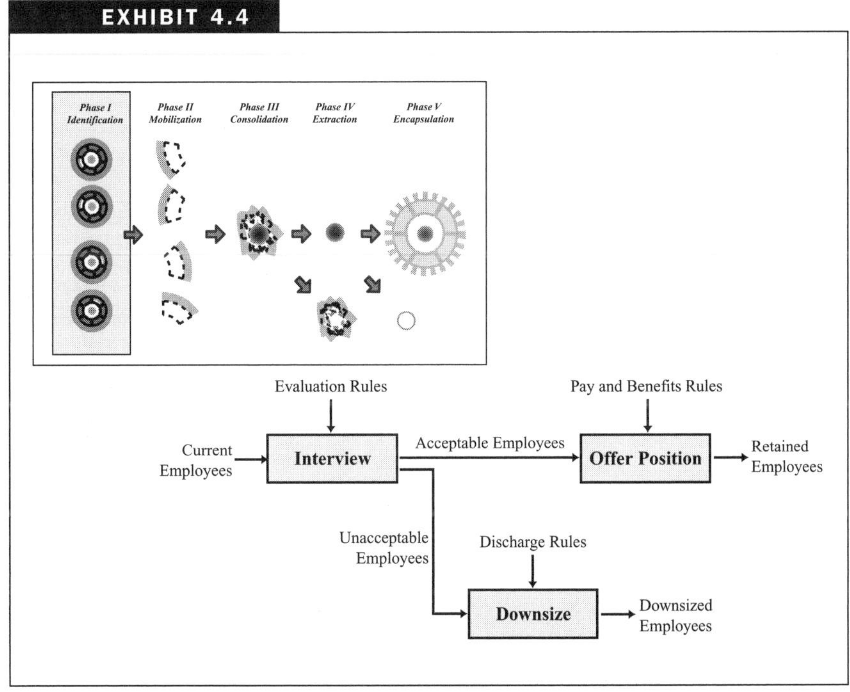

downsizing. Current employees of the HealthCare Partners network are interviewed, using evaluation rules established by the HR director. Those employees who fail to meet the standards codified by the evaluation rules or who don't want to move to the shared business unit are downsized in accordance with corporate discharge rules. For example, these rules may specify an economic package based on the number of years the employee has worked for the clinic or hospital and his/her current pay.

Employees found acceptable for employment by the shared business unit are offered positions by the HR director, using pay and benefit rules that may reflect an employee's seniority, pay, and position in their hospital or clinic. Those employees that are retained are subject to the activities in Phase II of implementation, as illustrated in Exhibit 4.5.

Phase II of the implementation process or Mobilization entails moving employees and other resources to a shared services center. Other key events in this phase are the downsizing of employees and determining overhead requirements. As shown in Exhibit 4.5, the transfer of

EXHIBIT 4.5

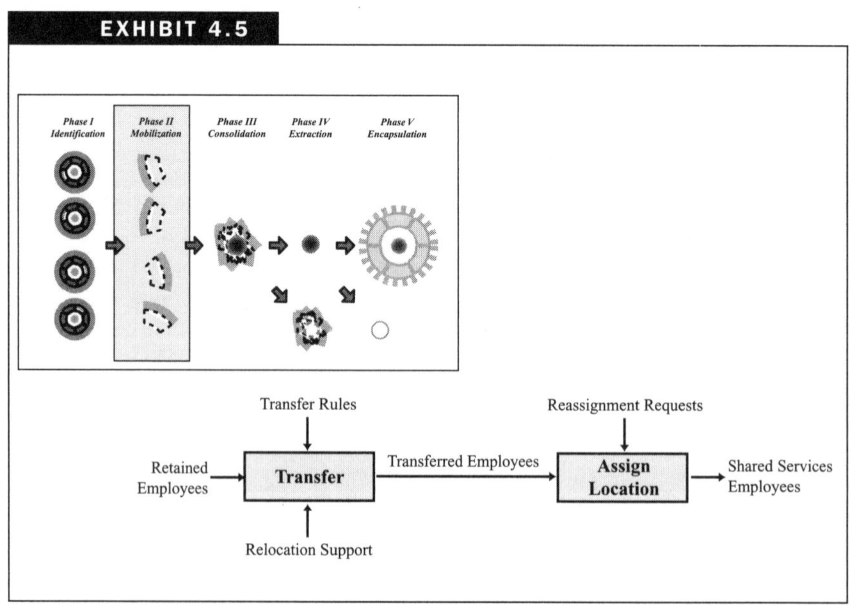

retained employees is aided by a corporate relocation support program, and is defined by transfer rules. Once employees are on site, they are assigned locations in their new work environment. They may also request reassignment to specific locations or positions within the new workplace.

Note that the process maps discussed in this chapter assume a particular perspective—that of the shared services consultant. Another perspective on Phase II might be that of the manager of Information Services, who might be more concerned with transferring PCs and other tools to the new office space.

The third phase of the implementation process, Consolidation, involves combining resources, downsizing, and improving upon existing business process. As shown in the process map in Exhibit 4.6, consolidation involves evaluating employee performance according to specific evaluation rules. Just as in the downsizing activities in Phase I and II,

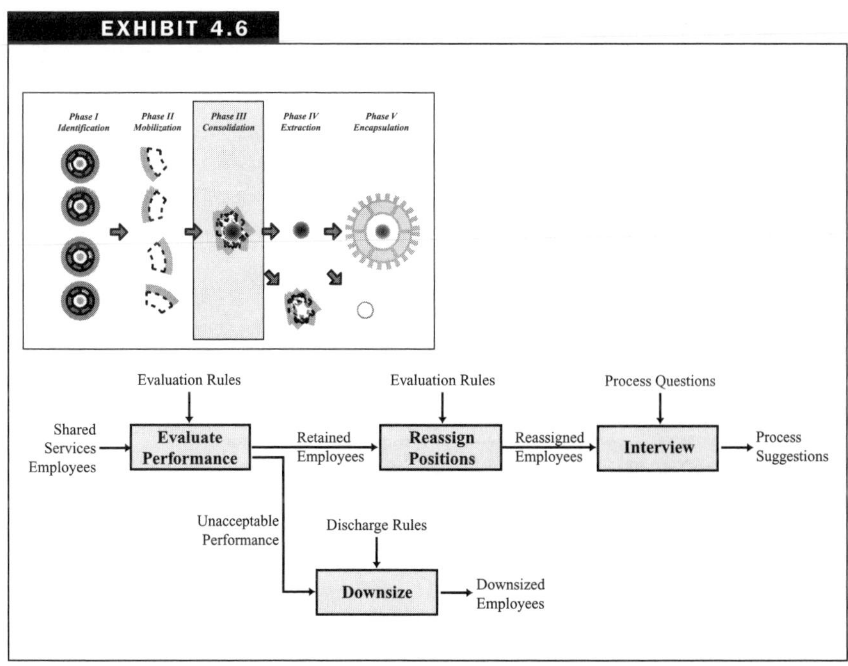

employees marked for downsizing are discharged according to a set of standard rules. However, by Phase III, the rules may be very different, because they may be established primarily by the HR director of shared business unit, and not, as in the previous phases, by the human resource department of the parent corporation.

As shown in Exhibit 4.6, those employees who have been retained are reevaluated and reassigned. Their new positions depend in part on the changes made in the work environment during the consolidation phase. More importantly, from the shared services consultant's perspective, these employees are interviewed to garner suggestions on how to improve the processes in the shared business unit.

Phase IV, Extraction, is concerned with establishing resources and procedures to support the shared business unit and with downsizing extraneous employees and managers. Following the process map in Exhibit 4.7, the current output of the shared business unit is assessed,

EXHIBIT 4.7

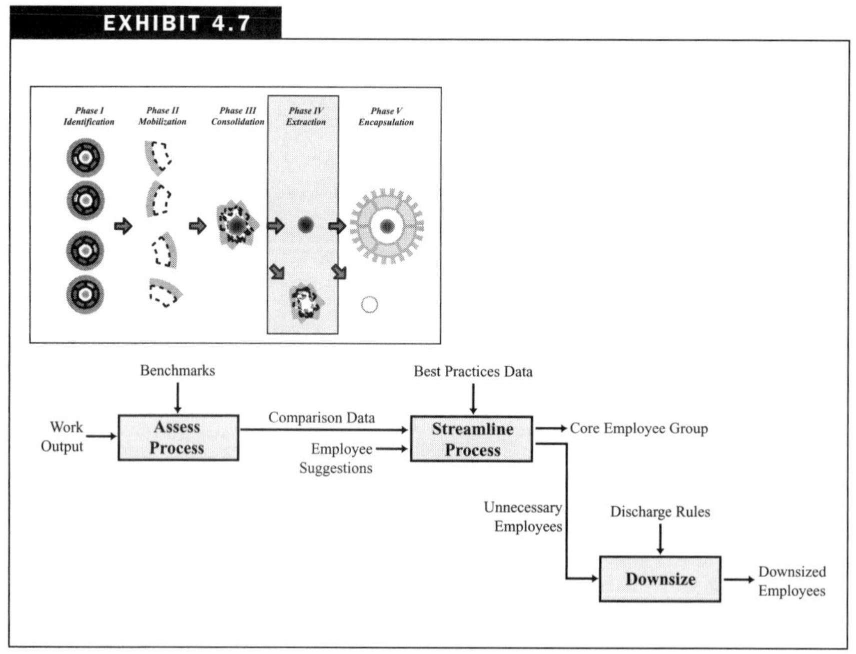

based on industry standards and from benchmarks derived from activities prior to the start of conversion. In the case of HealthCare Partners, the consultant made a point of establishing the work output figures of each payroll unit in every hospital and clinic in the network prior to the start of the shared services implementation.

With the comparison data from the process assessment and employee suggestions, the process is streamlined, creating a core employee group. Unnecessary employees are again downsized, using established discharge rules. Not shown in this perspective of the process map of Phase IV is the jettisoning of unnecessary hardware, software, furniture, leases, and other extraneous factors that don't contribute directly to the core competency of the shared services unit.

The final phase of shared services implementation, Encapsulation, supplements and supports the core competency of the shared business unit with back-end services and management (see Exhibit 4.8). For

EXHIBIT 4.8

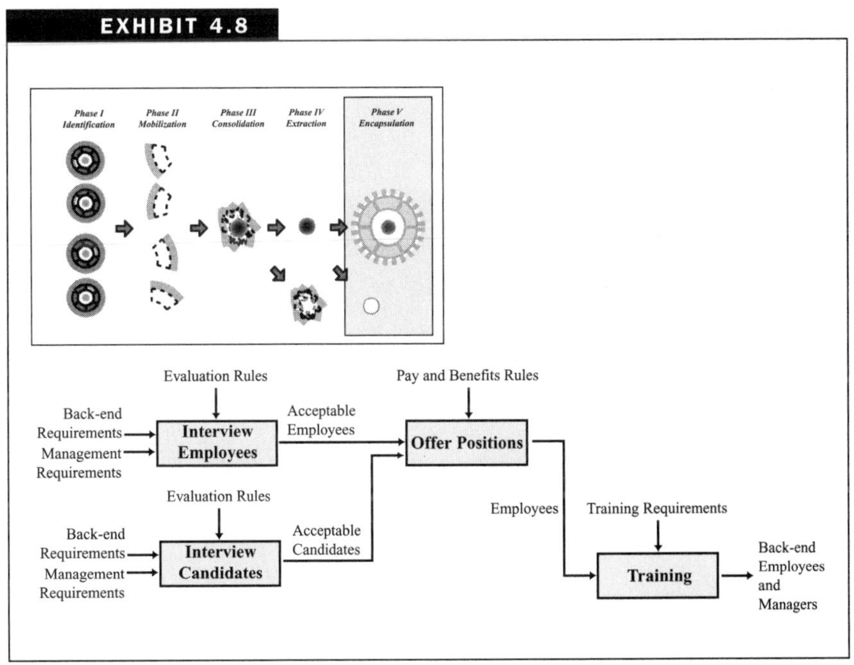

Management Styles

Operations management, charting techniques, and most other strategies and techniques, while important, ignore the real-world issues of management styles and the effect they can have on the effectiveness and efficiency of an organization. For example, managers typically follow one of four philosophies: they allocate resources, control resources, coordinate resources, or energize employees and other managers. These philosophies in turn reflect the manager's use of—and desire for—power.

In the shared services model, managers with different relationships with power typically cycle through the organization. At the birth of a shared business unit, there is a tendency for managers to use or acquire power through fear, especially fear of downsizing. This use of power is commonly seen in the transplanted or transitional manager who knows that he or she is in place to affect change and then leave. However, in the long term, employee morale inevitably suffers under such a regime.

In contrast to this use of coercive power is positional power, which is due to the manager's formal position in the organization. A manager who flexes his or her positional power through shared services policies and procedures is more apt to provide an efficient, effective work environment. Finally, there are managers whose power is derived from their knowledge, skills, and experience. These seasoned managers have the greatest potential to affect positive change in the shared business unit because employees and other managers respect them for the leadership and experience they bring to the organization. These managers are more appropriate for the long-term management of the mature shared services unit.

example, potential employees and managers of the human resources department are interviewed in light of evaluation rules, back-end requirements, and management requirements. Acceptable external candidates and internal employees are offered positions in the shared services unit's back-end departments. Many of these employees will need to be trained in supporting back-end activities.

Synergies

A shared business unit with three or four hundred employees has needs for payroll, human resource, accounts payable and receivable, marketing, and other services that likely don't add significant value to the service it provides to the parent corporation. Just as the parent corporation focuses on its core competency by creating a shared business unit to handle back-end processes, a shared business unit may outsource its own back-end process so that it can focus on its core competency.

Consider that even if the core competency of a shared business unit is processing payroll, several constraints may make outsourcing its own payroll an attractive alternative to handling the payroll in-house. For example, it may be less expensive to have an outside firm process a few hundred paychecks per month than to have the information services department of the shared business unit maintain a separate database and payroll application for internal employees.

However, there are situations in which in-house support of back-end services is the best option, such as when there are synergies possible between back-end and core processes of the shared business unit. Synergistic relationships between processes are characterized by mutual advantages that are multiplicative instead of simply additive.

For example, in support of its internal communications and problem tracking, the shared business unit may expend internal resources developing and supporting its own internal Web site. If the shared business unit is charged with providing customer support for the parent corporation, then expanding customer support from telephone and e-mail to an external Web site that lists frequently asked questions (FAQs) and other information could be accomplished at a very low marginal cost. Not only would the Web site provide an added service to customers of the parent corporation, but the information on the Web site would likely reduce the phone and e-mail traffic load on the shared business unit.

The potential synergies between back-end and core processes, shown in Exhibit 4.9, are primarily technical, managerial, or economic. Technical synergies include those related to information technology, research and development, and process improvement. For example, the data collection, data analysis, and database tools and techniques used to optimize core processes can be applied to back-end processes, and vice versa.

Supporting back-end processes in-house provides employees within the shared business unit with an opportunity to perfect technologies that can be applied on a much larger scale in the parent corporation. For example, assume that the core competency of the shared business unit is providing customer support and other customer relationship manage-

EXHIBIT 4.9

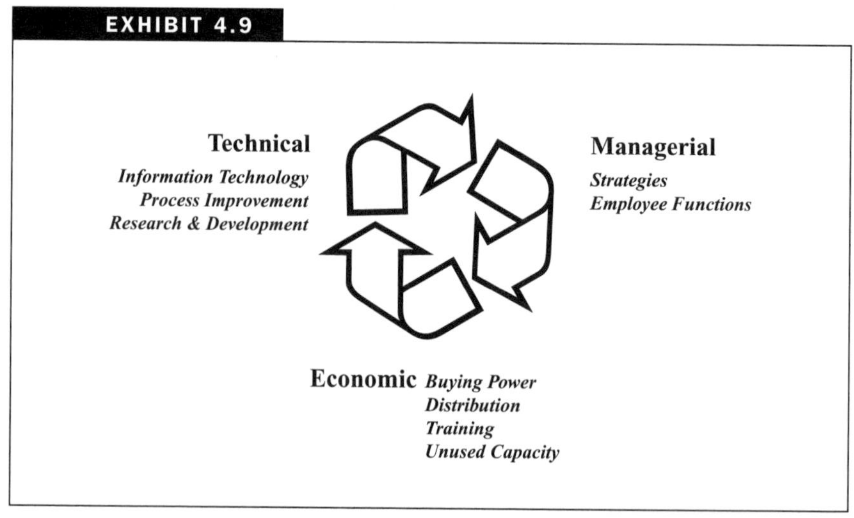

ment functions for the parent corporation. Management of the customer service unit may perceive a need for a Web touch point to supplement telephone, fax, and surface mail in the parent organization. However, it may not have the experience with what would be involved in developing, maintaining, and staffing an interactive Web site. An in-house Web site to support employees of the shared business unit can provide that experience.

One of the characteristics of information technologies is ease of duplication and, in many cases, negligible marginal cost. For example, once a Web site has been developed, the cost of supporting an additional viewer is virtually zero. The same interfaces and code have to be in place and functioning perfectly in order to support 50 shared services employees or 5,000 users in the parent corporation. Of course, although a standard desktop PC can serve 50 or 100 users on an internal network or intranet, supporting 5,000 users distributed across the United States will probably require a very modest investment in a dedicated server.

Using the Web as a means of internal information distribution can suggest process improvements within the shared business unit that transfer directly to the core competency of the unit. For example, once a Webmaster is in place in the shared business unit, adding the task of maintenance of content on the Web site used by employees and customers of the parent corporation may add negligibly to his workload. This is especially true if there is already staff employed in generating properly formatted content for distribution in print form, since posting the information to the Web may be as simple as copying content from the source files and pasting them into the Web tools.

Note that potential synergies are just that—potential. External factors, such as the cost of legal contracts, organizational inflexibility, and rapidly changing needs of the parent corporation or shared business unit may either negate or shorten the window of opportunity for taking advantage of potential synergies.

Streamlining the Core Process

The generic process depicted by process mapping above applies in some degree to most shared services implementation. However, this description doesn't address the specific evaluation rules used throughout the process or allow for specific process improvements. For specific components, the nature and area of the core process have to be considered in detail. It's important for management to consider the company's core competency, so that the shared business unit is enhanced and not weakened.

Streamlining the core process usually involves the application of a variety of management techniques, including:

- *Detailed process descriptions.* Following the process mapping examples applied to the generic translation process, a detailed process description for the core process can provide the manager with insights into potential sources of underutilized resources.
- *Information flow diagrams.* Tracking the flow of data throughout the organization may highlight inefficiencies and duplication of effort that can have a negative effect on the unit's bottom line.
- *Defining sources of error.* Interviews with employees, examining customer complaint logs, and other objective and subjective data can often identify sources of error in the existing processes. Removing these sources of error or compensating for them is one aspect of streamlining the core process.
- *Defining critical paths.* Relying on a variety of graphing tools, it's important to identify the critical paths associated with the core process—the processes that, if interrupted, could derail the core process.
- *Identifying potential enhancements.* With a critical description of the internal core processes in hand, it's usually possible to identify potential enhancements and their ultimate effect on

the company. A new computer program, new computer, or additional secretarial support for tracking customer complaints may be all that are need to bring shared services to near profitability.

- *Measuring ROI.* In identifying potential enhancements to shared business unit processes, the resulting expected and actual return on investment (ROI) should be used as the guide for capital and resource investments.

As shown in Exhibit 4.10, streamlining the core process in the shared business unit benefits from a detailed view of the underlying processes. For example, the teaching process in Phase V of implementation can be divided into steps of increasingly finer granularity. As shown in the exhibit, employees are evaluated for training based on the job specifications and standard evaluation rules. Additional training requirements are then defined for each employee. Then, the method of training is identified, based on a cost analysis and on employee constraints. Employees are given the option of onsite training, eLearning, or offsite didactic training, depending on their needs.

Managers who can't afford to leave the business to attend classes every other night would likely be assigned eLearning training, in which they use their computer and internet connection to take courses on the Web. Conversely, some of these same managers and employees may be so busy that this is the only way they can be guaranteed quality study time. For some employees and managers, onsite didactic training has its place in shared services as well.

Operations Management

Operations management, a quantitative or mathematical approach to analyzing and optimizing the production of goods and services, is particularly applicable to the implementation and long-term management of a shared business unit. Operations management techniques are

EXHIBIT 4.10

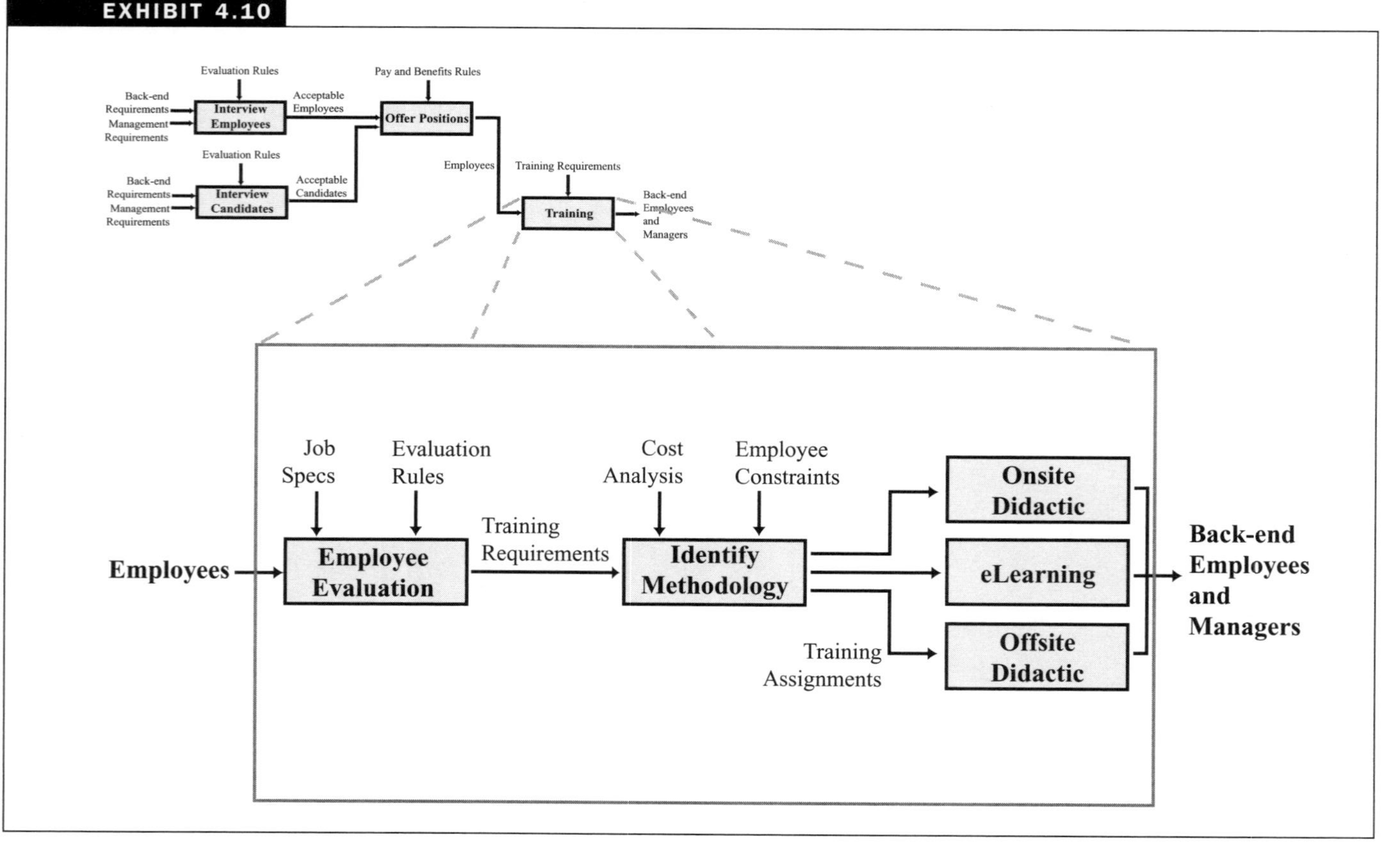
Evaluation Rules
Back-end Requirements
Management Requirements
Interview Employees
Acceptable Employees
Pay and Benefits Rules
Offer Positions
Evaluation Rules
Back-end Requirements
Management Requirements
Interview Candidates
Acceptable Candidates
Employees
Training Requirements
Training
Back-end Employees and Managers
Employees
Job Specs
Evaluation Rules
Employee Evaluation
Training Requirements
Cost Analysis
Employee Constraints
Identify Methodology
Training Assignments
Onsite Didactic
eLearning
Offsite Didactic
Back-end Employees and Managers

designed to decrease the degree of uncertainty associated with business decisions in one or more of five key areas: production capacity, production process, resource scheduling, inventory management, and standards. These areas are discussed in more detail here.

Production Capacity

In planning for potential expansion into outside markets, hiring or downsizing, whether or not there is unused capacity that can be redirected toward external markets or back-end activities, it's important for management to have a firm grasp on the production capacity of the shared business unit. The key questions regarding production capacity of the shared business unit include:

- How much service can the unit provide, in quantifiable measures? For example, what is the number of clients served per hour, number of problems resolved per day per call center operator, or number of checks that can be processed per hour?
- What is the marginal cost of additional output?
- Does staffing, technology, capital, process, the physical plant, or a combination of these factors limit production capacity?

Consider that in processing the payroll, the production capacity, as measured in the maximum number of checks that can be printed and stuffed into envelopes per hour, may be limited by the mechanical sorter and envelope stuffer. Since there may only be a 24-hour window between when the checks are "cut" and when they need to be mailed, the number of checks that can be printed by the equipment in a 24-hour period represents the maximum production capacity of payroll system—considering only the equipment. In reality, there are usually several limitations to production capacity. In this example, it is the number of employees available to manage the machines. If there are only two shifts of employees available to ensure the printing and stuffing

TIPS & TECHNIQUES

The Six Ms of Production Capacity

Traditionally, the production capacity of a business is described as a function of six factors: machinery, manpower, materials, messages, methods, and money—the so-called six Ms. In determining production capacity of a shared business unit, consider the following questions regarding each factor:

- *Machinery.* What is available, in terms of computers, telecommunications equipment, and other process-specific equipment, that can assist in production? Is the equipment up to date? What are the inherent limitations of the equipment, in terms of throughput, maintenance requirements, and mean time before failure?
- *Manpower.* What human resources are available to apply toward production? Do employees and managers require additional training? How will downsizing affect quality, time, and cost of work output? Is morale positive? Is there sufficient slack in employee and management time demands to allow for efficiency and effectiveness-enhancing innovations?
- *Materials.* Are the raw materials—whether paper forms or Web pages—needed to deliver service readily available and renewable? If the service is product related, such as a cafeteria service, then are the components of the product readily available?
- *Messages.* Is the communications infrastructure, including the computer and telecommunications networks, adequate for coordinating production?
- *Methods.* Is the production process as efficient and effective as possible? If not, where can it be improved, and

Tips & Techniques Continued

should it be improved? That is, what is the marginal cost of improving the current process?

- *Money.* Is there adequate capital to fund the current operation of the shared business unit? What about long-term financing? Is it necessary for the shared business unit to offer its services to outside businesses in order to become financially viable?

machines are operational and adequately supplied with ink and paper supplies, then at most the units can operate continuously for 16 hours. If the machinery is capable of printing, stuffing, and stamping 200 checks per hour, then the capacity of the shared services payroll unit is at most 3,200 checks (200 × 16 = 3,200).

In practice, there are multiple, interrelated constraints on production, and rarely are they purely technical. A motivated workforce can often overcome insurmountable technical challenges. Conversely, even the most advanced technology will lie dormant and useless without someone to push it to capacity.

Production Process

Creating an efficient core process in the shared business unit begins with examining the current production process to identify bottlenecks and areas that are out of control. Relevant questions to ask regarding the production process include:

- Is the current system functioning properly?
- How can the current production process be improved?
- What are the time, quality, and cost constraints?

- What is the variance in quality, cost, or delivery time from one day or employee to the next?
- Is this variance acceptable to customers and management?

The operations management focus on the production process, known as control, is concerned with controlling the production process to the point that operations are within a specified tolerance for accuracy and precision. For example, if the payroll system rounds time for hourly employees to the nearest 15 minutes, then the rules must be applied consistently to all hourly employees, and from one pay period to the next. That is, if 0 to 7 minutes is rounded to zero and 8 to 14 minutes is rounded up to 15 minutes, 8 minutes should always round up to 15, regardless of employee, date, or total hours worked in the pay period.

Resource Scheduling

Resource scheduling is about making the most of resources through scheduling the use of people, equipment, and other resources. Typical issues include:

- Is the ideal sequence of events in the process for delivering products and services on time and on budget?
- How can cycle time be shortened?
- What are the critical tasks—tasks that could hold up delivery of service if not performed?
- What is the critical path to delivery of service?
- What is the average wait time for service?
- How would the addition of more resources affect wait time?
- How would rearranging resources affect wait time?

In the shared services environment, resource scheduling is typically about how to make do with less. For example, a typical question is: "how much will the average time increase with each downsized employee?"

Inventory Management

In implementing a shared business unit, the amount of inventory on hand influences the unit's ability to respond quickly to sudden increases in demand and has an influence on the bottom line. As such, the primary questions that need to be addressed in inventory management are:

- What is the optimum level of inventory to keep on hand?
- How can inventory be minimized without interrupting the production process?

Inventory management is challenging because of the pervasive uncertainty in business operations. It's a challenge for management to determine how much inventory to have on hand when demand forecasts are uncertain. Too much inventory incurs a holding cost penalty, while too little inventory incurs an ordering cost penalty. Holding costs are warehousing and storage costs, including insurance and the financing of inventory. Ordering costs include the accounting, clerical labor, and other overhead associated with placing an order. In addition to ordering costs, there may be a holding cost penalty imposed by the supplier and shipper.

Consider that if the management of the shared services payroll unit decides to order blank check stock and envelopes on a monthly basis, there won't likely be much in the way of holding costs. However, the penalties associated with ordering checks every month include a degree of risk associated with the order not arriving on time, ordering costs, as well a higher per unit cost from the check supplier. Since the marginal cost of printing additional checks is minimal once a printing run is set up, it's often more economical to order several months or a year's worth of check blanks at a time. In addition, the cost of shipping and handling twelve separate orders of check blanks every month is likely to be significantly greater than that of a single shipment from the printer.

Standards

The performance of a shared business unit is typically measured relative to the performance of the parent corporation, industry standards, and similar businesses competing in the same or similar market. That is, the question that management must ask is: How do cost, quality, and delivery time and other benchmarks compare to those of the parent corporation, industry standards, and similar businesses?

Early in the life of a shared business unit, quality, price, time to delivery, and consistency standards are established and enforced by management of the parent corporation. In doing so, the parent corporation effectively controls every internal process in the shared services unit.

As discussed in depth in Chapter 5, these and other operations management techniques are accessible through affordable software packages available for the PC.

Summary

Transforming a back-end business operation in a parent corporation into the core process in a shared business unit is itself a process that has to be managed. Regardless of whether the service involved is payroll, accounting, or CRM, there is a generic process involved in the transformation that can be optimized through a variety of process analysis tools and techniques. One such technique, process mapping, has the advantage of displaying the transformation process to any level of detail and from a variety of perspectives.

Although it may seem paradoxical, one of the side effects of creating a shared business unit from a back-end service is to create the need for additional back-end services. The new shared services entity has many of the same needs faced by every other business, from payroll and accounting to copying and cafeteria services. Whether or not these back-end services are provided in-house by either training existing staff or hiring new staff or whether they are outsourced depends in part on the potential technical, managerial, and economic synergies that may exist between the back-end services and the core services of the shared business unit.

The transformation of the specific back-end process to the shared business unit represents the first opportunity for improving upon the processes used in the parent corporation. In this regard, operations management principles in the areas of production capacity, production process, resource scheduling, inventory management, and standards can decrease the level of uncertainty in re-engineering decisions.

> *Noticing small changes early helps you adapt to the bigger changes that are to come.*
>
> **Spencer Johnson, *Who Moved My Cheese?* (New York: G.P. Putnam's Sons, 1998)**

CHAPTER 5

Technology

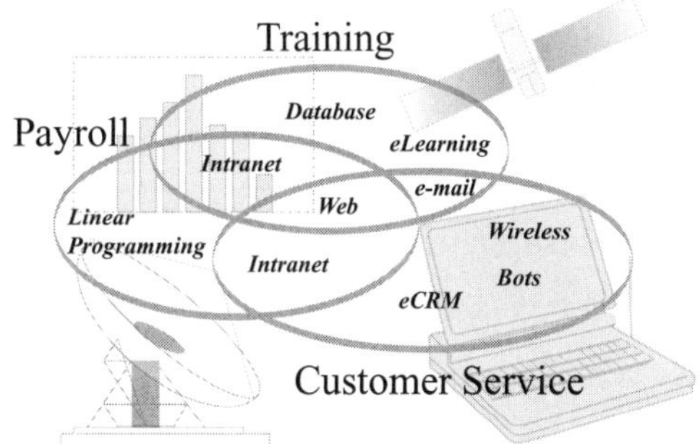

After reading this chapter you will be able to

- Understand how information infrastructure technologies form the basis for most shared services operations.
- Appreciate the general-purpose information technologies available for shared services operations, including communications technologies that facilitate communications between customers in the parent corporation and the shared business unit.
- Understand the application of process-specific information technologies in increasing the efficiency and reducing the staffing requirements of the shared business unit.
- Recognize the potential of disruptive information technologies on the future of shared services.

Unlike an accounting program for CPAs or a statistical analysis program for statisticians, there isn't a shrink-wrapped software package for managers of shared business units. Because the shared services model can be applied to virtually any activity in any industry, vendors haven't entered the field with specific "shared services" software and hardware. However, there are numerous general and process-specific information technologies that can be used to support shared services implementation and operation.

A wide range of information technologies, from communications networks to data processing, can be applied to virtually every shared services implementation. These tools serve as intellectual levers and provide the connectivity needed to efficiently transfer information between the shared business unit and the parent corporation. There are also specific information technologies that can be applied to a shared business unit to allow fewer employees to work more efficiently. Examples range from CRM software suites that enable shared services call centers, to database systems that can be used by human resources staff to track and evaluate employee performance.

Before delving into a description of these and other enabling information technologies, consider the challenges of implementing and operating a shared information services center for HealthCare Partners.

A Path for Information Services

The practice of creating a shared information services unit is increasingly common in a business environment characterized by acquisitions, mergers, and strategic partnerships. However, in addition to the human resources challenges highlighted in the previous chapter, there are numerous technological challenges. Foremost is the need to integrate disparate technologies in a way that preserves legacy data.

One approach is to create comprehensive communications links or computer interfaces between legacy computer systems so that data can be interchanged seamlessly between the patchworks of incompatible systems. A second option is to build or buy a homogeneous, enterprise-wide system, import legacy data into the system, and switch over to the new system in one operation. A third option is a multistep approach in which limited functionality interfaces are constructed between the disparate, incompatible computer systems from each institution so that a subset of data can be shared. Meanwhile, a new, enterprise-wide system is constructed and incrementally activated and fed with legacy data on a site or functionality basis.

Management's need to provide employees throughout the enterprise with continual access to legacy data favors the latter approach. That is, preserving some of the old system while simultaneously building a new one eases the cultural shock of change. In addition, management's need to cut costs and improve services favors the formation of a shared information services unit for the HealthCare Partners network.

As is typical of the technologically challenged health care system, the hospitals and clinics in the HealthCare Partners network each have incompatible computer systems. For example, the information system at State General Hospital is a combination of vendor-supplied systems and several in-house systems that use an assortment of incompatible hardware and software. What's more, the other two hospitals in the HealthCare Partners network each has their own unique combination of hardware and software systems and these are also incompatible with those in the other hospitals or clinics.

For example, State General Hospital's radiology department has a system that is incompatible with the system developed by a group of programmers for the pathology department. Similarly, the admission, discharge, and transfer (ADT) system is incompatible with both the radiology and pathology systems. Historically, this inter-system incompatibility arises because each department has its own operating budget from both the hospital and through external grants. Compatibility with external systems takes second place to developing and maintaining applications that directly affect the efficiency of the department. As a result, the reality of an integrated hospital-wide information system is still a novelty in most hospitals.

The status of information services at State General Hospital is replicated in the other two hospitals and in some of the clinics. For example, most of the clinics have only an ADT system and no automated means of tracking laboratory reports and nothing that would resemble an electronic medical record.

With the formation of HealthCare Partners network, the successful integration of information systems is clearly one key to success. However, integration is a non-trivial challenge. Not only must the existing systems be integrated and moved to a shared services center, but information systems have to be implemented from scratch at most of the clinics. In addition, continued support for existing services, including payroll, has to be considered in the overall development plan.

In order to start to move the disparate information services in the HealthCare Partners network to a shared services model, senior management identifies a transition team headed by a transitional CIO, director of human resources, the heads of Information Services at each of the member institutions, and several consultants.

Because it's critical to the functioning of the HealthCare Partners network that the flow of information within each hospital or clinic not be interrupted, the new shared services information system is brought online on an institution-by-institution and department-by-department basis. For example, in order to the support the payroll system described in Chapter 3, electronic interfaces to each of the payroll systems in the HealthCare Partners network are designed, tested, and deployed. As a result, employees in the shared services payroll unit can extract information from the payroll systems in each institution, while the employees of the shared information services unit develop the new enterprise-wide payroll system that they will manage. The rolling three-year implementation plan includes moving the software, servers, and other major computing hardware to the shared information services unit, and using the Internet to deliver applications to employees through an Application Service Provider (ASP) model. Using this Web-based technology, applications and data remain in the shared information services unit, allowing software and data maintenance to be performed by employees working in the unit. Other than a standard Web browser, there is nothing to maintain on the thousands of PCs throughout the network.

By the end of the three-year process, the senior management of HealthCare Partners intends to have a robust information infrastructure in place as well as a variety of general and process-specific programs that can support core health care functions. On the list is wireless physician order entry, as well as functions in the process of being moved to a shared services model, including customer service, payroll, billing, insurance claims processing, and sales and marketing. Part of the reason for a three-year plan is to have more time to assess potentially disruptive technologies, such as the wireless Web, in terms of vendor viability and return on investment (ROI).

While management of the shared information services unit is creating the information infrastructure for its network of hospitals and clinics, it's also supporting the management of the newly formed shared payroll system with its library of operations management and decision support tools. These tools are designed to help management streamline internal processes, decide whether or not to implement back-end services in-house or outsource them to a vendor, determine the optimum inventory supplies to keep on hand, and how to best grow the unit to maturity.

Several key issues are highlighted implementing a shared information services unit for the HealthCare Partners network:

- *Information technology can be critical in enabling a move to shared services.* Doing more with fewer employees requires better ways of doing things (process optimization) as well as technologies that allow organizations to leverage their intellectual capital.

- *Information technologies applicable to shared services fall into three categories: infrastructure, general-purpose, and process-specific.* Infrastructure technologies, such as networking, provide the foundation for all information sharing. General-purpose information technologies, such as data communications and storage can be applied to virtually all shared services operations. Process-specific information technologies, such as dedicated payroll, accounts payable, and training systems can enable fewer employees to work more efficiently.
- *Including an information technology overhaul in the process of creating a shared business unit can add significant time to the implementation process.* Consolidating a group of employees from several institutions or departments into a new space often requires less time than moving the equivalent information services components of their jobs to the shared business unit.
- *Information technology is no panacea.* Many of the information technologies promoted by vendors have yet to prove themselves economical or universally applicable in the shared services space.
- *Technology has a finite lifetime.* Today's new technologies, including leading-edge information systems, become tomorrow's legacy systems.
- Because of the dependency of most shared services implementations on information technologies, failure to select the most appropriate technology for the situation can be catastrophic.

This discussion of issues is expanded in the following sections.

Information Technologies: An Overview

Although the shared services model can be applied to manufacturing products, it's most often used with information-intensive services.

IN THE REAL WORLD

eLearning in Corporate America

Minimizing or eliminating loss of time from work during training is increasing the popularity of eLearning—the use of the Web, intranets, wireless computing, and other digital means of teaching and learning at home and in the workplace. Although eLearning, which is variably referred to as online learning or distance learning, and computer-based education or testing, has been used in a limited capacity in academia, the military, and in a few professional organizations since the early 1960s, it is now expanding rapidly into widespread use in the workplace.

The primary reason for this expansion is economics—eLearning can be more cost effective than traditional classroom instruction or attending seminars. Most businesses have cut back on air travel for safety reasons, the hassle of flying, and the expenses associated with sending employees to attend seminars. Traditional offsite training requires employees to take time off from work for travel and dealing with the logistics of scheduling—issues that aren't problematic with asynchronous, on-demand e-learning. Companies that offer eLearning programs to their employees include:

- *IBM.* Working with the University of Texas at Austin, IBM employees can earn an MBA in technology commercialization.
- *Intel.* Employees can earn an MBA from Babson College.
- *Microsoft.* Employees can take courses that apply toward a master's degree in software and hardware at the Oregon Health and Science University's School of Science and Engineering.

In addition to a more knowledgeable and capable workforce, an added benefit of these and other eLearning programs is increased employee loyalty and retention.

Typical shared services functions such as payroll, accounting, customer support, and logistics rely heavily on the storage, processing, and communication of data. Similarly, as described in Chapter 4, deciding exactly how to implement a shared business unit in a specific area, such as payroll, entails gathering and processing data in order to make the best business decisions possible. The ability to predict, with a fair degree of certainty, future demands on the services offered by a shared business unit can make the difference between a profitable venture and disaster.

Given the information-intensive aspects of most shared services operations, it's clear that information technologies are essential for an efficient, cost-effective business. As described in the scenario of the shared information services unit above, there are three general categories of information technologies that are relevant to the implementation and long-term operation of a shared business unit: infrastructure (including the wired or wireless network), general-purpose information technologies (such as a database management systems), and process-specific information technologies, (such as a payroll application).

As shown in Exhibit 5.1, these three categories of information technologies are interrelated by a functional hardware and software architecture in that process-specific tools generally incorporate aspects of general-purpose information technologies. In addition, both general and process-specific information technologies require a network or other infrastructure to facilitate acquisition and sharing of data. These three classes of information technology and their application to shared services are described here.

Information Infrastructure Technologies

Information infrastructure technologies include the hardware and software that comprise the backbone of computing and communications for the business. This means everything from the wires and cables that carry e-mail and Web content to the microwave links between office

EXHIBIT 5.1

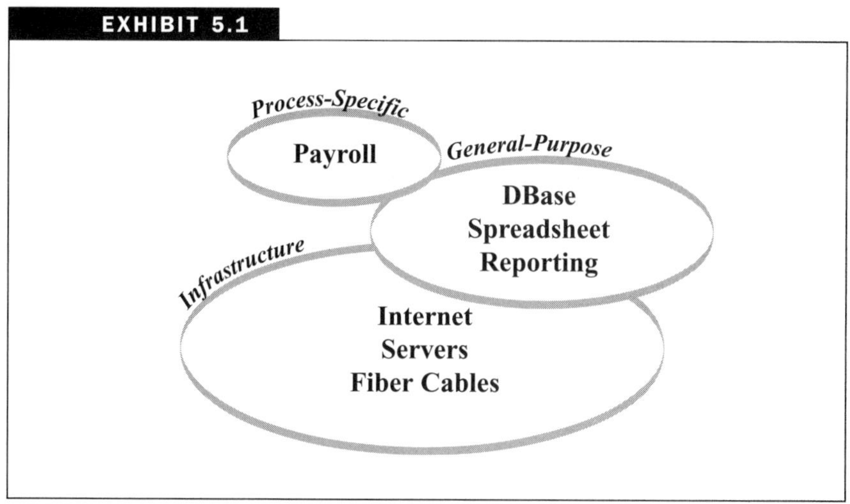

buildings located in different cities or countries. The technologies are listed in Exhibit 5.2. Infrastructure hardware includes network hardware, such as the copper and fiberoptic cables and the electronics—the switches, routers, and bridges—that connect the cables to each other and to devices on the network. Network devices include servers—

EXHIBIT 5.2

Infrastructure Technologies

Hardware

Network Hardware	Servers
Networked Peripherals	Wireless Networks

Software

Network Operating System

Systems

Internet	Security
Intranets	World Wide Web
Power	

mainframe computers, minicomputers, or high-end PCs—and networked printers, fax machines, optical scanners, and other networked peripherals. In addition to the wired infrastructure, there are wireless systems that work on either light or radio frequency signals to provide communications within buildings or, when satellites are involved, between continents.

When the cables, routers, bridges, firewalls, and other infrastructure hardware are coupled with a network operating system, the resulting network enables computers to connect to shared printers, databases, and to each other. These systems can take the form of an intranet, such as a private network contained within the shared business unit or an intranet that is shared by the parent corporation and a shared business unit. Alternatively, the infrastructure can be part of the global Internet and World Wide Web.

Part of the network operating system is a communications protocol that specifies encryption or encoding methods intended to prevent unwanted eyes from viewing confidential data. Encryption and other security measures implemented at the infrastructure level are especially critical for a shared business unit that processes payroll, billing, health care benefits, and other highly personal information.

Aside from security threats, the greatest problem facing a network system is loss of power. As such, virtually every network system includes some form of auxiliary power, in the event that the public power mains fail. A shared business unit with the responsibility of developing, maintaining, and hosting the parent corporation's Web site can't afford to be offline for three or four hours because of a local power outage, especially if the Web site is involved in order processing. When large Web sites such as Amazon and Yahoo go offline because of a power failure or a hacker's interference, the events usually make the business headlines. Backup power systems, including batteries and diesel generators, are part of every high-end Web hosting service.

Infrastructure technologies necessarily cover the continuum from predominantly communications technologies to those that are primarily computing related, given the continued blurring of what differentiates voice and data processing. The technology behind this trend, called Computer-Telephony Integration (CTI), is the real-time integration of voice and computer data. This technology allows e-mail and phone data from the same customer to be routed to a particular representative in a shared services CRM center, for example. The ability of customer support representatives to deal with customers who use e-mail and voice interchangeably provides continuity of support, reduced likelihood of errors, and uses the representative's time more efficiently, with the associated cost savings and shorter wait times for customers.

A shared customer support center is just as likely to use voice over the Internet in servicing customers surfing the company Web site as they are to use a more traditional telephone. Moreover, traditional telephony is increasingly likely to be a wireless digital headset that is linked to a central switching system in the customer support center.

Because of CTI and similar technologies, most CIOs are given charge of the telecommunications infrastructure as well as traditional data processing resources. However, someone unfamiliar with recent advances in information technology infrastructure might be surprised to walk into a modern computer center and find a few servers no larger than standard PCs instead of a mammoth water- or forced air-cooled mainframe. This scenario is increasingly common as more companies make use of programs delivered over the Web from Application Service Providers (ASPs), a model in which not only data, but the application that uses the data is maintained in the shared business unit.

Infrastructure technologies generally require the coordinated assistance of Information Services (IS) professionals who are fluent in the industry- and enterprise-wide standards of information systems. As the vignette above illustrates, a shared Information Services unit is likely to touch all aspects of the business, including communications between the parent corporation and all of its shared business units. In this regard, it's important to distinguish between Information Services that is resident in the shared business units, such as internal payroll, and Information Services that provides service to the parent corporation. As illustrated in Exhibit 5.3, there are three basic models of how Information Services can be configured in a corporation that relies on shared services.

One model of providing a shared business unit with information services is to simply use the parent corporation's resources (Exhibit 5.3, center), whether Information Services is run in-house or through a shared Information Services center. This model is especially applicable to newly formed shared services centers for several reasons. Foremost is that management of the parent corporation needs to be certain that the infrastructure installed in the shared business unit is compatible with that of the parent corporation.

As in the vignette above, the parent corporation can also supply information services to one shared business unit through a shared information services unit. For example, in the consolidation of payroll services for HealthCare Partners, a shared Information Services unit was

EXHIBIT 5.3

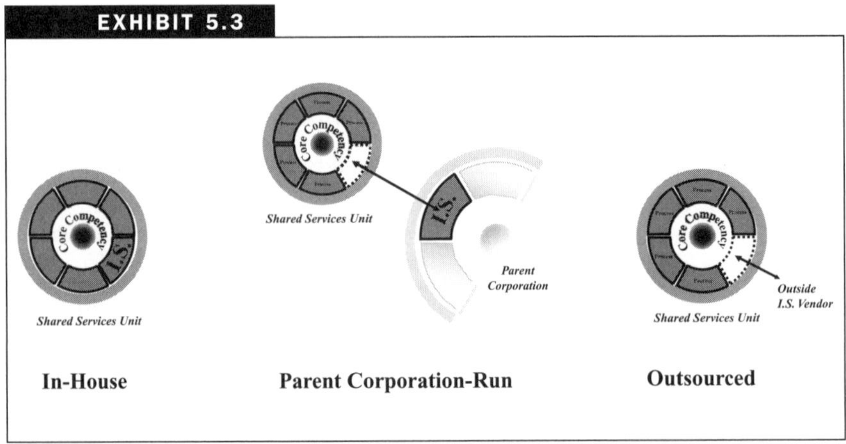

given the responsibility of coordinating the information infrastructure of the shared payroll system.

A second approach to providing Information Services to a shared business unit is to simply rely on an outside vendor. Outsourcing Information Services functions (Exhibit 5.3, right) has the advantage of freeing internal resources to work on the core competency of the business unit, such as payroll, and of minimizing the management resources required from the parent corporation. The third approach is to build an Information Services team in-house (Exhibit 5.3, left). This latter option is usually only feasible in shared business units with a hundred or more employees and deep pockets.

In each of these three scenarios, it's key for all of the Information Services professionals involved to establish a close and formal working relationship with each other so that there is agreement on standards, file formats, and other issues related to the efficient and effective sharing and processing of data, with a minimum of duplication of effort.

General-Purpose Information Technologies

A robust information infrastructure provides the platform for general-purpose information technologies, such as data storage, processing, communications, input/output, and analysis. As shown in Exhibit 5.4, general-purpose information technologies include hardware and software solutions that can be applied to virtually any shared business unit.

A distinguishing characteristic of general-purpose tools is that they can be applied to the core and ancillary processes of virtually any shared business unit. For example, a shared payroll services unit can use a database management system to maintain a record of employees of the parent corporation.

Another characteristic of general-purpose information technologies is that they can usually be acquired and used by individuals in small, independent groups within the shared business unit. For example, the

EXHIBIT 5.4

General-Purpose Information Technologies

Data Storage

Data Archiving	Data Warehousing
Database Management	

Data Processing

Data Aggregation	Localization
Data Encryption	Personalization
Data Mining	

Data Communications

E-mail	Paging Services
Messaging	Web Phones

Data Input/Output

Application Service Providers	Measurement
Interactive Voice Response	Reporting
Logging and Monitoring	Voice Portals

Decision Support

Decision Tree Software	Linear Programming Software
Forecasting Software	Modeling and Simulation Software
Gantt and PERT Charting Software	Statistical Analysis Software

manager might use a general-purpose decision tree application and a statistics program too, with little or no assistance from Information Services, especially if the tools are single-user applications that are on the user's desktop and don't need to be accessed through the network. However, Information Services can be of assistance when it controls the enterprise-wide licenses for, and provides training in, general-purpose applications, such as database use.

Examples of general-purpose information technologies in the areas

TIPS & TECHNIQUES

Know Your Limitations

Given the ready availability of affordable computer-based decision support tools, it's tempting to think that all there is to becoming fluent at operations management is plugging a few numbers into a program and then sitting back to marvel at the graphic output. However, all statistical and modeling techniques are based on assumptions in the data and how the results of the analysis are to be used.

Consider forecasting, a commonly used operations management tool that can help management plan production schedules, resource allocation, and to estimate future production costs. A commonly used forecasting technique is time-series forecasting, which is based on the assumption that future trends can be extrapolated from historical data. There's also the issue of which curve fitting formula is most appropriate for the data being used. Using the inappropriate curve fitting formula can result in a meaningless forecast.

Consider the two exhibits shown here, which illustrate the classic learning curve theory that production costs decline as an increased

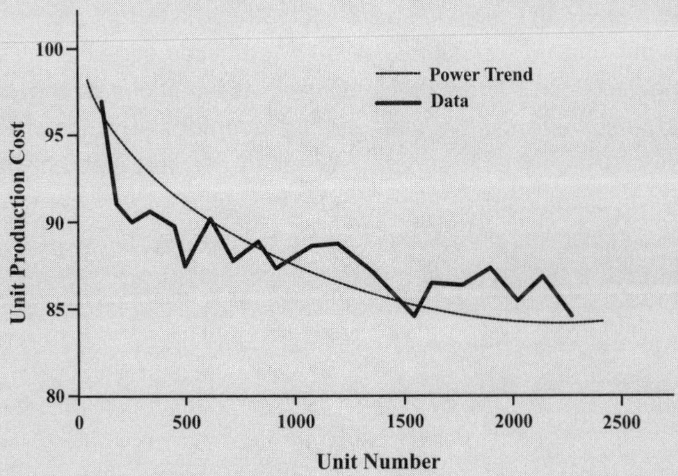

Tips and Techniques continued

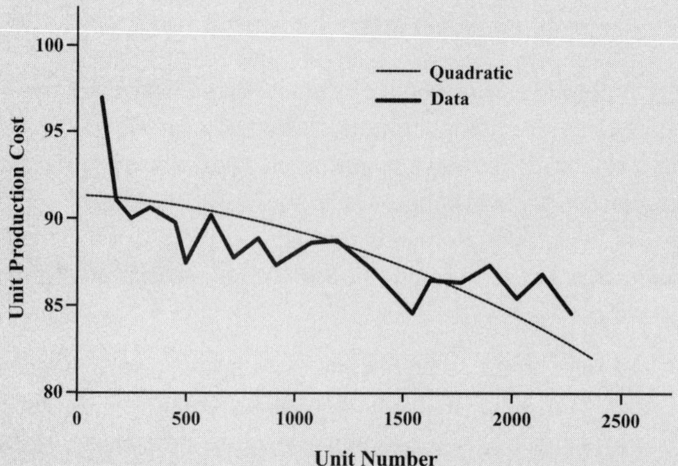

number of units are shipped, or the amount of service dispensed increases over time. This decline in production cost is often due to increased labor efficiency, improved processes, product redesign, or efficiencies of scale.

However, the predictive value of the historical production data depends on the curve fitting formula used. For example, in the first exhibit, a power trend curve is used to extrapolate the production costs, whereas in the second exhibit, a quadratic curve is used. Clearly, the two curves predict markedly different production cost per unit as the number of units produced increases. If the manager doesn't know the underlying assumptions of the data and the curve fitting formulas and the inherent limitations of forecasting, using a time series forecasting software package is a dangerous proposition. Every manager should know when to rely on his or her knowledge and familiarity with operations management techniques, and when to call on consultants.

of data storage, data processing, data communications, data input/output, and decision support are described in more detail here.

Data Storage

As a service organization, customer and process data is the lifeblood of the typical shared business unit. As such, archiving data, collecting data into a central repository, and managing data are key technologies. Data must be archived against disruption of business in the event of unforeseen destruction. Data must be collected so it can be quickly analyzed and searched for patterns in order to manage risk. The specific technologies and their applicability to the shared services model include:

- *Data Archiving.* Hardware and software technologies for archiving digital data range from automatic tape backup units to large disc farms that can be hung off the business unit's intranet to offsite, outsourced storage, accessed via the Internet.
- *Database Management.* A database management system (DBMS) is the software interface between employees and the data stored in a computer system. A DBMS simplifies and regulates the process of working with the records and files of a database, by providing tools for retrieving data, ensuring security, for querying relations between different data, removing duplicate data, and other housekeeping tasks.
- *Data Warehousing.* A data warehouse is a large, central database that integrates data from a variety of sources, such as a separate customer database, product database, order database, and inventory database. Data warehousing software isn't a single program, but is typically a suite of software tools that can be used to extract data from disparate databases, to check for errors and duplicate data, to aggregate the data, and then store it. The data warehousing software, which includes a DBMS, is the glue that ties the hardware and various databases together.

Data archiving and management are key to every service business. Data warehousing, in comparison, is typically necessary in only larger companies, or in smaller companies with several incompatible database systems. For example, a newly formed shared services information services center is often faced with the need to develop a data warehouse as a means of accessing and processing data from disparate business operations in the parent corporation and in other shared service units.

Data Processing

In most shared business units, the core competency is based on some form of data processing. For example, payroll, billing, insurance, logistics, and accounting are all business activities that data processing supports. In addition to these specific tasks, a number of general data processing activities are essential to the operation of the typical shared business unit. These operations include:

- *Data Encryption.* Customer data, whether medical records or payroll, has to be protected from the curious, the mischievous, and disgruntled employees. The standard method used to keep specific data confidential is to encrypt it such that only those with access to a decryption key can read it. Encryption software and hardware technologies are especially relevant when the parent corporation and shared business unit must exchange data electronically over Internet or telephone network.
- *Data Mining.* Data mining software supports the process of extracting meaningful patterns from customer data stored in databases and data warehouses. Data mining software identifies relationships and correlations in data. The results of data mining are used in marketing, for example, to derive customer preferences, and in operations management to predict future demand for services.
- *Localization.* When a shared services unit is charged with providing service to the parent corporation's internal customers

in multiple countries, localization software can be used to help identify the most appropriate language etiquette for customers. For example, an integrated caller-ID system can identify the origin of callers and route their calls to the customer service representative with the appropriate language skills. Automatic language translation technologies are also useful in providing a rough translation of text on the Web or in e-mails so that the recipient can read the content.

- *Personalization.* Software that helps compile customer-specific information, such as purchasing history and preferences, can be used to create a feeling of personal attention, and an increased likelihood of future business. For example, if a personalization software system in a shared services printing unit determines that a certain division in the parent corporation routinely orders business cards two weeks after a new employee has been hired, the printing unit can offer to automatically send cards two weeks after a new employee shows up on the corporate database. Personalization technologies are dependent on data mining and data storage technologies.

General-purpose data processing technologies, such as data mining, are typically combined with specific data processing techniques to provide increased functionality.

Data Communications

The efficiency, flexibility, and capacity of data communications within the shared business unit and between the unit and internal or external customers affect every aspect of the business. Communications technologies are changing both the nature of corporate communications and the ease with which immediate communications can be established. For example, with instant messaging, customers can contact support staff in the shared business unit and have a response within seconds of submitting a question. In addition, new wireless options, from cell phones

IN THE REAL WORLD

Security Speed Bumps

Wireless, one of the most promising technologies aimed at office automation and increasing the mobility and productivity of employees, has hit some adoption speed bumps because of security issues. The most prevalent wireless network technology, Wi-Fi, is growing popular in small and large businesses as an alternative to pulling cables between PCs, servers, and providing connectivity to the Internet. However, the technology is vulnerable to eavesdropping and hacking. As such, several high-profile companies and government agencies have either banned or restricted the use of wireless networks. For example:

- Lawrence Livermore National Laboratory in California, which conducts nuclear weapons research, banned all wireless networks from its grounds because of vulnerability to security breaches.
- The Los Alamos National Laboratory in New Mexico doesn't allow wireless networks in high-security areas.
- The M.D. Anderson Cancer Center in Houston cancelled a pilot program using wireless communications because of senior management's concerns that sensitive patient information could be intercepted.
- Aeronautical Radio, the company that provides communications services to the government and airlines, is replacing its wireless system because of security concerns. Given the increased scrutiny on airline security, the current system of bag matching using a wireless network is seen as a major vulnerability.
- The United States Department of Transportation is assessing the vulnerability of wireless systems in airports, based on the fear that hackers could alter passenger and baggage data.

As a result of these concerns, many Fortune 1000 companies are rethinking their use of wireless technologies, including the use of wireless handheld personal digital assistants.

to wireless handheld computers, are creating new opportunities for innovative managers to improve the efficiency of their shared services operations. The more prominent communications technologies useful in the shared services business include:

- *E-mail.* Virtually every business organization can benefit from text-based e-mail. In addition to supporting general communications, e-mail can be extended to improve the effectiveness of niche areas in a shared business unit. For example, it can be integrated with a problem-tracking database for customer support or an integrated voice and data system to handle orders from the parent corporation.

- *Messaging.* Like e-mail, text-messaging technology is becoming ubiquitous in business. It should be part of every shared services business that deals with real-time customer data and whose employees need to be constantly available to customers and coworkers.

- *Paging Services.* Shared services centers are like most other business operations in their need for providing a means of rapidly contacting managers and staff regardless of their location. Paging services can be used by shared services employees to communicate via pagers, cell phones, and personal digital assistants (PDAs).

- *Wireless Devices.* Wireless personal digital assistants (PDAs), Web-enabled cell phones, and standard cell phones provide the hardware platform for shared services employees and managers to use as the basis for voice and data communications. Wireless PDAs are especially popular for asynchronous text messaging and e-mail because they obviate the tedium of voice mail exchanges.

Efficient data communications depend not only on specialized hardware and software systems, but also on a high-speed, reliable communications infrastructure. In this regard, high-speed Internet access is the norm in most companies in the United States. In contrast, the domestic cellular network pales in comparison to wireless systems in Europe and Asia.

Data Input/Output

General-purpose data input/output technologies applicable to shared services operations include desktop, laptop, and handheld computers, handheld barcode readers to automate and reduce the errors in tracking customers, processes, and deliverables. There are also several key data input/output technologies that are especially suited for shared services centers, in part because they reduce the need for employees. Examples of these technologies include:

- *Application Service Provider.* Unlike the traditional approach of purchasing software from a vendor and either loading it locally on each PC or on a server located in the parent corporation, the ASP model offloads the software loading and maintenance task to an outside source—such as a business unit (see Exhibit 5.5). The cost savings of the ASP model, which is a form of remote data input/output, can be significant because activities such as data archiving, loading new versions of software, server maintenance, and other Information Services functions can be concentrated in the shared business unit.
- *Interactive Voice Response (IVR).* A voice-driven telephone interface to a computer system take the place of human telephone operators, allowing customers to retrieve information without the aid of employees from the shared business unit.
- *Automated Monitoring and Reporting.* Software tools for monitoring everything from Web site traffic to the number of phone calls handled by support staff can save time and free up employees for more core competency work.

In addition to these technologies, there are a variety of specialized input/output hardware devices, from voice recognition to synthetic speech generation, that can be used to facilitate more effective use of the

EXHIBIT 5.5

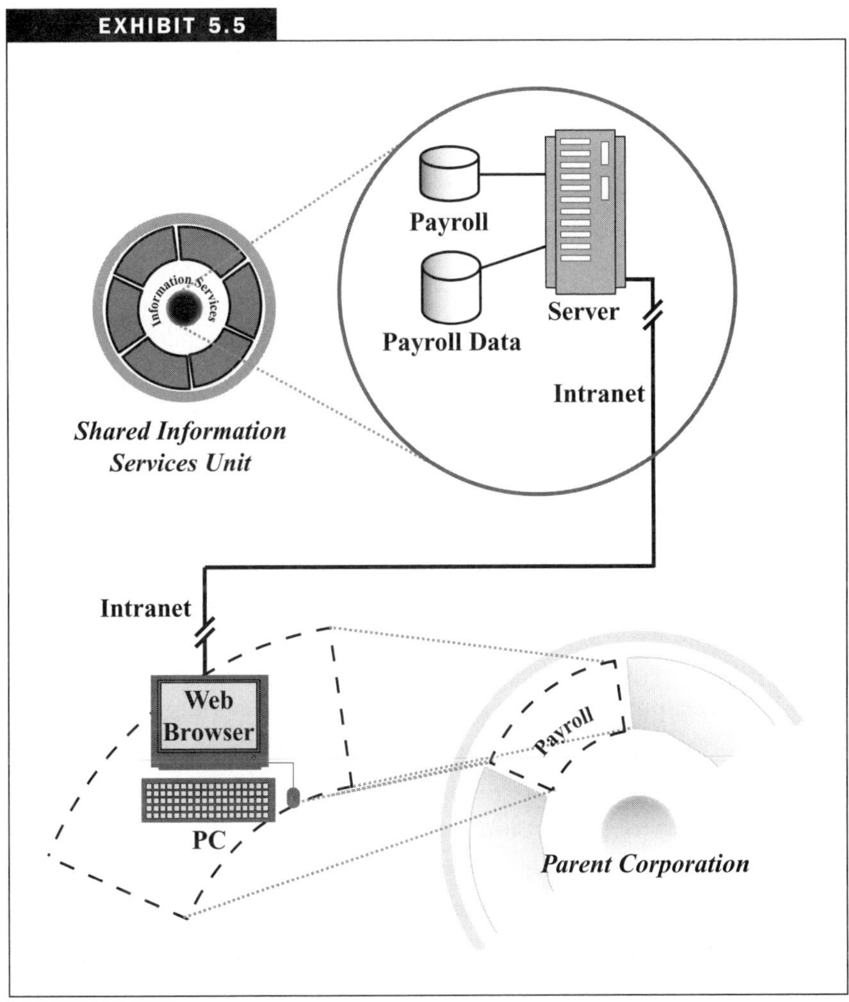

shared business unit's employee time while providing an enhanced level of service to customers.

Decision Support

Of particular value to shared services management is general-purpose decision support software that can help determine how to best position the unit for growth, determine the optimum number of employees that should be assigned to specific tasks, and help predict and monitor the quality of service provided to the parent organization or outside customer. Decision support software automates the tedium of operations management, allowing the manager to focus on the application of the results, as opposed to the minutia of, for example, solving multiple simultaneous equations in a linear programming problem. The key decision support software packages that can be used to facilitate the solution of operations management problems include:

- *Decision Trees.* Automated decision tree software allows a decision tree (see Exhibit 5.6) to be built in a matter of minutes instead of hours using a manual approach. This assumes, however, that the certain key factors are known, such as risk aversion, the complete set of options available, including their costs, and outcome probabilities. In reality, more time is usually spent finding and verifying these data than graphing the results.
- *Flow Diagramming.* Automated flow diagramming is an operations management technique that can help management answer production capacity questions by mapping out the workflow of a production process in a way that highlights potential inefficiencies. Flow diagram programs can pinpoint areas where production methods can change from inefficient sequential operations to parallel operations, for example. A flow diagram may show that a properly configured assembly

EXHIBIT 5.6

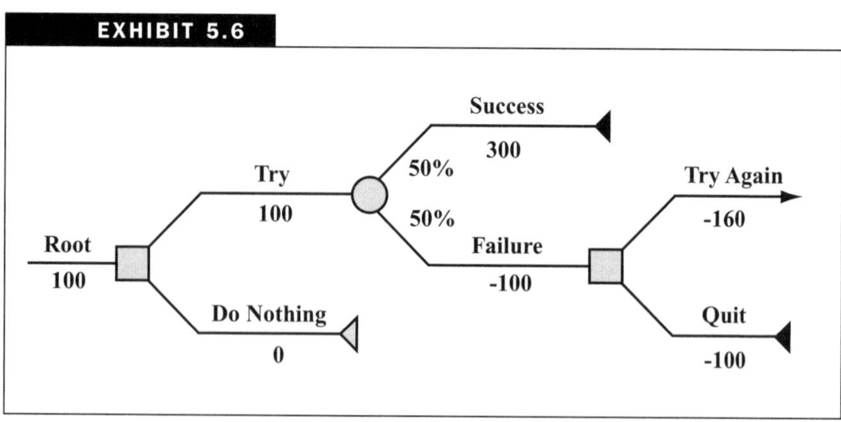

line with two employees working in parallel may outperform two employees performing sequential operations, for example.

- *Forecasting.* Automated forecasting programs use historical data to predict or forecast the status of a business process at some point in the future. The reliability of the forecast decreases as the prediction is carried farther into the future.
- *Gantt and PERT Charting.* Programs that use these two graphical representations of project management basics, included with virtually every project management software package, can help management determine how to use resources more efficiently.
- *Linear Programming.* Another software tool that can be used to explore production capacity and determine the optimum use of resources in the shared business unit is linear programming software. Instead of guessing whether three employees doing parallel tasks would increase production capacity at a lower overall marginal cost than, say, two employees working sequentially on production, but with better and more expensive computers, a linear programming application can solve for the optimum solution.
- *Modeling and Simulation.* Computer-based modeling and simulation techniques allow management to construct graphical models of current and potential production processes and then run the simulation to predict the outcome. In this way, management can experiment with a variety of production processes without interrupting the current process. The main downsides of using computer-based modeling and simulation techniques include the time involved in creating the models and the difficulty of validating the assumptions made in defining the models.
- *Statistical Analysis.* There is a plethora of software devoted to helping managers determining the mean, mode, median, and other quantifiable characteristics of a group of customers (or employees). Even inexpensive business calculators provide

statistical analysis functions that can be used to provide insight into, for example, the variation in quality of service provided by the shared business unit.

Software tools have evolved to the point that anyone with a passing familiarity with computers can perform what appears to be a reasonable analysis of corporate or shared services data. However, it's a mistake for a manager to trust a software package to solve a problem without first understanding the underlying assumptions of the methods used.

Process-Specific Information Technologies

At the highest level in the information technology hierarchy are process-specific tools that are designed to facilitate specific functions, such as customer relationship management, payroll, or logistics. The common characteristics of the thousands of process-specific tools available—a sampling of which is listed in Exhibit 5.7—are specificity and, at least in theory, the efficiency in supporting a particular business activity.

EXHIBIT 5.7

Process-Specific Information Technologies

- Administration Support
- Application Development
- Contact Management
- CRM
- Domain-specific suites
- Enterprise resource planning
- Finance
- Human Resources
- Inventory Management
- Material Requirement Planning
- Knowledge Management
- Payroll
- Professional Services Automation
- Real Estate & Physical Plant
- Sales and Marketing
- Training
- User Authentication
- Workforce Management

For example, although a spreadsheet and database management system might be used as tools in a shared services accounting unit, use of these and other general-purpose tools would probably not result in the most effective use of employee time. A much better approach would be to use a dedicated accounting package tailored to the needs of the shared business unit. The advantage of using a specialized accounting package is time savings, assuming that the package is compatible with the way employees in the shared business unit perform their accounting work. Time savings comes from predefined templates, preconfigured mathematical calculations, automated backup facilities, and the use of visual metaphors in the interface that decrease training time. For example, unlike a general-purpose spreadsheet, a dedicated accounting package may provide a chart of accounts, preconfigured time and invoicing databases, worksheets for tracking and billing for employee time on particular projects, and a database template for customers.

The disadvantage of using process-specific tools is that they may not match the processes used in the shared business unit closely enough to justify their added cost. There is always the option of building a custom application in-house or through a contractor, but this may be an expensive, drawn-out process. There is also the question of product lifetime, given that the operation of the shared services unit will likely be in flux, and any software developed to support current processes may be outdated in a year or two. Examples of the more significant process-specific information technology tools include:

- *Administration Support.* Software that addresses the specific needs of inventory, mailroom, printing, records management, and supply can be purchased separately or, in some cases, as an integrated administration support package.
- *Application Development.* A shared business unit involved in developing a Web site, providing information services support,

or modifying software in-house can make use of a variety of application development tools—editors, version control systems, and high-level authoring tools—that support rapid prototyping and development. In general, because the application needs will likely change in the lifetime of the shared business unit, low-level, time-consuming programming languages should be avoided.

- *Contact Management.* A suite of integrated tools designed to track and manage customer contact has a universal applicability in business. The typical full-featured contact management system includes a customer database; a method of recording the topic discussed with each call or e-mail—often with an automatic time and date stamp; a calendar with reminders; an integrated e-mail system; a phone dialer that dials the phone to automatically return a call; and a variety of tools to create reports, including lists of customers who have unresolved problems.
- *Customer Relationship Management (CRM).* A suite of utilities for customer relationship management typically includes modules dedicated to help desk management, field service, telemarketing, contact management, and territory management. Tools for eCRM—customer relationship management on the Web—include e-mail and Internet-compatible versions of CRM utilities.
- *Domain-Specific Suites.* Highly specialized suites of software applications, that address areas such as Hospital Information Services (HIS), when available, can greatly improve the efficiency of data collection, manipulation, and decision support. For example, a typical full-featured HIS package provides support for admission, discharge, and transfer functions, clinical reporting, and a medical transcriptions service. Domain-specific suites tend to be expensive, and the vendors that offer these packages tend to have very volatile business profiles because of the small number of customers. As such, the

domain-specific suites used in a shared business unit should be selected with caution.

- *Enterprise Resource Planning.* Software designed to improve the internal processes of a company, commonly referred to as ERP, is typically a suite of applications—database management, statistics and operations management tools—integrated by a vendor. As in the case of CRM, most ERP packages are in reality suites of loosely integrated general-purpose information technologies.
- *Finance.* Software suites that offer integrated general accounting, payroll processing, purchasing, taxes, and transaction processing can help streamline the financial process. As with other suites, the degree of integration limits the efficiency of the technology. In general, the tighter the integration, the less work there is for the employee working with the system.
- *Human Resources.* HR-specific application suites can automate the process of recruiting, relocation, staffing, training, and workers' compensation. Ideally, the HR director of a shared business unit can use these tools to leverage his or her abilities to the point that effective HR functions can be provided with significantly fewer staff than before.
- *Knowledge Management.* A variety of technologies for knowledge collection, storage, retrieval, dissemination, and application are available from any number of vendors. Because the focus of knowledge management tools varies so much from one vendor to the next, the challenge is to determine the knowledge management needs of the shared business unit before selecting the toolset.
- *Training.* Computer-based training or eLearning can be a major cost savings initiative, especially when the shared services staff is too thin to allow half of its employees to travel across the country to a seminar. At its best, teleconferencing technologies that provide two-way video links between teachers

and students can provide a more interactive, engaging teaching experience.

The challenge for a manager dealing with vendors offering process-specific solutions is to find a solution that is truly designed for the application it's sold for. For example, many tools marketed for CRM are minimally modified and repackaged ERP suites that may not perform as advertised when applied to CRM. Similarly, some Knowledge Management suites are simply loosely integrated general-purpose applications that provide very little added value over using independent toolsets.

Disruptive Information Technologies

Just as the electronic spreadsheet redefined the practice of accounting, there are a number of information technologies poised to change the way businesses—including shared business units—operate. These disruptive technologies include:

- *Bots.* Software robots or Bots have the potential to replace customer service representatives and other e-mail–based support functions. To the customer, a bot appears as a customer service representative or engineer replying to an e-mail question in real-time. As a fail-safe mechanism, most Bots used in customer support pass the customer on to the queue of a human customer service Rep after one or two failed attempts to handle the customer's question. In this way, customers are not left frustrated with their questions unanswered and with no human to turn to for help.
- *Language Processing (NLP).* This pattern recognition technology will allow a customer to converse in natural English sentences to a computer assistant, database search engine, or customer service Bot.
- *Voice Portals.* Voice portals allow customers to access the content on a Web site through any type of phone. In this way,

automatic services can reduce call-center costs, especially for package tracking, account status, and answering frequently asked questions.

- *Wireless Systems.* Wireless headsets, telephone systems, and PDAs provide freedom of movement without compromising connectivity. When tied in with the Web, wireless devices have access to a virtually unlimited store of data that can be used for customer support, materials tracking, or virtually any other data-intensive application. The main limitation of wireless systems is the added cost over wired systems, and a modest increase in the security risk because wireless communications can be intercepted.

Given the trend toward pervasive computing—the anytime, anyplace access to computer technology and data—it's likely that more disruptive technologies will soon appear in the marketplace. In addition, the increasing demand for service and cost-cutting measures will drive many shared services managers to explore the latest technologies that have the greatest capacity to realize these goals while assuming minimal risk.

The next chapter extends the discussion of information technologies to the evaluation of process and employee characteristics and their influence on a shared services business.

Summary

The premise of the shared services model is that it can save money and increase quality of service. However, to make this premise a reality virtually always requires an infusion of information technology, especially in data intensive services. Every CEO should at least be familiar with the general classes of information technologies available, their applicability to the shared services model, and their limitations. In addition, given the pressure for constant improvement, the CEO should be aware of information technologies on the near and far horizons that hold potential for enabling the shared business unit to operate at greater efficiency or at lower cost.

Technology intensifies the law of change.

Gordon E. Moore, co-founder, Intel Corp

CHAPTER 6

Evaluation

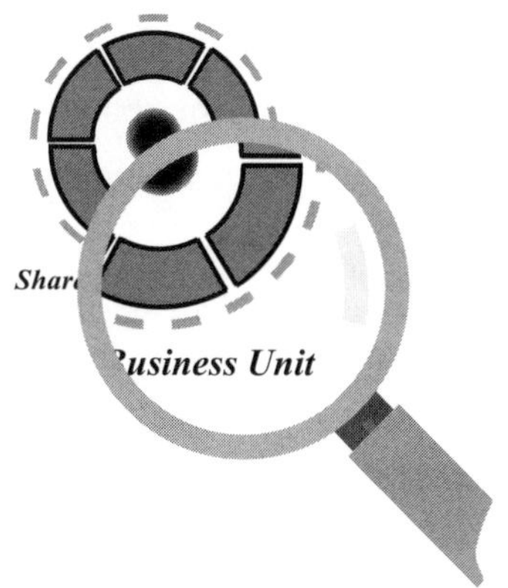

After reading this chapter you will be able to

- Appreciate the various approaches to evaluating shared services
- Understand the significance of benchmarking in evaluating and improving a shared services operation
- Understand the issues involved in evaluating the applicability of information technologies for a shared services business
- Appreciate the multiple perspectives from which a shared business unit can be evaluated
- Understand how to evaluate the issues involving people, processes, and technology in a shared service from management's perspective

The open market is mercilessly efficient at doling out feedback on which goods and services are acceptable. A profit-oriented company that fails to drive customers to its offerings and fails to keep them coming back for more simply won't survive. The shared business unit is unique in this respect because it is largely shielded from these Darwinian economics, as long the parent corporation is the source of the majority of revenue.

However, even if the shared business unit remains in a state of perpetual adolescence and doesn't venture into an open market dominated by profit-driven companies, it's nonetheless accountable to the parent corporation's senior management. Its customers are internal customers, and they too have a right to expect quality service. So too the management of a shared business unit, just like profit-making management, can reasonably demand employees and the technologies they use to perform up to or even exceed industry standards. As illustrated in the accompanying vignette, making these expectations a reality requires an evaluation process that is accurate, repeatable, and that generates actionable information.

Help for the Help Desk

It's now four years since HealthCare Partners implemented its shared business unit, information services unit—formally dubbed HealthCare Information Services or HIS. The challenge facing the current management is that the six full-time employees working at the information services help desk are operating in firefighting mode. The average problem resolution time has increased from two hours four years ago to over three days, today.

There are several reasons for the decreased responsiveness of the help desk. For example, the staff supports over 150 official applications, from an ASP-based payroll system to a networked statistical analysis program for the clinical and research staff. In addition, there are hundreds of software packages, purchased by the clinical and research staff for their own use, which disable or otherwise cause problems with officially sanctioned software installed on HIS-maintained PCs. There is also a continual demand for reloading and maintaining official applications because the stream of operating system upgrades causes them to fail. The demand for computer technician hardware repair time and software support is further compounded by the fact that the staff of the shared information services unit is charged with maintaining programs whose companies have failed, many of which are still relied on by HealthCare Partners staff.

Another reason for the increased demand on help-desk time is that HIS recently contracted its services to six outside clinics. These clinics, which pay HIS market rates for hosting their web site, hardware and software maintenance, and access to the ASP-hosted suite of office automation software, represent an added 25 percent workload on the help desk personnel. It also results in almost $600,000 in additional annual revenue for HIS. As such, the customers in the outside clinics are given priority over internal customers. When a call or written request from one of the paying clinics arrives, it's bumped up ahead of any internal customer requests already in the queue.

Because of the poor responsiveness of the help desk, internal customers are complaining, and frustration with HIS is general. Similarly, the HIS help-desk employees are complaining to management about the increased workload from the outside clinics with no additional hires or pay increases.

However, the senior management of HealthCare Partners is pleased with the new revenue source. More importantly, it views the dependence of the outside clinics on HIS as a means of politically maneuvering the management of the clinics to join the HealthCare Partners network of hospitals and clinics. HealthCare Partners senior management recently started talks with management of the outside clinics in an effort to solidify the relationship by offering them the option of investing in the HIS venture. With this lucrative business deal on the horizon, HealthCare Partners senior management is willing to put up with slower response from HIS in exchange for profitability, as long as the core business processes of the HealthCare Partners network are supported.

The HIS manager must deal with complaints from irate administrators from each institution while lobbying against the formation of independent pockets of rogue computer networks and software installations that are forming in response to frustration with HIS. He is faced with the conundrum of attempting to satisfy internal and external customers while moving HIS toward profitability in order to satisfy senior management's acquisition plans. In desperate need of a solution, the manager calls in a shared services business consultant that had helped establish HIS several years earlier and explains the situation.

The consultant and the HIS manager create a grid, dividing HIS into three management categories—people, processes, and technology—and evaluate each category separately (see Exhibit 6.1). In establishing benchmarks, they examine process first, and discover that, relative to industry standards for information service shops of the same size and with similar work load, HIS ranks in the lower third for help-desk complaint response time (response time) and about average for time to resolve issues (resolution time). More importantly, for internal customers, response time has almost doubled, compared to when the benchmarks were first taken four years earlier.

To address the process ineffectiveness, the manager and consultant explore the current process to identify areas of potential improvement. By interviewing and observing the help-desk employees, the consultant concludes that the workload is greater than the employees can handle, and that majority of employee time is spent handling printed requests involving mundane, low-level issues, such as request for passwords and password changes. In addition, most of the remaining requests involve support of third-party applications that were added by clinical, research, and administrative departments without first consulting HIS regarding long-term support obligations.

EXHIBIT 6.1

Original Benchmark Grid

Area	Benchmarks	Actions
Process	• Lower third for help desk response time industry-wide • Average for resolution time industry-wide	• Chargeback for third-part software support
Technology	• Minimal automation • Paper-based • Not considered best practices in the industry	• Buy/Install automated system • Add e-mail, Web touch points
People	• 6 employees involved, compared to industry average of 2 or 3	• Downsize to 2 employees • Service level agreements • Training online

Prior to the formation of HIS, the information services department in each institution had been overly permissive regarding support for third party applications. After all, the service was free—individual staff and their departments weren't charged for it since support was simply part of the overhead for the institution. Things are different with HIS, however, because information services is a billable service offered to institutions in the HealthCare Partners network. The consultant's recommendation to the HIS manager is that he immediately institute a chargeback policy for support of third party applications, using the pricing model developed for the external customers who are charged for HIS standard support. The chargeback mechanism will also provide the parent corporation's management with a means of allocating resources and of controlling its employees use and abuse of the shared business unit.

TIPS & TECHNIQUES

Training Helps

Making the shift to a customer-focused organization often takes more than a dictum from senior management. Often, lower management and employees need to show exactly what's expected of them. For example, British Columbia Hydro, a shared services electrical utility in British Columbia, hired training firms to work with its information technology staff on how to become more customer-focused.

Focusing on technology, the consultant suggests automating the help-desk function by installing a help-desk caller-ID application to automatically identify customers by their institution, whether they're internal or external customers, and the time they've been in the queue. With the system in place, customers can be juggled in the queue as a function of the criteria established by management. For example, external customers from hospitals may be given preference over customers from the external clinics.

In preparation for switching over to the automated system, the six employees staffing the help desk are interviewed for a second time, with the focus on compatibility with the new automated help-desk system. Two of the original six employees who are most comfortable and proficient with the computerized systems are trained on the automated help-desk application using an on-line eLearning system offered by the help-desk application vendor. Two of the remaining four employees are reassigned to other administrative tasks within HIS, and the other two are given a severance package and assistance from human resources in securing employment elsewhere.

With the automated help-desk system, management can decide in real-time whether to provide equivalent levels of service for internal and external customers. In addition, the system allows the two help-desk employees—who are now doing the work previously performed by six employees—to quickly resolve high-volume, administrative issues that formerly went to HIS. For example, help-desk employees can automatically assign passwords to new employees with a few keystrokes instead of taking the time to communicate the request to the appropriate technician in information services.

In order to encourage the two employees assigned to the automated help desk, the manager and consultant establish a service level agreement (SLA) between the employees and internal customers. The agreements, brokered by the manager, stipulate minimum response time and resolution time standards for internal and external customers, with specific timelines for escalation of standards over the next year, to be benchmarked every quarter. The manager, consultant, and help-desk employees accept the improvements, which are based on industry-wide standards of performance. All three agree that the improvements are realistic and achievable.

Three months after automating the help-desk system, the benchmarks are repeated (see Exhibit 6.2). Not only are administrative costs down by 30 percent, primarily because of the downsizing of help-desk staff, but also the average wait time for internal customers is reduced by nearly two thirds. With a newly trained staff, modified help-desk process, and automation, the new HIS help desk is operating in the top 10 percent, based on nationwide industry averages of response and resolution time.

The two employees eagerly anticipate the benchmarking every quarter because they have bonuses waiting for them as the benchmark goals are achieved or exceeded. As defined by the service level agreement, failing to meet the benchmark figures means no bonus for the quarter. However, since the benchmarks established by the service level

EXHIBIT 6.2

Updated Benchmark Grid

Area	Benchmarks	Actions
Process	• Response time in the upper 10 percent industry-wide • Resolution time in the upper 10 percent industry-wide • Administrative costs cut 30 percent	• Repeat benchmark in 3 months
Technology	• Automated, as per industry best practices • Electronic submission of problems	• Repeat benchmark in 3 months
People	• 2 employees involved, in line with industry average of 2 or 3	• Repeat benchmark in 3 months

agreement are realistic and achievable, employees don't feel unduly stressed by the challenges before them.

The experiences of the HIS manager and consultant illustrate several key issues related to evaluating a shared business unit:

- *The evaluation of a shared business unit includes both qualitative and quantitative measures.* The evaluation of the HIS help desk involves a quantitative analysis of response and resolution times, and subjective, qualitative evaluations from employees regarding process.
- *The evaluation approach reflects the perspective of the evaluator.* For example, in the vignette, the HIS manager focuses on the performance of employees in the unit. In comparison, the management of HealthCare Partners focuses on the strategic

importance of a profitable shared business unit as well as the performance of the HIS manager.

- *Investing the time and energy to measure results is only prudent when management intends to do something with the results.* For example, while measuring average response and resolution times is appropriate for resolving help-desk throughput issues, evaluating employee job satisfaction prior to automation is inappropriate just prior to a major process overhaul.
- *Service level agreements can be invaluable in establishing and maintaining standards for quality of service.* The service level agreement is a contract between providers and consumers of service that holds service providers accountable for the level of service they provide.
- *It's impossible for the shared business unit to completely fulfill every stakeholder's needs.* For example, the optimum approaches to CRM for internal versus external customers are at odds. In some cases, internal customers may be more likely than are external customers to be intentionally turned away, despite the relationship of the shared business unit with the parent corporation.

The significance of perspective in benchmarking is discussed in more detail here.

Evaluation Perspectives

The experience of employees, management, and the consultant faced with the HIS help desk challenge illustrates how a shared business unit can be evaluated from the perspectives of the primary stakeholders. The most important stakeholders in a shared business unit are:

- Internal and external customers
- Parent corporation and shared services management
- Employees
- Investors
- Competition

Customers

Internal customers tend to be primarily concerned with quality of service, including responsiveness; price is normally a secondary issue. In contrast, external customers are like typical retail consumers, in that they expect value for their money, as reflected in both price and quality of service. External customers are more price-sensitive than internal customers are because the shared services infrastructure at least partially insulates internal customers from actual costs, even if a chargeback mechanism is in place.

As shown in Exhibit 6.3, in evaluating the services of shared business unit, both internal and external customers attend to:

- *Clarity.* Customers expect an unambiguous trade of value for value, without hidden costs or required service add-ons.
- *Cost.* The cost of services is more important to external customers, who can easily compare prices of competing services.
- *Honesty.* Customers expect shared services employees to offer services that best fit their needs, without the influence of hidden agendas.
- *Personalized Attention.* Service is ideally anticipatory, reflecting

EXHIBIT 6.3

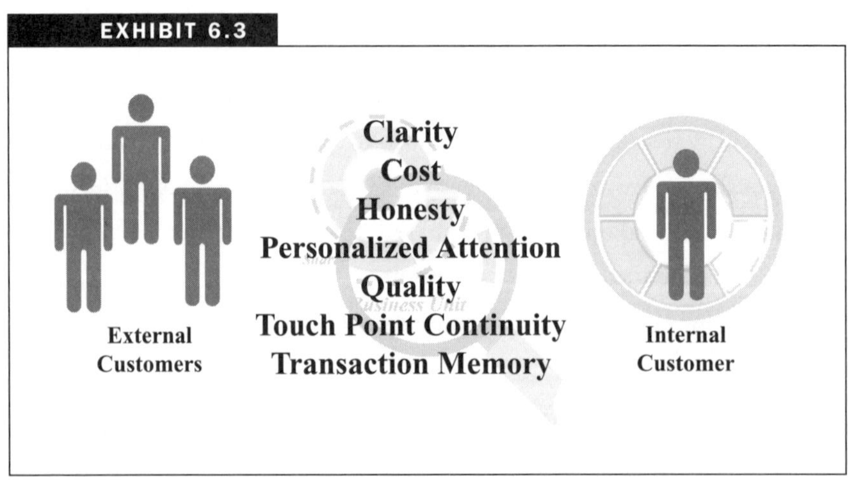

the individual needs of the customer. Both internal and external customers expect to be treated as valued consumers.

- *Quality.* The quality of service encompasses responsiveness and personalized attention.
- *Touch Point Continuity.* Customers expect the same level of service, value, and recognition, regardless of the touch point used.
- *Transaction Memory.* Customers expect the service provider to remember their needs after a reasonable period. A department that regularly contracts for copier service from a shared services copier repair center shouldn't have to describe the copier equipment to the help-desk operator every time the copier needs service.

Although most customers don't create formal metrics for benchmarking quality of service or price, their purchasing behavior provides an ad-hoc benchmark that can be used by management to evaluate shared business unit performance.

Management

Unlike customers, managers from both the shared business unit and the parent corporation base their assessment of the success of the shared business on definite benchmarks. As illustrated in Exhibit 6.4, parent corporation managers use more strategically oriented benchmarks, whereas management of the shared business unit is more concerned with tactical issues, such as internal process and customer behavior.

Shared services management is necessarily concerned with evaluating the internal operation of the shared business unit, focusing on people, process, and technology, as well as with customer trends, using market surveys, sales or chargeback figures, and changes in customer demand. In contrast, the management of the parent corporation is primarily concerned with evaluating cost, growth rate, and responsiveness to its employees' needs.

EXHIBIT 6.4

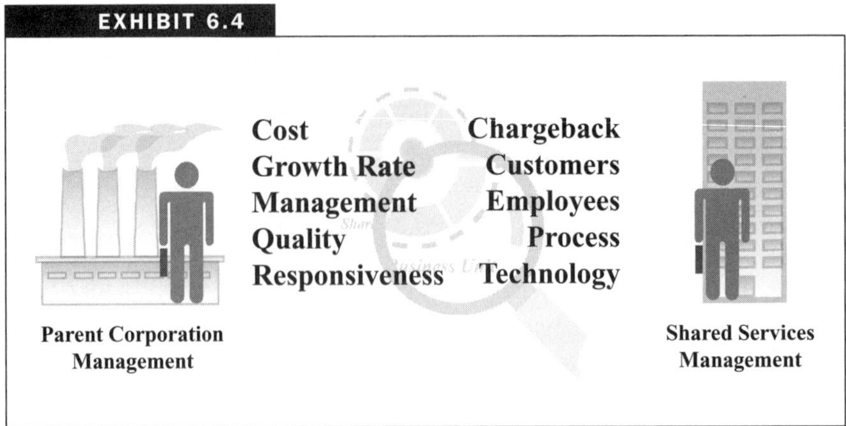

Typically included in the parent corporation's benchmarks are:

- *Cost.* One reason for implementing a shared services model is to reduce cost to the parent corporation for back-end services.
- *Growth Rate.* Related to cost and ability to provide services to internal customers, the growth rate of the shared business unit is an indicator of the cost of operation as well as demand for services.
- *Management.* The effectiveness of the interim or long-term management team is a key issue in evaluating the potential success of a shared services operation. Is it effective in implementing cost cutting measures? Can it deliver services on time and in the needed quantity?
- *Quality.* In addition to cost, the shared services model promises increased quality of service. Monitoring this quality is key to ensuring that internal customer expectations are being met.
- *Responsiveness.* Closely related to quality of service is the responsiveness of the shared business unit to internal customer needs. Deterioration in responsiveness, as was noted with HIS, may be due to a short-term distraction or it may represent a long-term trend.

Growth rate, quality of service provided to internal customers, and the ability to respond to internal customer needs are primary

IN THE REAL WORLD

A Return to the Nest

The real world can be overwhelming at times, even for adults. Competing goals and relentless pressure to live up to the expectations of others can make even the most hardened CEO long for the simpler life of their youth. Although this isn't a realistic option for most self-respecting CEOs, it isn't unheard of in the shared services arena. For example, after several years of operating as a mature, profit-driven shared business unit, Shell Services International turned back the clock and returned to an adolescent stage in which it dropped third-party customers and focused instead on the needs of the parent corporation, Royal Dutch/Shell. Instead of trying to serve two markets, Shell Services International reverted to a quality-driven shared services organization that focuses on the Information Services needs of the oil and gas company's business units.

benchmarks for parent corporation management. The benchmarks typically evaluated by the shared services manager are more tactical, shorter-term metrics, including:

- *Chargeback.* Monitoring the value-exchange, whether services are exchanged for chargeback or money, provides shared services management with hard metrics on the maturation of the unit and the unit's overall ability to deliver valued services to customers.
- *Customer Behavior.* The demand from internal and external customers for services provides a measure of the ability of the shared business unit to respond to and address specific customer needs.
- *People.* Evaluating the employees of the shared business unit provides benchmarks that can be compared internally over

time and to industry standards to track relative and absolute changes in performance over time. Relevant benchmarks include quantitative, objective measures of efficiency and effectiveness at particular tasks, as well as qualitative, subjective measures of flexibility and leadership potential.

- *Process.* Benchmarks are a critical component of process optimization, that is, the efficiency, effectiveness, cost, and management used to complete particular tasks, based on industry standards and prior employee performance.
- *Technology.* The competing goals of cost savings and increased service usually can't be achieved without the application of information technology, especially in the midst of downsizing. Whether technology is directed at improving the information infrastructure or provides general-purpose or process-specific support, it can usually be evaluated in terms of the benchmarks listed in Exhibit 6.5.

Because information technology is not only central to the benchmarking process but to the day-to-day operation of a typical shared business unit, more benchmarks are applied to this area of a shared services operation than any other. For example, benchmarks that evaluate a

EXHIBIT 6.5

Technology Benchmarks

Adherence to Standards
Compatibility
Customer Support
Growth Path
Installed User Base
Performance
Security Provisions
Suitability

particular technology product's adherence to standards are commonly applied to everything from the database engine, distribution media, and hardware platform, to network compatibility, operating system requirements, support for peripherals, software architecture, and ability to import and export data in popular formats.

Compatibility benchmarks are usually applied to existing systems, internal processes, and third-party support. Although customer support benchmarks commonly include training and documentation, the mechanism for reporting bugs and obtaining fixes typically ranks highest in any evaluation. Benchmarks concerning the growth path quantify the extensibility, flexibility, localization options, and scalability of the product.

Unfortunately, it's often the case that an information system that works on a small scale—such as in a department or workgroup—simply can't be used enterprise-wide because of inherent limitations in the operating system, bandwidth of the network connections, or the number of simultaneous users that can be supported by a particular software package. Scalability, the ability of a software or hardware product used on a large or small scale with little change in operation, is especially critical if management intends to grow the shared business unit significantly. Scalability is always a matter of degree, in that performance of capacity is virtually never a simple linear function of increasing hardware capacity or speed. Doubling the operating speed or storage capacity of a computer doesn't double the throughput of a payroll processing system, for example.

Benchmarks commonly applied to the installed user base include the number of successful installations in operation and, perhaps more importantly, the number of failures. These benchmarks may be difficult to validate, especially since most technology vendors don't make a habit of advertising their failures. Technology performance benchmarks include response time, in seconds or milliseconds, and reliability, typically measured in mean time between failure (MTBF) for hard drives, monitors, and other computer equipment. The lamps in an LCD (flat panel) monitor typically last 10,000 hours before failure, for example. The reliability of other devices, such as printers and fax machines, is generally expressed indirectly as the number of copies per month.

Technology benchmarks are usually established by the computer industry, in the form of magazine reviews. Magazines establish credible benchmarks for evaluating computer hardware and software because their readership is keenly interested in how the systems measure up to each other. Reviews offered by industry-specific and general-readership magazines are especially relevant for more subjective and qualitative benchmarks such as security provisions, suitability of the technology for the intended application, and the warranty. For example, an application may be ill suited for a given task because of problems with ease of use or lack of specificity. Because magazine editors frequently have access to every major competing product in a market, they are in the best position to offer qualitative assessments of subjective measures.

However, when large systems are involved, every installation is unique, and results differ from one implementation to the next, owing to the degree of custom work needed to get the system up and running. In this regard, standards established by the industry software and hardware-independent functions, such as average response time for an information services help desk, are more helpful in demonstrating the shared services performance to the organization's senior management. Regardless of whether a benchmark is quantitative or qualitative, the goal is to understand whether a particular technology improves the bottom line or simply increases complexity.

Employees

In the shared services model, employees are under considerable pressure to outperform their peers. They must meet or beat industry productivity norms. This pressure is especially pronounced during the early phases of a shared business unit, when downsizing operations are in full swing. Later, when the core employee group has stabilized, employees usually have more influence with management and some sense of job security.

Employees of a shared business unit evaluate their working environment in terms of conditions, culture, opportunity for advancement, pay, cash or stock incentives, recognition, job security, and respect from customers and management. Although employees may not complete a formal, quantitative evaluation, they vote with their feet. A large exodus of valuable intellectual property can profoundly affect the competitiveness of the shared business unit.

As shown in Exhibit 6.6, the top metrics used by individual employees and organized labor in evaluating a shared business unit include:

- *Corporate Culture.* The pervasive corporate culture can range from supportive, nurturing, and employee focused, to a bottom-line focus, competitive, and performance based. Most shared business units tend toward the latter culture, as reflected in the reward system.

EXHIBIT 6.6

Corporate Culture
Human Resources
Job Security
Management
Pay & Benefits
Schedule
Treatment by Customers
Work Environment

Employees

- *Human Resources.* The HR function in many shared business units tends to be one of culling less productive employees and of helping with job placement, especially during the implementation phase. Only later does the HR department tend to be directed primarily at resolving employee issues with benefits, promotions, and relationship with management.
- *Job Security.* Although labor unions can negotiate for job security, the expectation in a shared services model is that employees who don't materially add to the bottom line will be terminated.
- *Management.* The attitude of management usually profoundly affects the corporate culture and every aspect of the work environment. The typical shared services manager is fast-paced, results-oriented, and entrepreneurial, with high employee expectations.
- *Pay and Benefits.* A reason employees accept the more competitive work environment of a shared business unit is because of the potential increase in pay and benefits for those who can handle the pace and the competitive environment. Pay and benefits are hard metrics that individual employees can compare to geographical and industry norms.
- *Schedule.* In order to realize maximum output, some shared business units operate on a 24 by 7 schedule. This is especially true of shared customer service units that support the customers of multinational corporations. In these environments, shift work is often the norm.
- *Treatment by Customers.* Even though a service unit is necessarily customer-focused, there is the issue of treatment by internal customers, especially employees who serve former peers in the parent corporation. There is a common feeling of being treated as a second-class citizen, given the lowered status relative to former peers.
- *Work Environment.* The combination of the above factors define the work environment, which at best can be qualita-

tively defined within the range from pleasant and supportive to hectic and oppressive. The ideal work environment includes management that formally recognizes employee contributions through verbal and written acknowledgement and compensation, and gives employees permission to fail without threat of reprisal.

Just as the maturity of a shared business unit is defined by its ability to compete on the open market—even if it doesn't actually enter the open market—the relevance of benchmarking of the shared business unit by employees depends on their ability to exercise alternative employment options. Employees who are trapped in a shared business unit because there are no other employment options available tend to refrain from vocalizing their complaints with management. A multinational company establishing a shared services support center typically has the option of locating the center in India, for example, where wages are low and employees don't have much leverage against large employers.

Investors

Outside investors are typically concerned with evaluating the shared business unit in terms of timely return on investment. As a potentially profitable business, a shared business unit represents an investment potential for outside investors. An outside investment in a shared business unit is one way to solidify a service arrangement. It's much more difficult for a parent corporation to demand all of the output of a shared business unit when the external customers of the service are also investors.

Exhibit 6.7 shows the key issues that outside investors consider when benchmarking a shared services unit:

- *Financial Analysis.* Although there are many reasons for outside investors to pour capital into a shared business unit, including control and guarantee of future services, most investors base

EXHIBIT 6.7

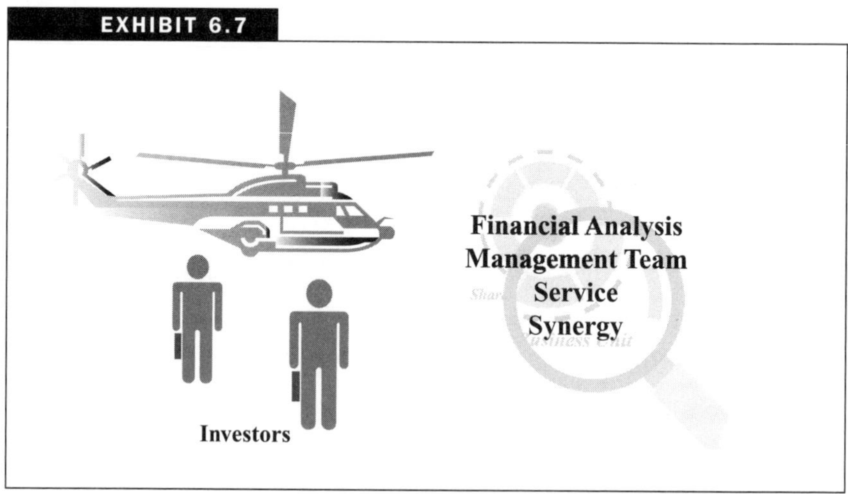

their decisions largely on the financial analysis of the shared business unit. For most investors, the potential for timely, significant return on investment, based on liquidity, debt, activity, and profit ratios, as well as information such as cash flow, profit margin, return on equity, and return on assets weighs heavily in the decision to invest.

- *Management Team.* The quality of the shared business unit management team in terms of past and current performance is an indicator of the potential success of the unit. The key management team includes the CEO and head of human resources.
- *Service.* The service area supported by the shared business unit largely defines the potential market for the service. For example, a strategic service, such as networking, or database, and software support may fair much better than, say, generic cafeteria services, in a given economy.
- *Synergy.* Since the outside investors may also be investors in the parent corporation, there may be synergy between the two investments. If the shared business unit costs the parent corporation less that the decentralized services model, then there is a net gain in value from the perspective of the entire enterprise,

even if the shared business unit isn't profitable as a stand-alone business.

In some shared services implementation, employees are also investors through stock options. Although employees may not use quantitative financial analysis tools to benchmark the potential of their stock options, an investment by employees often pays extra dividends to the company, in terms of buy-in and motivation to improve the bottom line.

Competition

Competing vendors in a market are always monitoring the movement of the real or potential competition. Every successful company, regardless of size or location, is keenly aware of the competition. Competitors to the shared business unit or the parent corporation are necessarily concerned about losing potential or current customers to a shared business unit that operates in the open market. In addition, even if a company isn't a direct competitor, because of either focus or geography, management is always interested in better ways of doing things if it means an improved bottom line.

Exhibit 6.8 shows the key benchmarks that competitors apply to shared business units:

- *Employees.* The number, composition, and attitude of employees provides a good indicator of competitiveness in the marketplace. A lean organization with positive, highly trained employees is on a much better footing than a bloated organization with poorly trained, disgruntled employees.
- *Management.* The quality of management, based on industry reputation and past experience, is a good indicator of current competitiveness.
- *Market Share.* A shared business unit that commands a significant market share is much more of a threat than is a unit that serves only closely affiliated companies.

EXHIBIT 6.8

Competition

Employees
Management
Market Share
Process
Profitability
Technology

- *Process.* In the competitive corporate world, any process improvements that can be borrowed from a successful shared business unit represents a competitive advantage.
- *Profitability.* A profitable shared business unit is a relative rarity. Not only does profit signify that the unit has successfully tapped a market, but that it has survived through significant changes in corporate culture, management, and employees. In practice, profitability figures may be very difficult for a competitor to come by, especially if the unit is privately held.
- *Technology.* Any technological advantage enjoyed by a shared business unit is necessarily of interest to the competition, especially if the technology can be readily purchased and applied. Technology vendors are invested in spreading the word as to how their system helps some corporation improve their bottom line or provide a service more efficiently or effectively.

Thanks to industrial spying and disgruntled employees, it's impossible to keep internal processes and technologies totally secret. For example, the free movement of employees and managers from a shared business unit to the competition is a primary source of information for the competition.

Benchmarking

Although the concept of benchmarking is straightforward, there's an art and a science to performing a benchmark and to using the results in a meaningful way. As an analogy, consider the benchmark commonly applied to sports cars—time from 0 to 60 mph. The value of a particular benchmark listed in a magazine advertisement, say, 6.2 seconds, depends on the reader and how he or she intends to use the information. To a naive customer comparing sports cars on a performance basis, the car may be more attractive than a competing car with an advertised benchmark of 6.9 seconds. However, to a sports car aficionado or engineer, the raw benchmark figure is relatively meaningless without documentation describing the process, standards, and tools used in creating the benchmark. Relevant questions include:

- *Was the benchmarking process based on an industry standard?* A figure based on the performance of a driver using an unorthodox method is much less meaningful than a figure based on a

IN THE REAL WORLD

Benchmarking Matters

Two of the most successful shared services implementations are the shared information services units of Bristol-Myers Squibb Company. One unit, Information Management Shared Services, manages 42,000 desktops, six international data centers, 2,000 applications, and the network infrastructure. The other shared business unit, Enterprise Systems and Processes, manages resource planning for the parent company's financial and manufacturing divisions. Each unit relies on benchmarking—its productivity and cost of service delivery, as well as service level agreements—to communicate how well the units are doing internally.

trained driver who evaluates the vehicles using industry standard protocols.

- *What were the composition, condition, and orientation of the test track?* Traction on asphalt and concrete can be significantly different. In addition, even a slight downhill grade can markedly decrease 0 to 60 mph acceleration time.
- *What was the configuration of the vehicle?* An empty vehicle, with spare tire, jack, and floor mats removed and one gallon of fuel in the tank can be expected to outperform a more realistic vehicle configuration with a full tank, tools and spare in the trunk, and mats in place.
- *Was the benchmark made with stock or racing tires?* Special, lightweight and high-traction racing tires would most likely result in a lower figure.
- *What was the tire pressure?* Over-inflating tires might improve the figure slightly, even though the increased pressure would be unsafe for the average consumer.
- *What type of fuel was used?* A high-octane, enriched fuel mixture that doesn't abide by environmental standards and that isn't available to the public will give misleading results.
- *How were time and speed measured?* Was the car's internal odometer and a manual stopwatch used, or a specially calibrated radar system with light-activated timer?
- *How was the final benchmark calculated?* Does the figure represent the average of three runs or the best of fifty runs?
- *What were the environmental conditions?* Altitude, weather, including temperature and humidity, like road conditions, can profoundly affect the 0-60 time.
- *How does the benchmark compare with those performed by those without a financial stake in the sale of the car?* Are there competing benchmarks performed by independent magazines?

Benchmarking a sports car illustrates that the four key factors that define a benchmarking effort are focus, standards, tools, and process, as described here.

Focus

The focus of a benchmark applied to a shared business unit is generally in one of five areas: customer satisfaction, operations, quality, finance, and employee satisfaction. Customer satisfaction can be evaluated in terms of repeat business, directed customer feedback, and the volume of calls to Support. Operations figures attempt to quantify operational efficiency and effectiveness, using metrics such as responsiveness and problem resolution time. Quality is normally evaluated in subjective, qualitative terms that reflect factors such as attention to detail and ease of use. Financial metrics are used to quantify business benefits, such as future cost savings associated with investments in infrastructure. Employee satisfaction metrics include turnover rate and direct feedback.

Standards

A benchmark means very little without reference to standards. These standards can be internal, based on comparing similar processes within the shared business unit. For example, call center operators with one shift can be compared to those from another shift. Standards can also be competitive, such as when comparing service level and processes of the shared business unit with those of the competition. They can be functional, focusing on processes, such as payroll, regardless of the industry. Finally, they can be industry-wide, based on national consulting or benchmarking groups.

The primary means of applying standards to the benchmarking process is with a Service Level Agreement (SLA) that specifies the level of service that must be delivered by employees and the service unit as a whole. To be useful, the service level agreement must be:

- *Affordable.* The cost of benchmarking must be such that it can be repeated as frequently as necessary. The most affordable benchmarking tends to be done automatically, by automated systems that continually update response rates and provide daily or even hourly statistics on efficiency and effectiveness.
- *Binding.* There must be a concrete reward or penalty associated with meeting or failing to meet the SLA, respectively.
- *Doable.* The benchmarks must be able to be carried out by employees. An overly complicated benchmarking scheme will be error prone.
- *Meaningful.* The data collected and the statistics generated must have practical applicability to the performance of the organization, normally as reflected in the bottom line. Meaningless benchmarks are worse than a waste of time, because they tarnish the image of benchmarking as a method of improving service quality.
- *Recognized.* Benchmarking standards must be just that—standards. The FAA evaluates airlines in terms of on-time departures and arrivals, for example. Benchmarks such as airplane tire pressure accuracy aren't going to be recognized by the industry, and will likely have little bearing on the performance of the airlines.
- *Verifiable.* Like any scientific measurement, a benchmark must be repeatable and verifiable by a third, unbiased party.

Tools

Even qualitative benchmarking requires the use of tools. However, when the focus of benchmarking is on process optimization and overall efficiency and effectiveness, there are specific tools that can be used to assist management. For example, statistical process control (see Exhibit 6.9) can be used to track benchmarks from month to month. A sudden increase in the error—as from March to April in Exhibit 6.9—

EXHIBIT 6.9

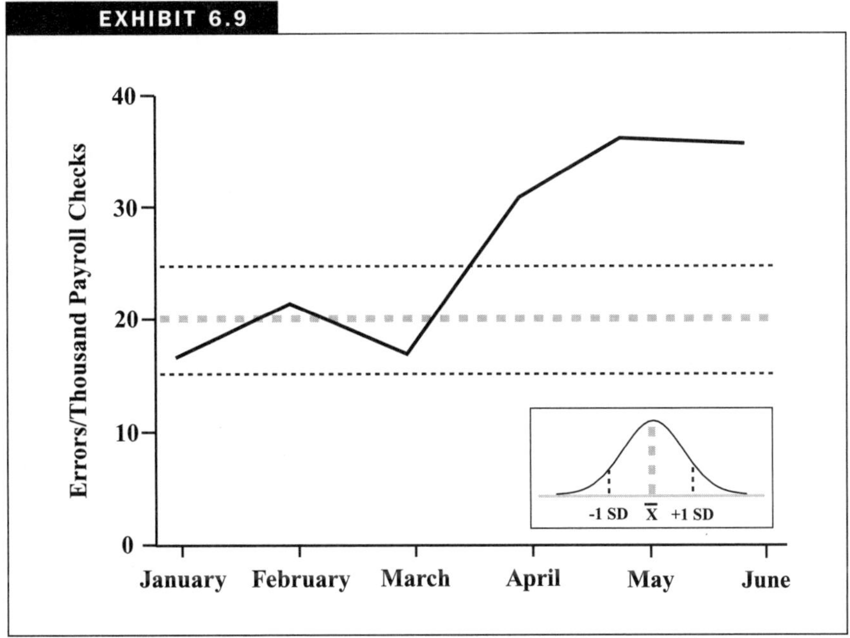

can suggest problems with employees, equipment, or some outside factor that adversely affects quality of service.

The inset in Exhibit 6.9, showing the limits of one standard deviation from the average or mean error rate (25 ± 5), illustrates how internal standards apply to benchmarking. Regardless of the industry-wide error rate, the issue is the relative change from the previous error rate achieved by the shared business unit.

Process

The process of evaluation is just as important as the standards or tools used. For example, returning to Exhibit 6.9, the figures collected for error rates are relatively meaningless without some notation about the process used. For example, were the measurements taken at regular intervals, and at peak or average workloads? What was the sample size, and how often were measurements taken? What is the repeatability of the process, and are the results certifiable by an independent observer?

Was the data derived from built-in software utilities, or based on independent third party audits by external consultants? What were the conditions of the benchmarking process? For example, was the sudden rise in error rates associated with a change in management or other external factor? The point is that a benchmarking process should be developed and codified in order for the values to have any real meaning.

A component of the process is making use of the results. However, although using benchmark values to improve quality of service or improve the bottom line may seem straightforward, in a shared services company there are often mixed messages from management at all levels, with the result that employees may provide less than what the customer expects. For example, the employees of the parent corporation and other customers may be most sensitive to service quality—in terms of time to delivery, personal attention, and the like. However, if management of the shared business unit is rewarded on minimizing cost to the parent corporation, then there are two orthogonal, competing goals. A shared business unit can't compete successfully based on both quality and price.

In addition to mixed messages, there is the issue of politics. There is a tendency of management to use benchmarking for political purposes instead of to assess and improve performance. In the shared services environment, this tendency to show parent corporation management a positive picture is especially prevalent, given the economic dependency of the unit on the parent corporation. The relevance of the economic connection between the shared business unit and parent corporation, and how this connection relates to the economic viability of the parent corporation are discussed in detail in the following chapter.

Summary

In business, feedback is unavoidable. However, when the source of feedback is controlled, the conditions are known, and the type of quality of data can be specified, the data are more valuable in reducing risk of failure and increasing the odds of success. A directed evaluation is a means of receiving feedback about business practices in time to make corrections before the customer decides whether the shared business unit is to survive. In this regard, benchmarks are standards that can be used to assess how a unit is performing over time relative to its previous performance, to similar businesses in the industry, or relative to norms established by independent evaluators.

> *Position yourself well enough, and circumstances will do the rest.*
>
> **Mason Cooley**

CHAPTER 7

Economics

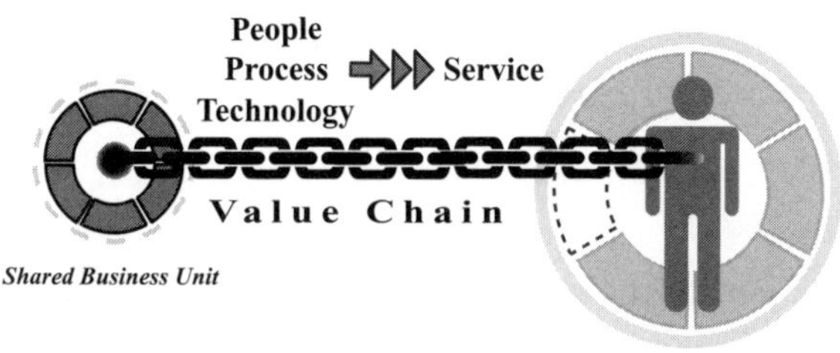

After reading this chapter you will be able to

- Appreciate the economic risks associated with starting and operating a shared business unit
- Understand the investment capital required to put people, processes and technology in place, for a shared services implementation
- Understand the factors affecting the return on investment associated with a shared business unit from the perspectives of both the shared business unit and the parent corporation
- Understand the relevance of investing in information infrastructure technologies for the success of the shared business unit
- Appreciate the legal aspects of a shared services model, including contracts, pricing models, service level agreements, billing, and the balance sheet

One of senior management's primary responsibilities is to increase the value of their corporation for stockholders. To this end, the shared business unit can be thought of as an economic engine that generates value for the parent corporation by assuming responsibility for the undifferentiated back-end processes and freeing the senior management of the parent corporation to invest its mental capital in developing its core competency so that it can be more competitive in the open market.

Ideally, the shared services model is a means for the parent corporation to increase its odds of success. However, simply creating a shared business unit doesn't guarantee the parent corporation freedom from distraction or risk. Like virtually every business venture, implementing a shared business unit is a risky endeavor, and one that requires knowledgeable stewardship to bring it to profitability and maturity.

To highlight the more significant practical challenges associated with the shared services business model, consider the evolving HIS shared business unit of the HealthCare Partners network.

Membership Has Its Privileges

Under the leadership of a capable manager, the HealthCare Information Services (HIS) shared business unit is operating in a for-profit mode, with the growing HealthCare Partners network members as its major clients. As such, HIS competes by bidding on all requests for proposals (RFPs) on a competitive basis. Thus far, only a few minor projects have been awarded to outside vendors, predominantly because HIS management didn't want to divert resources to address a small or a special project that had little or no strategic importance for either HIS or the parent corporation. In effect, the parent corporation saved HIS management the hassle of outsourcing the special project, had it been forced to handle the request.

Things changed suddenly when, in response to an open request for proposal for a major clinical pathology information system for all institutions in the network, a nationally recognized vendor suddenly appeared on the horizon. The out-of-state vendor offered the latest technology, including wireless tablets for data entry, an expansive list of add-on technologies, including voice recognition dictation, excellent references, and interfaces with the legacy systems in each of the member institutions. Since the system was in use in many of the top hospitals in the United States, the system was fully debugged. In addition, the vendor promised a very short installation time; the pathology system would be ready for testing within six months of signing the contract. However, the vendor asked for $4 million and nearly $500,000 annually for maintenance, upgrades, and limited on-site training.

In comparison, HIS can create a system that expands upon the existing system. Although it can't integrate wireless tablets or a voice recognition dictation option into its system without outside help, the pathology system will have the same "look and feel" of the current clinical system that physicians and nurses are accustomed to. As a result, training time on the new system should be minimal. However, since the system would have to be constructed in-house, with the present staffing, the project will require two years of work at an internal cost of $4.5 million, with a recurring $200,000 for annual maintenance and upgrades. On the basis of features and delivery time, the commercial pathology vendor is clearly the superior option. On the basis of purchase price, the differences are less clear. Going with the commercial option would save HealthCare Partners $500,000 up front but incur an additional $200,000 annually.

From the perspective of the clinical staff, the HIS home grown system is attractive because the training requirements associated with the it should be significantly less than that for the commercial system. However, some of the functionality provided by the commercial system, including the wireless options, could make the clinicians more productive, saving time in the long run. In addition, since the commercial system is popular with pathologists in hundreds of hospitals throughout the United States, odds are that if a pathologist leaves HealthCare Partners after using its own system, he or she will be forced to learn a completely new system, perhaps even the very one HIS rejects.

On the basis of price and functionality, there is no clear winner. Senior management of both the HealthCare Partners and the HIS Unit consider the strategic and tactical implications of going with the outside vendor for the clinical pathology system. HIS management is faced with minimizing losses. If it matches the vendor's price, it will lose $500,000 over two years, some of which it will gain back later in maintenance fees. Similarly, if HIS loses the contract, it will have to invest resources working with the vendor to integrate the commercial and HIS systems.

The expansion plans of HealthCare Partners, which include becoming a statewide presence in the health-care community, is one incentive for it to go with the less capable HIS-developed clinical pathology system. With a custom clinical pathology system of its own, HealthCare Partners can approach other hospitals and clinics in the state and offer the clinical pathology application as part of the suite of clinical tools. Within five years, with two or three additional hospitals in its network, HealthCare Partners should be able to recoup its original investment in the pathology system development. Even though awarding the contract to HIS represents a short-term loss for the shared business unit, it also represents a longer-term gain for both it and the parent corporation, in terms of license fees and political leverage.

Given the strategic importance of an in-house clinical pathology system, HealthCare Partners decides to have HIS develop a system according to the competitive proposal it submitted in response to the RFP. On the basis of price alone, one advantage that HIS management has over the commercial vendor is that the annual maintenance costs reflect should be less than the vendor's. The HIS costs are reduced because the support staff that is already on-hand that will help service the new system. In addition, since training classes are already established for clinicians and others in the HealthCare Partners network, the marginal cost of adding a course on how to use the new system should be minimal.

The relative payoffs and liabilities of using a shared services approach versus outsourcing the development of the clinical pathology system are summarized in Exhibit 7.1. The advantages of going with HIS shared services implementation of the system are the long-term cost savings to the parent corporation, the flexibility afforded by an in-house development, and relatively small maintenance costs. The major liability is the need for external resources, including consultants, in order to provide some of the leading-edge technologies, such as voice recognition dictation, that the commercial system offers.

In favor of outsourcing the clinical pathology project to the commercial vendor are short-term cost savings, a time savings of nearly 18 months, and availability of the latest technology. A significant downside, from the perspective of HIS management, is that the project will require

EXHIBIT 7.1

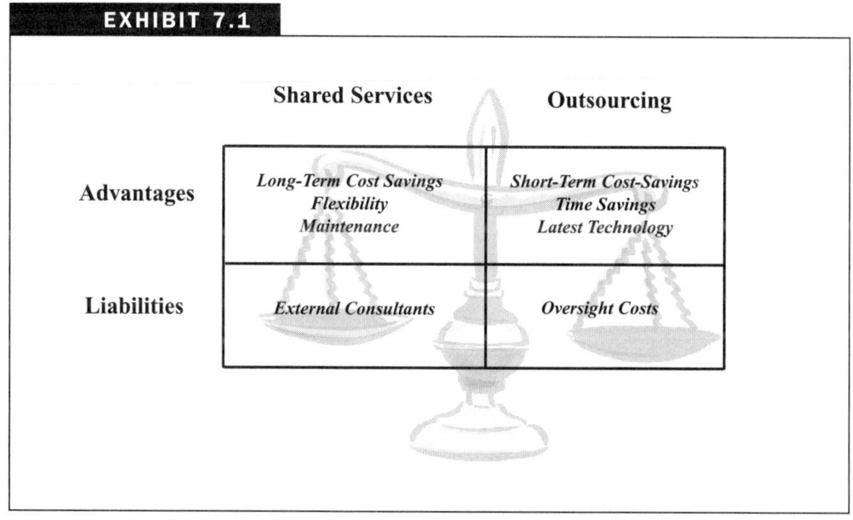

	Shared Services	Outsourcing
Advantages	*Long-Term Cost Savings* *Flexibility* *Maintenance*	*Short-Term Cost-Savings* *Time Savings* *Latest Technology*
Liabilities	*External Consultants*	*Oversight Costs*

internal oversight to verify that the deliverables are within specifications and to assist in the integration of the clinical pathology system with the HIS system.

With the internal contract between HIS and HealthCare Partners signed, senior management of HealthCare Partners reactivates its expansion program. It contacts an advertising agency for advice on how to initiate an advertising campaign directed at hospitals and clinics throughout the state that are potential customers of expanding HIS services.

The issues highlighted by the experience of HealthCare Partner's senior management include:

- A shared business unit, especially one that is located in or near the parent corporation, has several advantages over outside vendors. If it is on site, management has access to the parent corporation's senior management for advice, information, and networking. There is also the water cooler networking with customers and management that allows employees and management of the shared business unit to maintain relationships within the parent corporation. These and other communications opportunities provide the shared business unit with an intimate, unique understanding of the parent corporation's objectives that an outside vendor can't even begin to approach.
- A successful shared services implementation typically requires a significant investment in people, processes, and technology.
- In assessing the return on investment (ROI) of a shared services implementation, the overall short- and long-term effect of the investment on the parent corporation must be considered. An investment with a short-term negative ROI for the shared business unit may have a long-term positive ROI for the parent corporation.
- Comparing costs and ROI of a shared business unit with internal processes or other business models can be challenging or misleading because internal processes have hidden costs and

IN THE REAL WORLD

Companies With Shared Services Initiatives

About one quarter of Fortune 500 Companies have shared services initiatives. The roster of companies includes:

AlliedSignal	Glaxo SmithKline Beecham
American Express	Hewlett Packard
Amoco	IBM
Arco Oil and Gas	ITT Industries
AT&T	Johnson & Johnson
Avon Products	Lucent Technologies
Bristol Myers Squibb	Texas Instruments
General Electric	Thompson International

Although most companies that fail at implementing a shared services initiative don't advertise their experiences, the ones that do report annual savings in the 20 to 30 percent range. Results, of course, vary from one implementation to the next, as a function of the number of employees that can be downsized while maintaining output, the constraints imposed by organized labor, and the economic environment.

revenue sharing that may not be readily apparent. In addition, each activity may describe itself with different metrics, and with a unique set of assumptions that don't apply to the other models or processes.

The following discussion considers these issues in more detail.

Stakeholders

As shown in Exhibit 7.2, the primary stakeholders in the successful operation of a shared business unit are management and labor. The

EXHIBIT 7.2

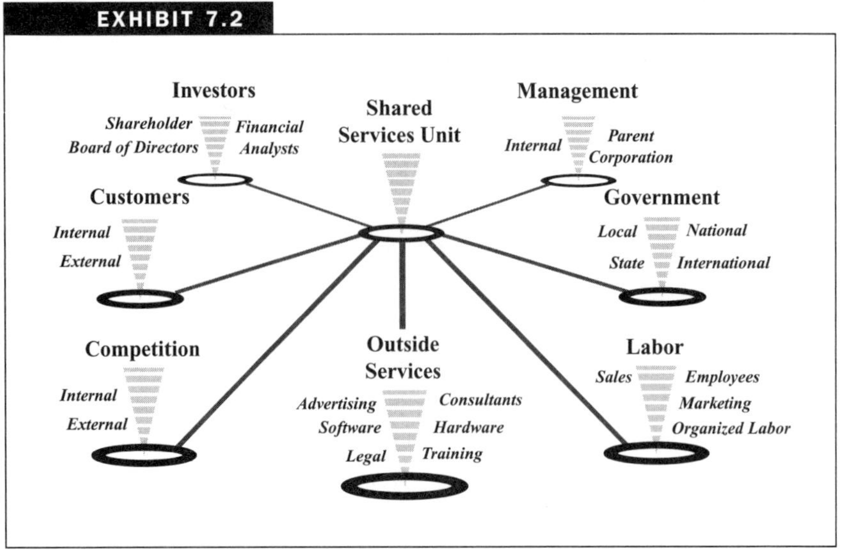

management of both the shared business unit and the parent corporation are stakeholders, and so are individual employees and organized labor. Customers, both internal and external, are also primary stakeholders in the successful operation of a shared business unit. The government, outside services, investors, and purveyors of outside services are also significant stakeholders, as described here.

Management

- *Parent Corporate Management.* The management of the parent corporation has obvious professional and personal career interests in the success of a shared services initiative. Not so obvious are the political issues that may be related to moving certain management outside of the parent corporation. For example, a senior manager threatened by an up-and-coming CIO may help orchestrate a move to make corporate information services a shared business unit, thereby removing the CIO physically and politically from the inner circle of senior corporate management.

- *Shared Services Management.* The career trajectory and income of the shared services senior management is obviously affected by the success or failure of the unit. Often, senior management undergoes a transition from a more radical changeover CEO during early implementation to a more conservative, entrepreneurial CEO as the unit approaches maturity.

Customers

- *External Customers.* Ideally, customers in the open market develop loyalty and dependency on the services of the shared business unit. In addition, as in the case of the external clinics considering investing in the HIS shared business unit, external customers may become investors in the unit.
- *Internal Customers.* The employees of the parent corporation who depend on the services of the shared business unit are major stakeholders in the success of the venture. As the shared business unit matures and management looks to outside sources of revenue, the needs of internal customers may be compromised.

Government

As a business operation, a shared business unit necessarily involves the government and *government regulations.* Shared business units must abide by government regulations regarding everything from employee pay to termination procedures, working conditions, and payment of taxes. Whereas domestic companies have to deal with local, state, and national rules, regulations and accounting practices, multinational companies have to deal with international labor and employment laws as well as different sets of accounting practices. Fortunately, many offshore governments are actively engaged in attracting employers, and are willing to provide major tax incentives in the short-term to increase employment of local citizens.

Outside Services

- *Advertising Agencies.* Creating advertising campaigns for back-end services targeted at internal and external customers is new to most former employees of the parent corporation. Advertising agencies can provide expertise and services that position the shared business unit advantageously in the customer's mind.
- *Consulting Firms.* CEOs typically don't go it alone in implementing a shared business unit—or any process overall. As the vignettes involving HealthCare Partners illustrate, external consultants can help reduce the risks of moving to a shared services model.
- *Equipment Manufacturers.* In addition to computer hardware, a variety of office automation equipment, from high-speed digital copiers to mail sorting and handling equipment, can be used to empower fewer employees with the ability to maintain or increase the productivity of a shared business unit.
- *Computer Hardware Vendors.* Creating a shared business unit is a technology-intensive venture. Virtually every implementation requires additional computer hardware.
- *Insurers.* A shared services implementation, like any other business operation, is a risky business. Insurers are normally happy to share the risk of a shared services initiative—in exchange for higher premiums.
- *Legal Counsel.* Creating and operating a shared business unit entails contract negotiations, labor agreements, tax laws, and a variety of intellectual property issues that demand competent legal counsel.
- *Marketing.* Creating a marketing campaign for external and internal customers may be a new concept for the employees of a shared business unit who were once engaged in back-end operations as employees of the parent corporation. An internal marketing group, assisted by consultants from an advertising

agency, or an autonomous outside marketing and communications group are two common approaches to marketing used by a resource-limited shared business unit.

- *Outside Service Providers.* Outsourcing payroll, copy services and other back-end processes may be time and cost efficient for a shared business unit, especially if employee resources are limited.
- *Sales.* As a shared business unit matures to a profit-oriented business, external sales support—in the form of new hires or consultants—becomes critical for success. For large internal customer accounts, a sales force may also be needed. In many cases, the unit's CEO doubles as a sales professional.
- *Shareholders.* Investors in the parent corporation, and, less often, the shared business unit, are betting that the endeavor is successful.
- *Strategic Partners.* These are external vendors that provide back-end services, companies that provide services or products that work symbiotically with the shared business unit's services. A company with complementary needs or products may be able to partner with the shared business unit to reduce costs or increase revenue. For example, a shared information services business unit may have a software product that requires a particular hardware device, and the device manufacturer stands to gain if it can interest customers in the potential of a package that contains the software developed by the information services business unit.
- *Suppliers.* Like most other businesses, a shared business unit requires a constant supply of office supplies, services for the upkeep of the physical plant, and a variety of raw materials involved in the day-to-day operation of the unit.
- *Training Companies.* A fast-paced shared business unit typically needs to bring employees up to speed on new processes and technologies, without sending employees across the country to

a meeting. E-Learning and on-site training are two popular training options.

Competition

The *competition* is directly affected by the success or failure of the shared business unit, whether it competes with the parent corporation or directly with the shared business unit.

Labor

- *Employees.* As virtual pawns in the shared services implementation game, employees of both the parent corporation and those on the payroll of the shared business unit typically experience a high degree of volatility. This upheaval in normal operations is greatest early on, when employees associated with the back-end services are destined to be moved to a

TIPS & TECHNIQUES

Too Much of a Good Thing

Moving from an ineffective, understaffed and under-trained help desk to an efficient shared services customer support unit is a mixed blessing. Customers will quickly come to depend on the new service, escalating the staffing and other resource requirements to potentially unmanageable levels.

One way to pre-empt an inevitable flood of employees seeking help is to invest in problem avoidance. One solution is to fix whatever is broken with the system so that employees won't need to call for help. If that's impossible or uneconomical, then alternative forms of support, such as lists of FAQs (Frequently Asked Questions) can be posted to the corporate intranet and Web site and added to the company newsletter.

shared business unit and either downsized or retained in a new, highly competitive environment. Employees retained by the shared business unit can face transfer to a new location, retraining, and a compensation package tied to productivity instead of seniority. This form of compensation isn't unique to the shared services model, but it is indicative of highly competitive companies in the open market.

- *Organized Labor.* Since downsizing in virtually mandated by the shared services model, organized labor is typically involved in negotiating the transition of employees from the parent corporation to the shared business unit. In some cases, preexisting organized labor contracts may limit the rate and degree of downsizing. This limitation may not affect the shared business unit directly, but may force the parent corporation to retain employees and distribute them to other locations in the parent corporation where they can either be retrained and absorbed or downsized when the time limit expires.

Investors

- *Board of Directors.* Members of the board of directors are motivated by stock options or pay keyed to the overall profitability of the shared business unit or the parent corporation. Alternatively, they may be motivated by the political merits of acting on the board, in terms of networking with other board members. In either case, there is usually significant motivation to have the organization succeed under their watch.
- *Financial Analysts.* Wall Street has a keen interest in the effect of a shared business implementation to the degree that it might affect productivity and profits of the parent corporation.

In addition to these primary stakeholders, an active shared business unit has hundreds of minor stakeholders. For example, the activities of large shared services operations, such as American Express or Lucent Technologies, affect their industries and the communities in which the managers and employees live and work. When the financially troubled Lucent Technologies restructured in 2001 it laid off thousands of employees, disrupting entire communities, and negatively impacting everyone from the corner coffee shop to the local bank.

Value

The typical CEO views back-end operations such as payroll, information services, or billing as a cost. However, for the manager of a shared business unit, these same operations, now considered core competencies for the unit, represent a potential profit-generating value chain. For example, a shared business unit charged with processing payroll for its parent corporation generates value through a multi-stage process that involves people, processes, and technology, as illustrated in Exhibit 7.3.

The primary people involved in payroll processing (top row, Exhibit 7.3) include the operators of computers, printers, and other office equipment that comprise the technology (bottom row, Exhibit 7.3) involved in processing the payroll. The actual process steps, from collecting employee data, validating the data, and computing pay, to printing checks, folding and metering the envelopes, and finally mailing

EXHIBIT 7.3

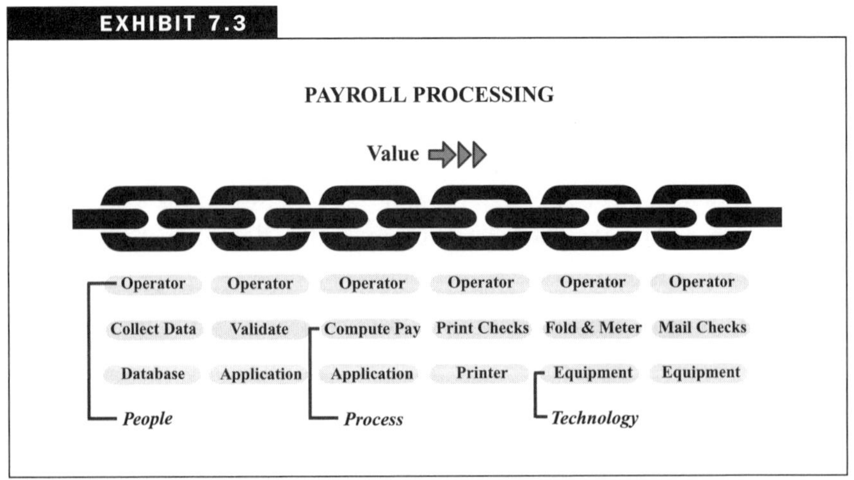

checks to employees (middle row, Exhibit 7.3) creates value at every step.

A shared business unit can outsource one or more stages in its internal value chain, just as a parent corporation can outsource or create a shared business unit to handle back-end processes that represent a distraction from its core competency. However, deciding which part of the value chain, if any, to outsource should also reflect the incremental value of processing from step to step. Value, as measured in terms of revenue, chargeback, or profit is derived from controlling the interdependent links between process steps.

Some of these interdependent links are responsible for generating considerably more value than others, as shown in Exhibit 7.4. In this example, value added between collecting and validating data represents as much value along the payroll processing value chain as do the following five process steps combined. This suggests that shared services

EXHIBIT 7.4

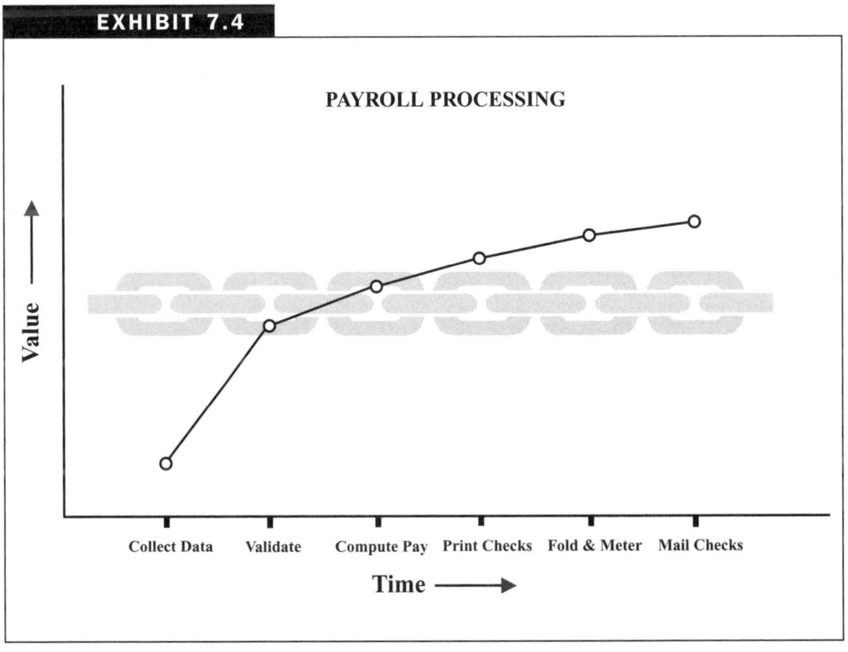

management should only consider low-value steps for outsourcing. In this example, printing, folding, metering, and mailing checks could be outsourced with very little change in the overall revenue for the shared business unit. In addition, outsourcing the mechanical operation of printing, folding, metering, and mailing checks obviates the need for operators of the special equipment, as well as an investment in the specialized mailing equipment itself.

The differences in increases in value along the value chain are due to multiple factors, including administrative costs, competing services, economies of scale, inefficiencies of processing, labor costs, overhead, and process. These factors are described in more detail here.

Administrative Costs

Some processes incur greater administrative costs than others. In the example of payroll processing, there is the administrative overhead of managing inventory, supplies, machine maintenance, and scheduling labor.

Competing Services

The value of alternative services creates an upper boundary on the value of a given process in the value chain. For example, after computing pay, a competing process is to simply send an electronic message to each customer's bank for electronic deposit. As a result, the folding component of the folding and metering process would be obviated, assuming that the deposit notice is a slip that can be inserted into a windowed envelope without folding. Similarly, an all-electronic system, with notification of pay details posted to a secure Web site obviates the need to print notices or generate a mailing. The web-based payroll notification process represents a disruptive technology in that it obviates the previous manual process, including the equipment and employees needed to operate it.

Economies of Scale

Printing, sorting envelopes, and other human resource–intensive processes associated with back-end services such as payroll are much more sensitive to economies of scale than are automated processes such as computer-mediated data collection and verification. Automated data processing is generally less sensitive to volume changes than are manual processes, such as handling forms or copying. For example, whereas doubling the amount of payroll data that must be processed may not require an upgrade in computer hardware, doubling the number of checks that must be folded, stuffed, and metered may require an expensive upgrade of the associated equipment.

What's more, when computer systems have to be upgraded, the cost of the much more powerful and effective replacement hardware is generally the same or less than that of the original computer equipment, especially for PC-based applications. For example, as illustrated in Exhibit 7.5, assuming volume to be handled increases over several years, upgrading to a PC with a more powerful, next-generation processor generally costs no more that the original investment in the technology. Incrementally upgrading from a PC with a 25 MHz Intel Pentium processor to a 2 GHz Pentium IV, for example, provides several orders of magnitude increased processing power, at the same or lower purchase price.

In contrast, manufacturing equipment, such as check folding and sorting machines, don't double or quadruple in power or effectiveness every year or two, and the prices for a given handling capacity don't drop as precipitously as they do for the PC. As such, the economies of scale are different for typical manufacturing equipment associated with many back-end processes (see Exhibit 7.6). Upgrading to a more capable model of equipment incurs a significant cost, diminishing the profitability associated with scaling up to a greater handling capacity.

EXHIBIT 7.5

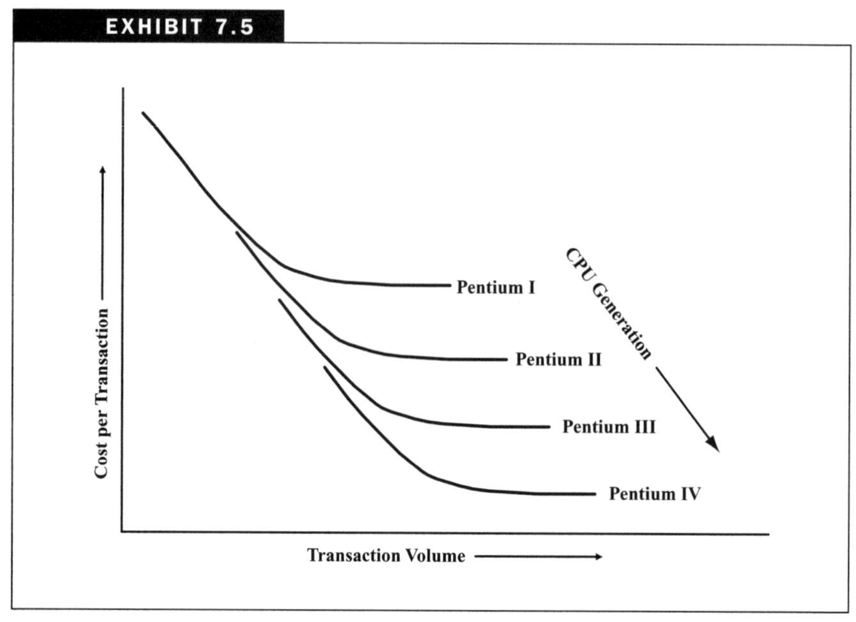

EXHIBIT 7.6

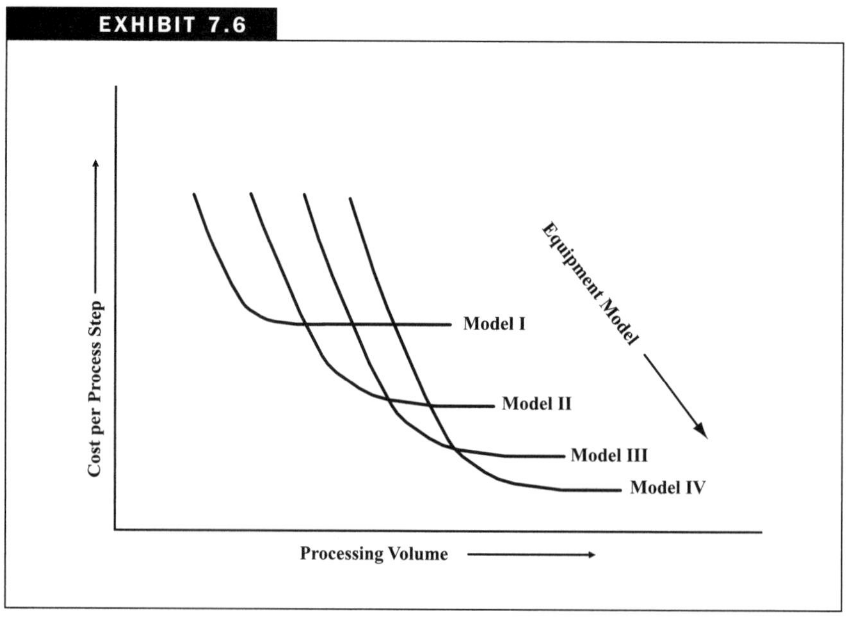

Inefficiencies of Processing

Some processes are inherently less efficient than others. For example, doubling the number of operators at a help desk doesn't produce a doubling of throughput because of the cost of additional interpersonal communications, a more sophisticated phone and CRM system, phone and e-mail queuing systems, and the need for a greater management role. In comparison, a software program that runs a series of data validation routines on customer data typically needs very little attention from human operators. For this reason, computer and communications automation is a key component in any shared services implementation, in that it allows a downsized workforce to handle more workload than the original workforce.

Labor Costs

The cost of labor varies for different professions, areas of expertise, and the demand for particular workers in the general economy. A process within the value chain with a relatively high labor cost may provide a relatively low incremental increase in value. The high cost of labor with little or no accompanying increase in value decreases the value attributable to that stage of the value chain.

For a service such as a cardiac bypass operation, the high labor cost of a cardiac surgeon is associated with a comparable increase in value along the value chain. However, when labor costs are temporarily elevated for relatively unskilled employees who are expected to learn on the job, their contribution to the value change is usually minimal. For example, during the dot-com boom, Web programmers were in such high demand that secretaries and anyone else who could type on a keyboard were recruited—often at insane salaries—despite their very low productivity. With the dot-com correction, the cost of labor returned to reasonable levels, and the programming positions were replaced with

A Technology Boost for Bean Counters

Starbucks, the Seattle-based company that seems to have outlets on virtually every street corner in major cities throughout the United States, uses an automated request processing system in its shared Information Services operation. The computer-based system not only reduces customer wait times by more than two-thirds, but computer technology has reduced the need for employees as well. With the technology in place, two employees handle the front-end functions of the Information Services help desk—a task that required six full-time employees before it was automated.

seasoned professionals, with a concomitant increase in value of that stage in their company's value chain.

Overhead

The incremental cost of utilities, furnishings, equipment, and the technology infrastructure can adversely affect the processing at each stage along the value chain, limiting the increase in value possible at each step in the process.

Process

The very nature of the processes involved in the value chain can limit the incremental and total value generated at each step. Rearranging or dropping processes may improve upon an ineffective process. For example, it may be possible to increase the efficiency of a stage in the value chain by performing some tasks in parallel or by using information technology to replace some of the workforce.

All of these interdependent factors affect the return on investment associated with the shared business unit, as described here.

Return on Investment

Regardless of the process used, the economics of the shared business unit boils down to a return on investment (ROI) figure for the shared business unit, the parent corporation, and outside investors. ROI, the tool most commonly used to evaluate business performance in terms of earnings returned on a capital investment, is a generic concept that is calculated as:

ROI = Return / Capital Invested

where "Return" is the profit, income, or gain and "Capital Invested" is the amount of capital invested during a specified period to produce the return. The ROI for a successful shared services implementation is typically in the 20 to 30 percent range, meaning that the return is 20 to 30 percent of the amount of capital invested to produce the return. The major investments in a shared services implementation are in people, processes, technologies, and infrastructure, as shown in Exhibit 7.7.

Many of these investments are common to any new business operation, but they differ by a matter of degree in a shared services implementation. For example, since downsizing is a major part of most shared services implementations, investment in severance packages is typically greater than for a stable company, given the same external economic conditions. Conversely, although a shared business unit may have to assemble a sales and marketing team, it's typically much smaller than that of a company of comparable size because many—if not all—potential customers are employees of the parent corporation.

Investments in processes include the creation of new back-end processes for the employees of the shared business unit, such as payroll,

EXHIBIT 7.7

Shared Service Unit Investments

People

Consultants	Recruiting
Employees	Relocation
Management	Sales
Marketing	Severance Packages
Professional Services	Training
Programming	

Process

Back-end Functions	Process Optimization
Contractual Obligations	Re-engineering
License Arrangements	Vendor Selection

Technology

Ancillary Utilities	Interfaces to Legacy Systems
Applications	Maintenance
Conversion	Peripherals
Customization	Security
Employees	Software
Hardware	Upgrades
Implementation	Web Hosting

Infrastructure

Communications	Facilities
Equipment	Network

human resources, and billing. The return on this investment, which is typically measured in reduced cost, increased quality, and increased productivity, may not be easily calculated up front, because the overall effects may take years before they are apparent.

The technology investment is typically in line with that of a comparably sized company that has been newly acquired or merged with another company. Since virtually all shared business unit implementations involve an investment in new computer and communications hardware and software, a means of evaluation ROI for an investment in information technology is one of management's primary concerns. Given the difficulty in providing hard metrics for returns on technology investments, it's not surprising that the average lifespan of a CIO is on the order of 18 months—well below the average tenure for a typical senior manager of a corporation.

Infrastructure investments are generally aimed at consolidating facilities into a single shared business unit, thereby decreasing rent and providing the parent corporation with room to expand internally. Other investments include the communications system and computer network that can support the technology, processes, and people in the organization.

Doing the Math

ROI is a generic term that encompasses more specific evaluation tools, including return on assets (ROA) and return on equity (ROE). ROA, the ratio of operating earnings to net operating assets, is a test of whether a business is earning enough to cover its cost of capital. ROE, the ratio of net income to the owner's equity, is a measure of the return on investment for an owner's equity capital invested in the shared business unit.

Different ROI measures apply to evaluating a shared business unit, depending on how it is established and run, and whether or not there are outside investors. For example, assuming the outside clinics in the HealthCare Partners network invested $900,000 in the HIS shared business unit they would receive a return of $30,000 for the first year:

$$\text{ROE} = \$30{,}000 \;/\; \$900{,}000 = 3.3\ \%$$

If equally or less risky investments are returning 8 percent, then the investment in HIS is a poor one—at least from a short-term investment perspective. However, if the primary reason that the clinics invested in

HIS was to exercise control over the fate of the shared business unit, especially regarding continuation of service, then the relative loss attributable to the strategic investment is simply the price management is willing to pay to guarantee service from HIS.

The ROI calculation is complicated by the reality that a shared business unit may never produce a profit, especially if it is kept under the control of the parent corporation and never enters the open market. A related challenge associated with calculating or predicting ROI for a technology investment is that many measures are qualitative. For example, consider the challenge of quantifying the security of the HIS shared business unit. It's possible to calculate the ROI for a secure information services system from any number of formulas, such as:

$$\text{Predicted ROI} = \text{Recovery Cost} - \text{Cost of Intrusion}$$

where "Recovery Cost" is the cost per year (or other specified period) to recover from any number of intrusions, including installing data and applications from archives. The "Cost of Intrusion" figure represents the predicted loss during the same period associated with a successful hacker. Although a quantifiable dollar figure can be generated from this formula, the value for ROI as calculated can swing significantly, depending on the assumption of the number of intrusions per year, and exactly what is classified as an intrusion. For example, it can simply be a hacker breaking into the system for the fun of it, or a professional industrial spy who is looking for trade secrets, employee lists, and other assets that can significantly affect the future profitability of the HIS unit.

Legal

The economic fate of a shared business unit is inherently linked to the legally binding obligatory and consensual agreements and obligations made between management of the shared business unit, the parent corporation, investors, and employees. The most significant legal issues are related to the government, control, accountability, and the contract—the document that specifies these and other aspects of the relationship.

Government

The government, the silent partner in every business operation, is a primary consideration in the creation of every shared business unit. For domestic companies, the shared business unit is typically created as a separate legal entity in the form of a C-corporation. A variety of government regulations, including tax laws, come into play when the parent corporation begins to resemble a holding company if it spins off a significant portion of its operations as semi-autonomous shared business units.

The legal issues related to the government are even more complicated when international corporations are involved because of constantly shifting tax, insurance, and outright grant incentives offered by offshore governments for companies willing to locate and hire employees overseas. A multinational corporation with the intention of creating shared business units requires the advice of counsel with knowledge of international tax and government regulations.

Control and Accountability

Assuming a domestic operation and a C-corporation, control and accountability are typically defined by the corporate charter and the contractual arrangement between the parent and the shared business unit. The board of directors, officers, and stockholders all have responsibilities and benefits, as defined by statutes, the Articles of Incorporation, bylaws, and the decisions of the Board of Directors.

A shared business unit is unique in that the parent corporation and the shared business unit both desire control. As such, rules are generally explicitly defined for common shared service activities. For example, the parent corporation may enter into the bylaws of the shared business unit that senior management of the unit may not outsource internal back-end services without permission of the parent corporation. The parent organization may also exercise control over the unit by designating a specific number of seats on the Board of Directors as permanently allotted to the parent corporation. Similarly, on the issue of accountability—for severance packages for downsized employees, for example—joint accountability is often beneficial to the shared business unit because many of the issues either are under the control of the parent corporation or reflect decisions made by the parent corporation prior to the formation of the shared business unit.

Although shared business units located offshore may have tax advantages over domestic companies, they also often have complicated accountability issues, such as who is legally responsible for upholding local statutes. Accountability issues often make the clean separation of parent corporation and shared business unit difficult because of the inequity of having the management of a shared business unit legally responsible for inappropriate activities over which it may have no or little control.

Contract

Given two business entities, each legal in the eyes of the government for accountability and tax purposes, the day-to-day operational relationship between the parent corporation and the shared business unit must be clearly defined. The service contract, a legally binding agreement, defines this relationship. This contract between the shared business unit and the parent corporation, referred to here as the parties, typically specifies:

- *Accountability.* The fiscal responsibility of senior management for safety and statutory violations by either party
- *Billing.* The frequency and nature of billing for services rendered by the shared business unit

- *Competitive bidding procedures.* How requests for proposals (RFPs) will be communicated from the parent corporation to the shared business unit. The procedure for evaluating bids according to specific criteria and clarification and comparison should also be specified.
- *Contingencies.* The fate of the shared business unit under typical business operations, such as mergers, acquisition, divestitures, spin-offs, bankruptcy reorganization, strategic alliances, and joint ventures. For example, if the parent corporation enters into a joint venture with an outside company, the effect on the shared business unit should be specified *a priori.*
- *Current and future pricing models.* The planned evolution of the pricing model. If charge back is to be used initially, followed by a cash exchange, the timing of the transition must be known.
- *Duration of the relationship.* The initial contract may specify a one- or two-year renewable relationship between the two parties.
- *Employee benefits.* The pension, benefits, seniority credits, incentives, and wage rates for employees of the newly formed shared business unit. Employees retained from the parent corporation will be especially sensitive to seniority credits and any increase or decrease in wages.
- *Expected lifecycle.* The expected maturation pace and maturation endpoint of the shared business unit. For example, if the goal is to have a shared business unit competing as a profitable entity in the open market within five years, then the timeline for specific milestones leading to that end should be identified.
- *Expenses.* Responsibility and procedure for handling expected and unexpected expenses. For example, the party responsible for leasing facilities and for replacing an antiquated communications infrastructure should be specified.
- *Funding the shared business unit.* The party expected to cover operating costs of the shared business unit. Prior to becoming

a self-sufficient, profit-oriented company, the parent corporation will likely assume funding responsibility of the shared business unit.

- *Governance.* The party responsible for governance. Normally the parent corporation is charged with governance responsibilities, especially as the shared business unit evolves to maturity. One of the key characteristics of a shared business unit is that it is not involved with governance.
- *Handling of intellectual property.* Transfers and licensing of patents, trade secrets, trademarks, and other intellectual properties. A common scenario is to have mutual cross licensing of intellectual properties, especially if the shared business unit is involved with R&D activities.
- *Human resource management.* The entity responsible for resolving human resource issues. A small shared business unit may use the parent corporation's human resources department or outsource the activity to a third party.
- *Personnel transfer.* The practical and legal aspects of employee transfer, including the responsibility for transportation and relocation costs
- *Regulatory considerations.* Local, state, national, or international regulatory obligations for each party, including tax liabilities
- *Remedies.* Compensation or recognition that either party has failed to abide by the terms of the contract. Depending on the nature of the relationship between the two parties, the remedies specified by the contract may be limited to non-performance, but may also extend to defining punitive damages for fraud or violation of fiduciary duty.
- *Risk management.* The liability of each party for financial and legal obligations, including insurance for senior management and the board of directors.
- *Tax issues.* Responsibility for managing and paying local, state, federal, and international tax liabilities

- *Terms of renegotiation or termination.* In the unlikely event that an impasse is reached by the two parties, the terms of renegotiation or termination of the contract
- *Transition date, duration, and process.* The transition date specifies the date that specific business activities are transferred from the parent corporation to shared business unit. The evolving obligations of each party during the transition period should be clearly specified.

Service Level Agreement

The service level agreement (SLA), while not necessarily a legal document, defines the practical aspects of the relationship between the shared business unit and its parent corporation, such as the service to be delivered, timeline, and quality standards. The typical components of a service level agreement are:

- *Billing.* The frequency (e.g., weekly or monthly) and method (e.g., paper invoices or e-mail) of billing. An overly complex billing system can negate the benefit of shared services.
- *Contingencies.* The bonuses and penalties associated with delivering a quality service on time and on budget
- *Pricing Models.* The method of pricing, which can be on a project, transaction, or hourly rate. Cost-based pricing is internally focused and against the principles of shared services. Price-based billing, which uses open market pricing, can be either customer or competition-centric.
- *Quality Standards.* Standards that the shared business unit must meet in terms of responsiveness to customer demands, the frequency and nature of benchmarking, measures such as cycle time, and how employee performance will be tracked
- *Responsibilities.* Defines who is responsible for what in the relationship. Normally, the shared business unit is responsible for

all activities relating to its core competency, as defined by the parent corporation.

- *Service to be delivered.* A clear description of exactly what services will be delivered by the shared business unit
- *Timeline.* The expected timeline for stages in the evolution of the shared business unit. The timeline may also specify exclusive supplier status for the shared business unit for specified period.

Unlike the contract between the shared business unit and the parent corporation, the SLA is intentionally an accessible document that can be understood by an average employee without the help of an attorney.

Risky Business

Fundamentally, a shared business unit is a business within a business, and a means of adding value to the parent corporation, shareholders, and investors. However, in business, there are no sure bets. Although risk can't be avoided, negative outcomes can generally be contained.

One way to minimize risk is to spread it around through an insurer, in exchange for a known loss or premium. Another approach is to avoid unnecessary risk, which involves first learning to recognize the various forms of risk. For example, key risks associated with the shared service model include:

- *Cost overruns.* Misuse of consultants and consulting firms ranks high in this category
- *Customer rejection.* Internal or external customers may simply reject the service, based on cost, quality, or both.
- *Disruption of service.* Avoiding this source of risk involves knowing the weak points in the process and having alternative processes and technologies available if the need arises. For example, installing backup power supplies in the event of a plant-wide power failure. The ill effect of disruption of serv-

ices depends on the service. If accounts payable is shut down for a week or two, few, if any, internal customers will complain. However, if payroll is cut off for a week, every employee in the organization will know about it.

- *Disruptive technologies.* A disruptive technology can potentially obviate the need for a shared business unit overnight. For example, a shared CRM service that employs hundreds of customer service representatives to assist Web-based customers could potentially be replaced by a single PC running a bot or software robot. Using a variety of artificial intelligence techniques, the system could respond to several hundred e-mail messages at a time.
- *Evolving standards.* A shared business unit established to handle third party billing for medical expenses, for example, might suddenly find the majority of its paper-handling process worthless if the third parties suddenly standardize on Web-based forms. The solution to avoiding risk from evolving standards is for senior management to invest time in studying trends in the back-end industries they're considering moving to a shared business unit so that they're not blind-sided by a change in standards.
- *Finances.* Inadequate funding from the parent corporation and external investors is a major risk, especially when revenues from the parent corporation are down.
- *General economic slowdown.* A constrained economic environment is a risk for every business.
- *Management.* A manager with poor project management skills, lack of vision, little or no experience with risk management, conflict resolution, managing expectations, or risk avoidance is a recipe for disaster.
- *Loss of intellectual property.* The downsizing characteristically associated with a shared business unit can result in an exodus of the best and brightest, as opposed to the deadweight.

Incentives, open communications, and listening to the needs of star players earmarked as eligible for transfer to the shared services can reduce the risk of intellectual property walking out the door.

- *Strong competition.* A lean and mean shared business unit may not be able to compete successfully with a much larger, leaner, and meaner competing company. Risk avoidance includes assessing the competition before starting out on shared services development.
- *Unrealistic and shifting expectations.* Senior management of the parent corporation may simply have unrealistic expectations of what a shared services implementation can provide.
- *Timing.* Often success isn't so much a function of whether a particular service can be of use to various groups within the parent company as it is a matter of timing. The introduction of a new service just as a series of massive job cuts is made in the parent corporation is simply bad timing.
- *Vendor failure.* It's always possible that key vendors of enabling technologies will fail. The downside associated with vendor failure can be minimized by identifying and working with a backup vendor. In this regard, it's a good idea for management to try out the vendor on a small project that allows management to fully assess the vendor's capabilities and corporate culture.

In some regards, the level of risk increases with the size of the shared business unit and parent corporation. The larger both entities are, the greater the potential savings and the greater the risk of failure due to increased complexity. For example, with a parent corporation with tens of thousands of employees, and dozens of business deals in process, timing the creation of a shared business unit so that it occurs with minimum disruption is nearly impossible. Similarly, the exodus of hundreds of employees during a major downsizing related to a shared services implementation may result in a significant flow of irreplaceable intellectual property directly to the competition.

The next chapter ties together the issues presented here and in the previous six chapters and offers advice on how to implement a shared services with minimum risk to the parent corporation or the management of the shared business unit.

Summary

The economic reality of a shared business unit is defined by a complex set of governmental, legal, and accounting constraints. The challenge for management is to operate within these boundaries to maximize ROI while moving the unit along the growth curve toward maturity. A well-designed service contract between the shared business unit and parent corporation, as well as a less formal service level agreement, are two means of maximizing the odds of success. However, even with the best possible agreements and legal arrangements, the success or failure of a shared services initiative is in the hands of the unit's senior management. A manager that invests time in learning about the field, pays attention to potentially disruptive technologies on the horizon, and leads employees through what can be a demoralizing downsizing period, is in the best position possible for successfully moving the unit forward.

The key to winning is skating first to where the puck will be next.

Wayne Gretzky, Hockey Player

CHAPTER 8

Getting There

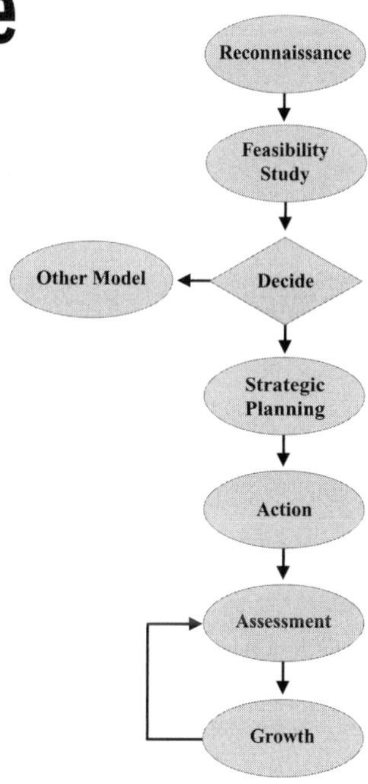

After reading this chapter you will be able to

- Develop a practical seven-step process for a shared services implementation
- Appreciate and recognize the risks involved in shared services and how to avoid them
- Understand the significance of the request for proposal process in defining needs internally and in working with external vendors
- Identify positive predictors of a successful shared services implementation
- Appreciate the psychosocial aspects of change management
- Predict the likely future of shared services, and how it will affect your organization

For the abstract concept of a shared services business model to take on practical significance, there has to be a need for change, an awareness of the potential benefits of shared services, and a vision of where the company is going. To this end, this chapter provides an implementation roadmap to illustrate one possible path to success, based on the shared services model. By focusing on the practical perspective of the implementation process, the reader can decide whether the prospect of gain, the associated risks, the timing, the corporate culture, and personal ideals warrant investing resources and time in the process. As in previous chapters, the following vignette is offered to illustrate several poignant issues related to shared services, continuing with the story of the HealthCare Partners network.

Offshore Interests

In medicine, one of the greatest impediments to moving to an efficient, paperless system of clinical record keeping is the backlog of paper medical records. The basements of most hospitals and clinics are filled with musty medical records that date back for decades. These records can't be discarded while the patient is living because they may contain irreplaceable information on a patient's past health, including specifics of surgical procedures, life-threatening allergies, medication history, and past diagnoses.

From a process optimization perspective, paper-based medical records represent a bottleneck in the flow of information in what could otherwise be an efficient, automated, computer-based operation. The paper medical record is especially problematic when patients move from one health care provider to the next because of delays and errors involved in transporting the records to the new health care provider. Several days prior to a scheduled patient visit, clinicians must generally request a patient's paper medical record from medical records department and after medical records personnel hunt it down, a dog-eared folder anywhere from one to eight inches thick appears on the clinician's desk.

The clinician then has the responsibility of manually reviewing the records to the detail necessary. An extensive review of the patient's medication history might be appropriate before major surgery, for example, whereas a cursory review might suffice for an annual office visit. However, when an unconscious, critically injured patient is admitted to the emergency room following a major motor vehicle accident, there is no time to retrieve a written medical record. As a result, decisions have to be made without any historical information about the patient, and the quality of patient care suffers. In either case, failure to note a significant finding that results in an unfavorable clinical outcome for the patient often results in a malpractice suit against the clinician as well as the medical institution. If the patient data were part of an electronic medical record, then the information on past medications could be called up with a few keystrokes.

Unfortunately, many patients who are part of a large medical services network, such as HealthCare Partners, can't make full use of the medical expertise in the network, especially in acute and emergency situations. Even though the infrastructure for electronic medical record system may be in place, the data aren't there. Older patients and younger patients with extensive medical histories have paper-based records that must somehow be moved into the electronic medical record system.

In an effort to increase the quality of medical care and reduce losses due to malpractice suits, the senior management of HealthCare Partners asks the management of its HIS shared business unit to conduct a series of tests. The goal is to determine the resource and time requirements that would be required to move paper medical records over to digital form so that the data could be made available to clinicians over the network's electronic medical record system. The cost figure, based on hand-feeding paper into an optical character recognition (OCR) system is

TIPS & TECHNIQUES

Avoiding Disruption of Service

Disruption of service is one of the most costly risks associated with transitioning to a shared services model. Leaving the legacy system in place and operational, dismantling it only after the new shared services system has been up and running satisfactorily for several months, can minimize the risk of disruption of service, especially when mission-critical functions are involved. The added cost of maintaining a dual system is inexpensive insurance.

about $50 per record, not including the necessary computer hardware. In addition, HIS management estimates that the system would only be able to handle about 20 records per day with a full-time staff of four employees.

To HIS management, the conversion of paper records to digital files is a major detour from its core competency. In addition, the cost is too high for HealthCare Partners. However, HealthCare Partners can't fully recoup its investment in its newly installed electronic medical record system without making all legacy patient information available to its clinical staff online.

Charged with exploring the options, the senior management of HIS explores the cost of having the medical records manually re-keyed overseas. Including secure transport of records to and from a service center in India, the cost of manual re-keying is less than $5 per record on average, with a throughput of about 100 medical records per day. In addition, the companies guarantee a greater accuracy than what is available through automated OCR-based conversion. With about 100,000 paper-based records in its medical records department, the cost differential of $42 per record is significant.

HIS management works with senior management of HealthCare partners to break down the costs of transferring this work overseas. They determine minimum response time, allowable error rate, provisions for security and privacy, transport of the records, and other relevant issues in creating a comprehensive request for proposal (RFP) document. HIS management issues the RFP to the top six conversion companies in India, working through representatives in the United States. With the help of domestic counsel and one with international contract experience, a contract is negotiated and signed with the vendor with the best proposal. At the suggestion of the attorney experienced in international contracts, HIS management also negotiates favorable rates with two additional services in India, as a backup in the event that the original company folds or is otherwise unable to deliver as promised. The decision is to limit overseas outsourcing to India instead of exploring additional options in China, Russia, or the Philippines because of India's reputation for quality, government support, British-based educational system, and over four decades of uninterrupted service.

A year into the three-year medical record conversion process, HIS management decides to act as a value added reseller and offer the conversion service to hospitals and clinics outside of the HealthCare Partners network. Because the use of electronic medical records provides hospitals in the network with a competitive advantage over competing hospitals in the area, HIS management reaches a compromise with HealthCare Partners and limits the service offer to non-competing hospitals and clinics. Several contracts are signed between HIS and outside hospitals, many with hospitals in adjacent states, at a reasonable profit margin for HIS.

With the exception of a few minor glitches in the handling and shipping of records overseas, the system works flawlessly, and HIS enjoys what appears to be an expanding, profitable business venture. However, the international environment changes suddenly when India and its long-time rival Pakistan become involved in a skirmish over nuclear proliferation. Each government claims the other is involved in terrorist activities against the other.

The United States government, in a move to control the escalation, issues a boycott on goods and services from both India and Pakistan. The immediate effect is to halt the electronic delivery of converted medical record data from the conversion company in India. By the end of the first month of the boycott, managers from the outside hospitals are threatening to sue both HIS and HealthCare Partners over breach of contract. What's more, the hospitals are demanding return of over a thousand original medical records being held by the conversion company in India.

Unfortunately, the contracts that HIS signed with both the offshore service provider and the domestic hospitals makes no provision for boycotts from the U.S. government. HIS is unable to collect damages from the offshore service, and is being sued by the hospitals that were once eager and willing customers. At least the management of HealthCare Partners is somewhat understanding, and simply delays its move to an all-electronic medical record system. HIS and HealthCare Partners settle out of court with the external hospitals. They agree to reimburse the outside clinics and hospitals for the previous work performed as well as for all legal and contract-related fees related to the business deal. Working with the U.S. State Department, HIS also manages to have the original medical records returned. When the boycott is finally lifted four months later, HIS returns to the business of orchestrating the conversion process for HealthCare Partners, but doesn't venture to external customers until it has secondary contracts established with companies in Russia and China.

The experience of HealthCare Partners and its shared business unit, HIS, illustrates several issues regarding the management of shared business units, especially as they relate to risk:

- Growing a shared business unit isn't an ad-hoc process. Successful growth is usually part of a well thought out implementation plan that involves feasibility studies, strategic planning, and continued assessment.

- Relationships between the management of the parent corporation and its shared business units and outside service providers should focus on the preparation of a request for proposal. The RFP helps establish the expectations and requirements of management and provides vendors with explicit issues that they must address in order to win a contract.
- The growth of a shared business unit, like initial implementation, requires skillful management of change. No business model is impervious to unforeseen changes in the market, political environment, or legal attack.
- Risk management through contractual agreements and redundant systems is an essential component of continued success.
- Predictors of success include a solid plan, provision for multiple contingencies, insightful leadership, knowledgeable and experienced outside consultants, and a management team who knows when to accept added responsibilities and when to outsource projects.

This discussion of issues is expanded in the following sections.

TIPS & TECHNIQUES

Marketing Matters

A successful shared business unit requires an effective marketing effort, even if doesn't venture into the open market. When the shared information services unit of Blue Cross/Blue Shield of Florida in Jacksonville, Florida, created a marketing group, it worked directly with employees, generating awareness of its network and desktop support services.

Implementation Overview

Implementing a shared business unit requires that senior management have an understanding of the corporation's needs, the characteristics of the business models available—including shared services, the technologies involved in enabling the process and of sustaining growth, the processes involved in operating a unit, as well as the legal, contractual, and economic implications of shared services. Addressing these requirements systematically through an established process maximizes odds of success and provides senior management with flexibility in modifying the approach to meet their needs.

The process offered here is a seven-step roadmap that addresses the implementation of a shared business unit from the perspective of the parent corporation's senior management. The phases of the seven-step process are:

1. *Reconnaissance.* Collect data about the company and the business environment.
2. *Feasibility Study.* Determine if a shared services implementation is feasible.
3. *Decide.* Move forward to implementation or explore other options.
4. *Strategic Planning.* Create specific milestones for success.
5. *Action.* Implement the plan.
6. *Assessment.* Apply benchmarks to assess progress.
7. *Growth.* Move toward a value-based system and freedom from the parent corporation.

A prerequisite to starting the implementation process is to establish an Implementation Committee. Politically, the composition of the committee can affect the ultimate outcome of the committee's recommendations. As such, a major task is to identify the most reasonable representatives of the primary stakeholders who should be invited to work on the team. Minimally, the team should include a senior manager and a consultant who is knowledgeable and experienced with shared services.

The demands on the parent corporation are necessarily greater during the first five phases of the process, after which operational responsibility typically shifts to shared services management. If the intention is to move the shared business unit to a for-profit business, which competes in the open market, then the responsibility of the parent corporation's management is eventually limited to oversight. Conversely, if the unit is destined to be a closely held unit that provides services only to the parent corporation, then the role of the parent corporation's management is much greater. Regardless of the relative contribution of shared services and parent corporation management, the growth and assessment phases are in a positive feedback loop, in that the results of the assessment phase are used to maximize the odds of success in the growth phase.

Consider the players and factors influencing successful outcomes in each of the seven stages in a shared services implementation in more detail.

Reconnaissance

With the Implementation Committee in place, the first phase of the implementation process involves data gathering, both within the company and from external sources (see Exhibit 8.1). Internal to the parent corporation, the main questions for the committee to answer include:

- Who is behind the initiative behind a shared services implementation?
- What is the map of political landscape, including primary stakeholders?
- Who should have a say in deciding on the details of the implementation approach?

EXHIBIT 8.1

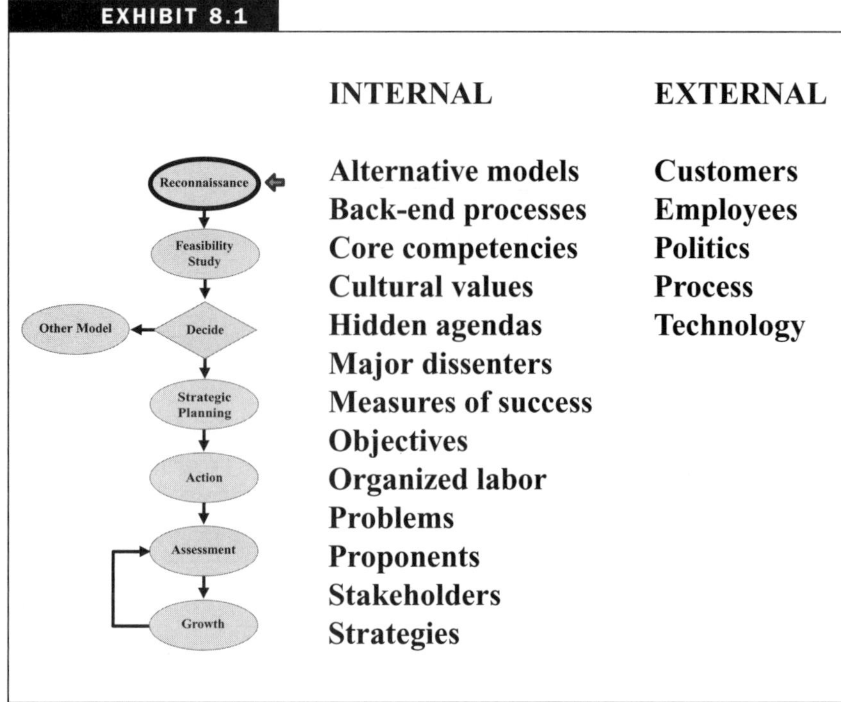

- Are there any major dissenters in senior management?
- Will there be resistance from organized labor?
- If labor resists, is the resistance surmountable?
- What problems do proponents of the initiative hope to solve?
- What are the objectives and strategies of those involved in the implementation?
- Why is a shared services model preferable, at this stage of the business lifecycle, to other business models?
- Are corporate cultural values compatible with a shared services implementation?
- What are the measures of success?
- Are there any hidden agendas?
- What back-end processes are eligible for shared services?

- What are the parent company's core competencies?

Externally, relevant questions that should be answered during the reconnaissance phase of the implementation process include:

- What are the best business practices in the industry?
- Which enabling technologies are available?
- What companies in similar industries have benefited from shared services?

Site visits can help facilitate external data gathering and provide the implementation team with a perspective on exactly what is involved day-to-day in an implementation effort. Sending a representative from

IN THE REAL WORLD

Resistance to Change

In 1991, AlliedSignal Inc., a manufacturing conglomerate, had three major business sectors, 32 strategic business units worldwide, 17 North American data centers, 32 different ways to calculate overtime pay and over 100 different pension plans. In a move to cut costs, reduce head count, and improve customer service, the shared services business unit, AlliedSignal Business Services (ABS) was formed. By 1994, ABS had consolidated over 75 business functions in the areas of finance, human resources, and information services, using 1,000 employees instead of the original 1,600, and at an annual savings of $70 million.

Although the transition to shared services was a victory for the company, the transitional process was especially challenging because of employee resistance. At one point during the implementation, for example, some employees were so fearful about losing their jobs that they barred ABS teams from entering their buildings.

the committee to attend seminars, networking with colleagues in other businesses, and consultancies can also help in the data gathering process. Similarly, an outside consultant with distance from the company and the ability to talk freely with employees and managers at every level in the company can be especially helpful in the internal fact finding process.

For the implementation project to move past data gathering, senior management must be fully behind the initiative, and with the right motivation. Reasonable motivations to explore a shared services model include cutting costs, increasing the quality of the back-end service, and freeing management to focus on the company's core competencies. Less reasonable motivation behind the initiative may be to move part of the management team away from the core business unit and send it into political exile. Similarly, since the shared services model lends itself to innovative accounting practices, the model may be appealing to members of senior management who are under pressure to move their company to a more profitable position in the market. However, given the accounting changes enacted since the Enron bankruptcy, the chances of showing profitability using nontraditional accounting practices are relatively low.

Feasibility Study

With internal and external data in hand, the next phase of the implementation process is to determine if shared services is economically, politically, and culturally feasible for the company (see Exhibit 8.2). Key questions that should be addressed during the feasibility study phase of implementation include:

- What are the alternative business models that would satisfy the needs of the corporation?
- What are the immediate and long-term capital requirements?

EXHIBIT 8.2

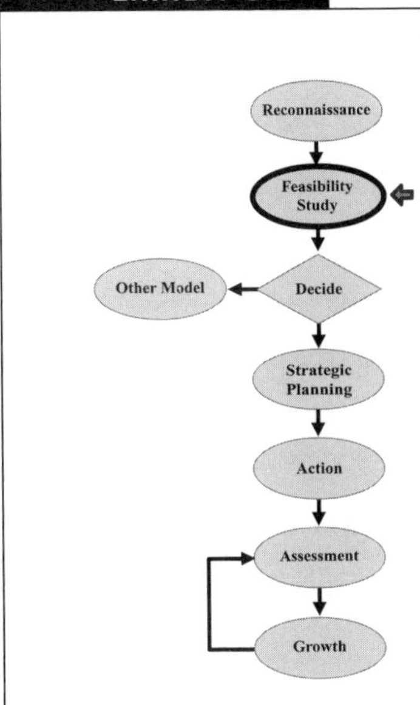

Alternative models
Capital requirements
Cost of alternatives
Employees
Financial analysis
Projections
Quality control
Real estate
Redundant systems
Resource requirements
Security
Technology
Timeline
Training

- What are the long and short-term costs associated with alternative models?
- What is the company's relationship with employees, and how central are they to defining corporate culture?
- What are the results of the financial analysis of moving to a shared services model, including return on investment (ROI) studies?
- What are the projections for growth of the parent company, the industry, and the need for back-end services?
- How will quality control be implemented?
- What are the implications for corporate real estate, including pressure to relocate?
- Are there requirements for redundant systems, and if so, can the company afford them?

- What additional resource requirements are associated with a shared services implementation?
- How will security measures be enacted, and at what cost?
- What is the projected investment in technology over the life of the shared business unit?
- Is the timeline for implementation reasonable and compatible with other corporate activities?
- Will additional training be required for employees and management, and at what direct and indirect cost?

In exploring the feasibility of a shared services implementation, due diligence on the part of management includes exploring options including traditional outsourcing or simply staying with the status quo. This determination depends on the short- and long-term capital requirements of each business model, as well as the scope of the planned implementation. How disruptive will it be to the normal operation of the business? For example, if the company prides itself on its close relationship with employees, then a significant downsizing may be unacceptably disruptive to the corporate culture.

The feasibility of moving to a shared services model also depends on projections for the company's need of back-end services, and whether specific back-end services warrant investment in a shared services model. For example, some back-end services may be so strategic that the potential increase in quality of service is worth the investment in a shared services model. As with all business endeavors, given the investment of time required to accomplish a transition, timing will likely be a critical issue, especially relative to planned mergers and acquisitions. Unlike simply outsourcing the services to an external vendor, a shared services implementation can take years and involve significant restructuring of business processes, employee and management relocation and training, and a sizeable investment in information technology.

Decision

Second only to the decision to initiate the shared services implementation process is the decision of how to move forward after the feasibility study (see Exhibit 8.3). A consideration of whether to move to a shared services model or to explore other models in more depth necessarily weights the following factors:

- *Adequacy of resources.* Are there sufficient in-house resources to create a shared business unit, or will some amount of outsourcing be required? A shared services implementation doesn't normally entail a buildup of employees, other than perhaps management and a few essential staff.
- *Capacity constraints.* What is the capacity of the company, and does growth potential warrant or require spinning off back-end services?
- *Desire to integrate operations.* Is there enough interest, at all levels in the organization, to integrate operations into a shared business unit?

EXHIBIT 8.3

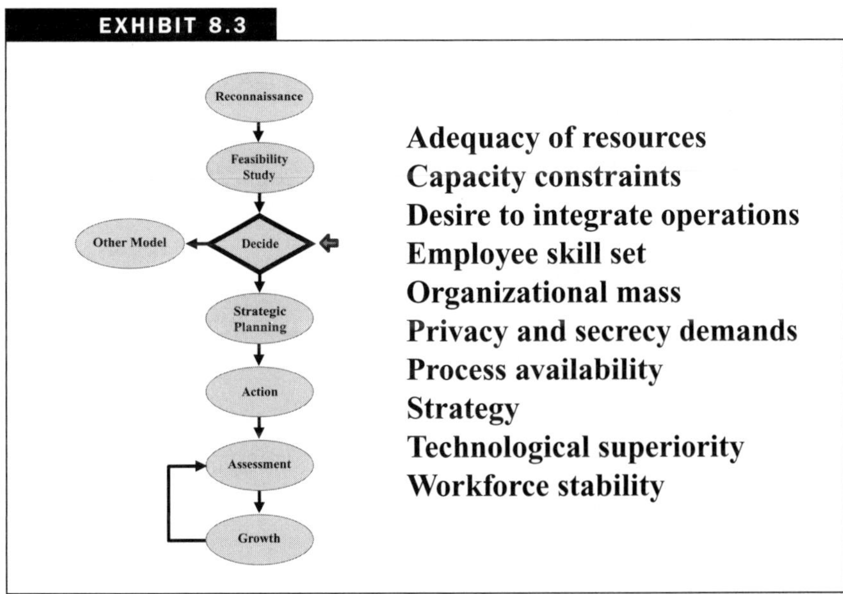

- *Employee skill set.* Does a move to shared services and the associated technology infrastructure represent a major shift in employee skill set requirements?
- *Organizational mass.* Is the company large enough to benefit from shared services? The larger the company and the greater the transaction volume of back-end services, the greater the potential benefit of a shared services model.
- *Privacy and secrecy concerns.* If the company is involved in government contracts or deals with sensitive records (e.g., patient records for an AIDS clinic or financial records from a bank), then it may be impossible to move to a shared services model or outsource back-end services.
- *Strategy.* How well does shared services fit with the overall corporate strategy?
- *Technological superiority.* Does the company enjoy technological superiority in any area, and will a shared services implementation leverage this superiority?
- *Workforce stability.* Are employees likely to submit to downsizing and retraining, or simply find employment elsewhere?

The decision to move forward with a shared services implementation or explore alternative business models should be made by senior management, based on information presented by the implementation team.

Strategic Planning

Strategic planning is about defining a flexible plan with specific, verifiable milestones (see Exhibit 8.4). Key factors during this phase of the implementation process include:

- *Establish business benchmarks.* For the current system as well as those to be used to evaluate the planned system
- *Anticipate contingencies.* Including problem management, slips in timelines, and disaster recovery

EXHIBIT 8.4

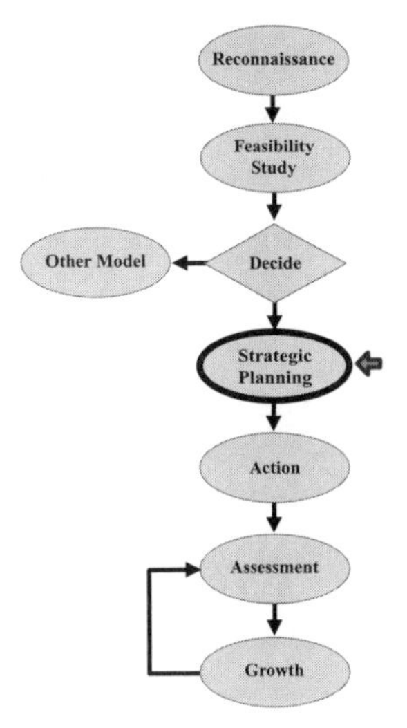

Benchmarks
Contingencies
Control
Functional specifications
Lifecycle
Performance expectations
Project management
Request for proposal
Requirements specifications
Technology
Timelines
Transition team
Transitions
Vendor evaluation

- *Plan management controls.* The relative control of parent corporation management and shared services management
- *Write and review functional requirements.* Including hardware and software requirements, in terms of performance and standards
- *Anticipate the company lifecycle.* The flow of resources and revenue over the lifetime of the shared business unit
- *Establish reasonable performance expectations.* In terms of return on investment, quality, and service
- *Design the project management.* Including resource management
- *Write an RFP for outside services, especially technology.*
- *Write a requirements specification* to define operational constraints of technology.
- *Implement new technology.* Normally a separate implementation project championed by information services

- *Draw up timelines.* For technology infrastructure improvements
- *Appoint a transition team.* For employees, technology, and business processes
- *Plan resource shifts.* Includes plans to shift resources and focus at the start and end of implementation
- *Evaluate vendors for outsourcing work* mentioned in the RFP

One of the key tools at this stage of implementation is the request for proposal (RFP). The RFP, which documents much of the strategic planning thinking, is essential if external vendors are involved. For example, an RFP defines the functional and requirements specifications for a technology vendor who will provide networking and computer-based applications to empower a downsized workforce.

Action

Taking action on the strategic plan developed in the previous phase takes on an added dimension with the addition of management either currently or soon to be engaged in managing the shared business unit (see Exhibit 8.5). From the perspective of management from the parent corporation, the key action items are:

- Write the contract, that is, the legally binding agreement between the parent corporation and the shared business unit.
- Downsize, train, and recruit new employees.
- Write a service level agreement, the working document that specifies expectations of both the shared business unit management and the parent corporation.
- Transfer assets, physically and legally—these can include employees, furniture, equipment, and intellectual property.
- Select vendors for technology and other needed resources that for the implementation.

From the perspective of shared services management, additional action items are:

EXHIBIT 8.5

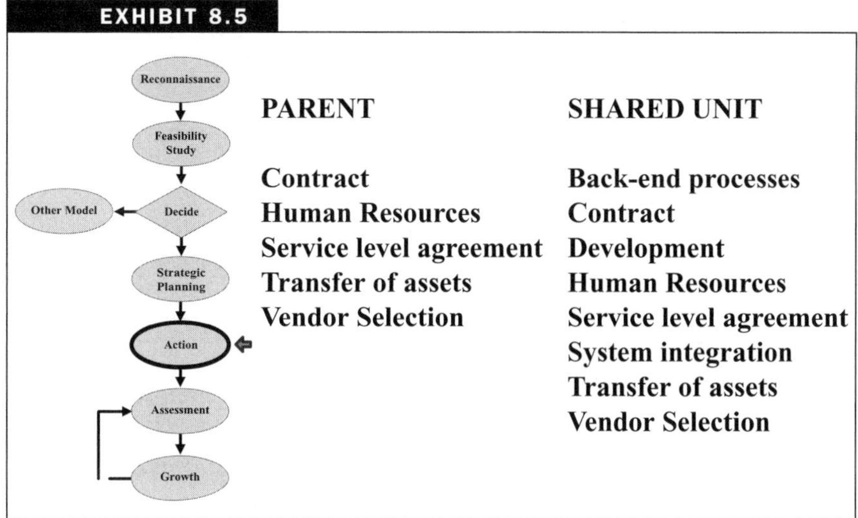

- *Identify back-end processes that are candidates for outsourcing.* The shared business unit may need to outsource payroll, accounts payable, and other relatively small back-end processes if internal resources are insufficient to support them or they detract from the unit's core competency.
- *Write contracts with outside vendors.* Agreements between the shared business unit and outside vendors
- *Manage development.* Oversight of outsourced technology projects, employee training, and other external and internal projects
- *Integrate information systems.* In the context of information services, combining existing and new information systems
- *Select vendors.* Outside vendors that report directly to the shared business unit

Clearly, most of the action items require coordinated effort from management in both the parent corporation and the shared business unit. For example, in selecting outside vendors for technology, both the parent corporation and the shared business unit have a stake in the vendor chosen. Management of the parent corporation needs to be certain that technology selected is compatible with legacy systems, and management of the shared business unit needs to be certain that they're not stuck with supporting antiquated systems. The ease or difficulty with which this first major collaboration is exercised should provide both managers with an idea of what's to come.

Assessment

For both the parent corporation and the shared services unit, the key tasks during the assessment phase (see Exhibit 8.6) are:

- Apply benchmarks established earlier in the process to assess the performance of the shared business unit and outsourced services.
- Manage the inevitable problems in timing, cost overruns, and resources.
- Sign off on vendors who have delivered within specification and according to any service level agreements.
- Assess service level and either adjust the work to fit the agree-

EXHIBIT 8.6

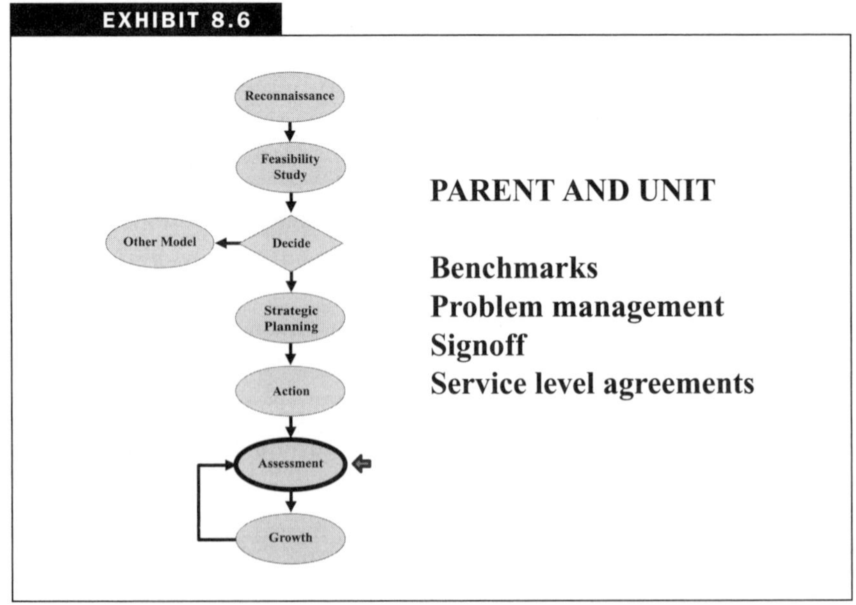

ment or alter the agreement to reflect the reality of what can actually be delivered.

Assessment isn't simply a phase of the implementation process that is traversed once, but a continuous process that involves reexamining the benchmarks at regular intervals and adjusting processes accordingly. Management of both the parent corporation and the shared business unit have benchmarks that must be assessed. For example, the shared business unit has to be responsive to benchmarks agreed to in the service level agreement it has with the parent corporation. Similarly, the shared business unit has internally monitored benchmarks as well as service level agreements with outside service providers.

Growth

The growth phase of a shared services implementation is an extended process that is linked with assessment in a positive feedback loop (see Exhibit 8.7). Whether or not growth involves actually attaining profitability in the open market and freedom from the parent corporation, it minimally involves increased service quality and value for the consumer of the service. From the perspective of the parent corporation, the key issues and responsibilities in the growth phase are:

- *Repairing the corporate culture and work climate.* These can be adversely affected by the prospect of other services being moved to a shared services model, and uncertainty in the business environment. After a shared services implementation, surviving employees may have to rely on former coworkers for back-end services.
- *Correcting delivery timelines and service level agreements.* Management may have to modify the service level agreement with the shared business unit, and make other corrections suggested by benchmarking and feedback from the assessment phase of implementation.

EXHIBIT 8.7

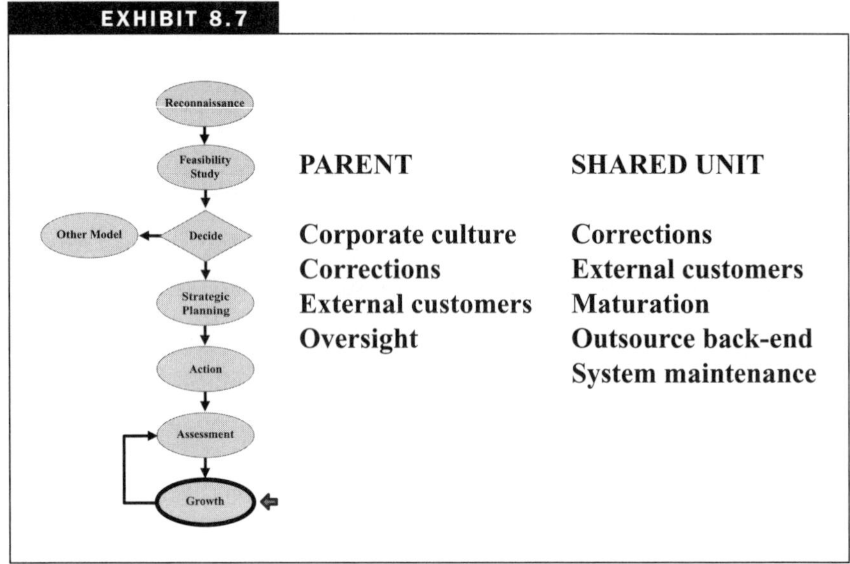

- *Acquiring external customers.* With proven reliability of its shared business unit, management of the parent corporation may offer services that build on or even rely directly on the contribution of the shared business unit in the open market.
- *Changing management oversight.* The nature of oversight typically changes as the shared business unit matures.

From the perspective of shared services management, the key issues and activities in the growth phase of implementation are:

- Correcting timelines and service level agreement adjustments with outside vendors
- Making direct sales to customers outside of the parent corporation, on a for-profit, cash basis
- Expanding to charge back for internal customers and cash transactions for external customers
- With maturation and a focusing of the shared services unit on its core competency, back-end processes such as payroll and billing may be outsourced.
- Maintaining and modifying information systems takes an

increasingly significant role as management of the shared business unit focuses on providing increased value in its services.

The growth phase can continue indefinitely, linked with assessment, to provide for the inevitable changes that will be needed to address a changing market, improvements in technology, and fluctuations in the workforce.

Request for Proposal

The strategic planning phase of a shared services implementation revolves around the request for proposal (RFP). On a superficial level, the RFP can be viewed as a written call to vendors to propose solutions to the corporation's challenges. In reality, the RFP is a multi-faceted internal change agent and an external communications vehicle. For example, financial representatives can focus on return on investment (ROI) projections. In many respects, the process of creating an RFP is as valuable as the final document. The RFP authoring process is an interactive forum that can be used by management to address ambiguity, political perspectives, and concerns.

An RFP should address vendor assessment, pricing, market requirements, functional specifications, development and deployment timelines, licensing and contractual issues, as well as management's criteria for evaluating each vendor proposal and response schedule. These topics are outlined in more detail here.

Vendor Assessment

The most important predictors of the long-term success of any collaboration are the vendor's market and financial status. A vendor's qualifications and record of accomplishment are more important than the technology or service it offers. The most important points to include in the vendor assessment component of an RFP include:

TIPS & TECHNIQUES

Getting Help

In the post-ENRON era, selecting a consulting firm to help sort out the tax and accounting implications of moving to a shared services model of doing business is no longer a simple matter of contacting one of the top five consulting firms. Regardless of whether the consultancy is a top 5 or top 500, the same selection criteria should be applied:

- *Experience.* How many shared services projects has the consultant or accounting firm been involved with and in what capacity? Were the size and scope of the projects comparable to those of the proposed project? Does the firm have experience with international shared services operations?
- *Success rate.* How many shared services implementations were successful? What were the reasons for success? How many were unsuccessful? Why? What has the consultancy or firm learned from its successes and failures that can be applied to the current implementation?
- *References.* What do the references have to say about the consultancy or firm's communications skills? Adherence to the timeline? Ability to work with others, from consultants in human resources and senior management to employees and organized labor?
- *Deep pockets.* If the consultancy fails because of gross error or neglect, does it have sufficiently deep pockets to cover related losses if found liable in court?
- *Rate.* Consulting rates vary considerably throughout the industry. Shop around and don't accept the first rate quoted, but negotiate a rate that is compatible with current industry standards.

- *CEO's record of accomplishment.* The CEO should have a record of achievement as well as a sound reputation in the industry.
- *Corporate composition.* The vendor should supply an organizational chart that lists the number of people assigned to customer support, R&D, installation and marketing; the percentage of work assigned to subcontractors; and the relative numbers of permanent, temporary, contract and overseas employees.
- *Country in which the majority of work will be performed.* If a large portion of the work is shopped out overseas, there may be an issue of quality control. There is also risk of international boycotts and other political interruptions.
- *Employee qualifications*
- *Financial stability of the company.* A certified copy of the vendor's bank account and credit references should be provided to verify that the vendor is financially sound.
- *Percentage of gross revenues derived from the vendor's top three clients.* In general, the lower this number, the greater the stability of the company, and the more likely that it will survive the loss of a top client.
- *Vendor experience.* The installed user base of organizations that actually uses (vs simply own) the vendor's product or service, backed up with verifiable references.

Pricing

Common pricing models include *per-hour fees, pay-for-performance, fixed price,* and *cost plus* pricing. Pay for performance pricing involves bonuses for the vendor when it meets its own agreed-upon performance objectives. Fixed cost pricing involves a fixed price for the duration of the project, regardless of external conditions. Cost plus pricing, in comparison, results in a fluctuation in price, depending on cost. With fixed cost pricing, the vendor assumes the risk and benefits of price fluctuations.

Regardless of the pricing model selected, the RFP must clearly define the initial, up-front, and continuing or long-term costs, such as annual maintenance contracts. In particular, the vendor must specify incidental costs that could otherwise swing wildly in the future.

Requirements Specifications

The requirements specification component of an RFP describes, in operational terms, what management expects the product or service to do for the parent corporation or shared business unit. Since requirements specifications are highly application-specific, exactly how the functionality is established is addressed in the functional specifications component of the RFP.

Functional Specifications

The functional specifications document incorporates and crystallizes the requirements specification document, the existing and optimal processes in the corporation, industry standards, and management's vision of where the shared business unit is headed. Assuming a software product, typical functional specifications issues include:

- Functional capability
- System software
- Database software
- Back-up facilities
- Hardware requirements
- System capacity
- Expansion capabilities
- Documentation
- Installation and training
- Project management

- Support
- Stability and security

Other products and services, such as a hardware-intensive network, have similar issues.

Development and Deployment Timelines

The vendor should specify the time required, in exacting detail, for every step from contract acceptance to signoff. Timelines should be included for training, testing, deployment, and conflict resolution. Ideally, timelines should be keyed to a process flowchart that depicts the milestones along the way, alternative routes to completion of the project, and final contract resolution.

Licensing and Contractual Details

The RFP should detail the procedures for management's signoff and acceptance of the vendor's work, including the acceptance of the test procedure and schedule. The vendor should supply its primary contact for all contract issues and disputes, the warranty period, remedies the vendor offers if the system can't meet performance specifications during the warranty period, and the price of work after the warranty period expires.

Evaluation Criteria

The company's objective evaluation criteria, including the contribution of up-front costs and the use of subcontractors to the overall evaluation score, provide vendors with a clear idea of where they need to be competitive. Internally, objective evaluation criteria that are determined before any vendor proposals are received are helpful in overcoming personal biases and emotional attachments to a particular vendor.

Since a vendor's response to an RFP isn't legally binding, it's prudent to fold the original RFP and the vendor's proposal into the final contract.

Risk Management

For most corporate managers, managing risk is a continual process that involves rethinking strategies and employing tactics to minimize the odds of failure and maximize the likelihood of success. One of the primary tactics in managing risk is learning to predict where problems can arise, and to recognize them as soon as possible. The key areas of risk associated with a shared services implementation are related to management, politics, finance, law, technology, and marketing, as listed in Exhibit 8.8.

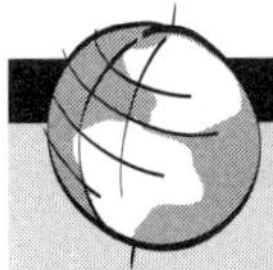

IN THE REAL WORLD

Too Great Expectations

One of the hallmarks of a shared business unit is a competitive work environment. Employees and managers are expected to pull their weight every day, or face being downsized. However, unrealistic expectations under threat of being let go for sub-maximal performance can create a culture in which employees and managers fear losing their positions more than they fear breaking the law.

For example, employees and managers at Enron, the huge energy broker that filed for bankruptcy in early 2002, were expected to increase their output by 15 percent a year—or else. Employees and managers who made their quota every year were rewarded handsomely for their overtime at the office, while those who failed to measure up were quickly excised from the company. With this culture, everyone from employees to upper management was motivated to use "creative" accounting practices that eventually lead to the largest bankruptcy in the history of the United States.

International Risks

Of particular importance in risk management is addressing the specific cultural, political, financial, technological, managerial, and legal issues

EXHIBIT 8.8

Risk Areas for Shared Services

Management	
Implementation strategy	Resource requirements
Leadership	Reward system
Market volatility	Shared services unit focus
Marketing and sales	Vendors
Reporting structure complexity	
Politics	
Domestic regulations	Standards organizations
International regulations	
Finance	
Creative accounting practices	Lost opportunity costs
Competition	Strategic partnerships
Economic environment	Time pressure
Infrastructure investment	
Law	
Customer privacy	Intellectual property
Fraud	International risks
Technology	
Archiving	Scalability
Capacity	Security
Interfaces	Standards
Responsiveness	Usability
Marketing	
Heightened expectations	Limited touch points

associated with doing business internationally. Specific areas of risk internationally include:

- *Domestic law.* Special U.S. tax rules apply to intellectual property used offshore. In addition, there are constantly changing laws regarding the export of information technology and trade secrets. For example, the United States places restrictions on computer processor power in systems that can be exported to certain countries.
- *Hidden international issues.* The need for special permits and licenses may not be known until penalties and fines are imposed.
- *Inability to enforce a contract.* An unenforceable contract is valueless.
- *Intervention of foreign government.* May define the rights of overseas employees, such as compensation upon severance, even if employees from a parent corporation are moved directly to its shared business unit
- *Legal privacy and intellectual property protection.* Including restrictions to international transfer of data, personnel, and goods
- *Political sanctions.* As in the vignette, sanctions and boycotts can result in restrictions on imports.
- *Supra-national sources of law.* Unilateral organizations, free-trade unions, and bilateral treaties, such as the European Union (EU) and NAFTA (North American Free Trade Act), may adversely affect international contracts.

Change Management

Managing change in an organization means managing people; technology and operating principles are useless without an effective work force. In creating a shared services workforce from selected parent corporation employees, managing employee expectations and the cultural change process are clearly the greatest challenges to management. In this regard, attention to specific psychosocial heuristics, which are rooted in group dynamics, can be critical to effective change management. These heuristics, and their relationship to managing the changes in the workforce inherent in a shared services implementation include:

- *Acknowledgement.* Most employees want to be acknowledged for their contribution to the corporation.
- *Consistency.* Employees crave consistency in their work lives. The constant threat of an impending restructuring or reassignment within the shared business unit can quash productivity.
- *Emotions.* Employees are emotional, not logical creatures. The cold logic of why they were moved into a shared business unit doesn't hold as much weight as an emotional appeal from management for employees to work together against a competitor.
- *Fairness.* There is a subjective concept of fairness within a group, such as pay for seniority instead of job performance, which must be addressed by management.
- *First impressions.* Initial impressions of management are lasting impressions. The first steps that management or human resources take that employees perceive as affecting their life in the company largely defines the tone of the future employer employee relationship.
- *Herd mentality.* Employees fear exclusion from their group. This fear adds to the pressure to conform, and often drives employees to accept and take part in activities that they wouldn't have normally considered. However, this behavior can also result in an unwillingness to be ejected from the parent corporation.
- *Peace of mind.* Since employees seek peace of mind, any uncertainties in employment status or working conditions should be resolved as quickly as possible.
- *Relative value.* Employees tend to base their decisions, judgments, and impression on relative values—what the employee

in the next cubicle is making, and what the employee made last year, for example—and not on absolutes. A significant increase in uncertainty and responsibility without a commensurate increase in pay won't be readily accepted.

- *Simplicity.* Employees embrace simplicity. A complicated restructuring of reporting hierarchies adds to employee stress and decreased productivity.
- *Structure.* Employees crave structure. Free-floating in a dynamic reorganized shared business unit can be unduly stressful for some employees.

A prudent manager considers these and related group dynamics before making major decisions that can adversely affect the productivity of the corporation.

Predictors of Success

Given a newly operating shared business unit, managers and investors are necessarily interested in indicators of future performance. In addition to the numerous operations management tools available to senior management, predictors of a successful shared business unit include:

- *Effective leadership.* A CEO and other senior managers with an entrepreneurial spirit, positive outlook, excellent communications skills, flexibility, tolerance for ambiguity, clarity of purpose, an ability to clearly articulate a vision for the company, competence with analytical tools, and experience with change management.
- *Effective workforce.* Availability of skilled employees, a supportive business culture, high employee morale, and an open employee communications.
- *Market opportunities.* An attractive industry, significant barriers to entry for competitors, significant business growth potential, a clearly defined market, profit potential, and a strong economy.

- *Operational excellence.* A resource management plan, explicit strategies for marketing, production, finance, and R&D, a significant diversification potential, the regular monitoring of performance through benchmarks, positive benchmark results, advantageous logistical alliances, an organizational structure that facilitates the business process, a stable parent corporation, and outsourcing back-end functions that can't be efficiently and economically handled internally.
- *Technological superiority.* The most appropriate systems and infrastructure that will support the company's processes.

IN THE REAL WORLD

A Smooth Transition

In 1992, Tenneco, a $7 billion global manufacturing company with 50,000 employees worldwide, was faced with the erosion of revenue and earnings. This erosion accelerated as non-energy divisions failed to generate sufficient cash flow to make up for the losses created by the plummeting price of crude. The company had an immediate need to improve its bottom line. With six data centers, over 20 accounting systems, and more than 100 payroll systems, an internal analysis revealed that Tenneco was spending double what its competition was spending on simply generating an invoice.

In 1995, Tenneco launched Tenneco Business Services (TBS), employing 350 employees to consolidate human resources, information services, and finance operations into one shared services business unit. One of the first wins of the shared service transition was the ability to renegotiate copier service plans, travel agency rates, utility rates, amounting to tens of millions of savings annually. Tenneco was able to smooth the transition by publishing a quarterly newsletter to keep the process in the open and circumvent potential turf wars.

As in all endeavors, luck—when preparedness meets opportunity—is also critical for success.

Future of Shared Services

Looking to the future of the shared services model, the most likely change is an increased reliance on information technology, especially the Internet and associated technologies, such as Application Service Provider (ASP) services and the Great Global Grid. These and similar enabling information technologies have the potential to support shared services, in the form of Virtual Shared Services (VSS), divorcing them from the time, hassle, and cost associated with physically combining facilities or relocating staff.

Because of the ease of reconfiguring an information-based back-end process such as payroll, virtual shared services becomes more of an accounting and tax issue than a structure-limited process. In a virtual shared services model, companies—even competitors—work together to create products and deliver services. Since each company contributes its core competency to the mix, each participant concentrates on the processes that it performs best. In this scenario, coordination is key, and that's where Internet technology and, more importantly, cultural change come into play. Having companies engage in cooperative competition, where one company provides services to several competing companies, raises issues of trust, cooperation, and partnership.

Regardless of the future of the shared services business model, today's economic reality dictates that management exploit every opportunity for increased competitiveness. As a result, the business environment will increasingly be one of constant improvement—and change. As such, the primary role of the senior management will remain one of providing leadership to a workforce that is inherently risk averse. A CEO or other senior manager with a clear vision, a repertoire of alternative business models, and sensitivity to the needs of employees and customers is ideally positioned for success.

Summary

Implementing a shared services model is a major endeavor, and one fraught with risk and uncertainty. However, by following a reasonable implementation process, such as the one offered here, the odds of success can be maximized. Once senior management—under the advisement of knowledgeable consultants—decides to move forward, its success is in the details of implementation, from attention to RFPs, contractual negotiations and agreements, to developing service level agreements, and spreading or avoiding the risk of failure.

For readers contemplating the move to shared services, the best advice is to "know thyself." With a clear vision of personal career goals, and the knowledge of the demands of stockholders, the needs of employees, and the expectations of customers, a leader can effectively maximize the performance of the corporation.

Those who approach life like a child playing a game, moving and pushing pieces, possess the power of kings.

Heracleitus

Further Reading

Business Models

Chapman, R. *Insourcing after the Outsourcing.* New York: AMACOM Book Division, 1997.

Donnahoe, A. *What Every Manager Should Know about Financial Analysis.* New York: Simon and Schuster, 1989.

Geaver, M. *Strategic Outsourcing.* New York: AMACOM Books, 1999.

Hays, R. *Shared Services Excellence.* Sarasota, FL: Summit Executive Press, 1996.

O'Grady, T. *Implementing Shared Governance: Creating a Professional Organization.* New York: Mosby-Year Book, 1992.

Quinn, B., R. Cooke, et al. *Shared Services: Mining for Corporate Gold.* Harlow, Great Britain: Pearson Education Limited, 2000.

Schulman, D., R. Dunleavy, et al. *Shared Services: Adding Value to the Business Unit.* New York: John Wiley & Sons, Inc., 1999.

Customer Relations

Anderson, K. and R. Zemke. *Delivering Knock Your Socks Off Service.* New York: AMACOM, 1998.

Bergeron, B. *Essentials of CRM: Customer Relationship Management for CEOs.* New York: John Wiley & Sons, Inc., 2002.

Blanchard, K. and S. Bowles. *Raving Fans: A Revolutionary Approach to Customer Service.* New York: William Morrow and Company, Inc., 1993.

Greenberg, P. *CRM at the Speed of Light.* New York: McGraw-Hill, 2001.

Kessler, S. *Measuring and Managing Customer Satisfaction: Going for the Gold.* Milwaukee: ASQC Quality Press, 1996.

Newell, F. *Loyalty.com.* New York: McGraw-Hill, 2000.

Nykamp, M. *The Customer Differential.* New York: AMACOM, 2001.

Swift, R. *Accelerating Customer Relationships: Using CRM and Relationship Technologies.* Upper Saddle River: Prentice-Hall PTR, 2001.

Organizational Change

Harvard Business Review. *Harvard Business Review on Organizational Learning.* Boston: Harvard Business School Press, 2001.

Bolton, R. and D. Bolton. *People Styles at Work.* New York: AMACOM Books, 1996.

DeMarco, T. *Slack: Getting Past Burnout, Busywork, and the Myth of Total Efficiency.* New York: Doubleday, 2001.

Horibe, F. *Managing Knowledge Workers.* Etobicoke, Ontario: John Wiley & Sons Canada Limited, 1999.

Willingham, R. *The People Principle.* New York: St. Martin's Press, 1997.

Process Optimization

Brown, M., D. Hitchcock, et al. *Why TQM Fails and What to Do About It.* Burr Ridge, IL: Irwin Professional Publishing, 1994.

Hammer, M. *The Agenda: What Every Business Must Do To Dominate the Decade.* New York: Crown Publishing, 2001.

Harry, M. and R. Schroeder. *Six Sigma.* New York: Doubleday, 2000.

Hunt, V. *Process Mapping.* New York: John Wiley & Sons, Inc., 1996.

Minoli, D. *Analyzing Outsourcing: Reengineering Information and Communications Systems.* New York: McGraw-Hill, 1994.

Porter, M. *Competitive Advantage: Creating and Sustaining Superior Performance.* New York: Free Press, 1985.

Pryor, T. *Using Activity Based Management for Continuous Improvement: 2000 Edition.* Arlington, TX: ICMS, Inc., 2000.

Sanders, G. *Data Modeling.* New York: Boyd & Fraser Publishing Company, 1995.

Silbiger, S. *The Ten Day MBA.* New York: William Morrow and Company, 1999.

Technology

Aktas, A. *Structured Analysis and Design of Information Systems.* Englewood Cliffs, NJ: Prentice-Hall, Inc., 1987.

Bailey, K. and K. Leland. *Online Customer Service for Dummies.* New York: Hungry Minds, Inc., 2001.

Bergeron, B. *The Eternal E-Customer: How Emotionally Intelligent Interfaces Can Create Long-Lasting Customer Relationships.* New York: McGraw-Hill, 2001.

De Looff, L. *Information Systems Outsourcing Decision Making: A Managerial Approach.* New York: Idea Group Publishing, 1997.

Hartman, A., J. Sifonis, et al. *Net Ready: Strategies for Success in the E-Conomy.* New York: McGraw-Hill, 2000.

Humphries, M., M. Hawkins, et al. *Data Warehousing Architecture and Implementation.* Upper Saddle River, NJ: Prentice-Hall, 1999.

Johnson, S. *Interface Culture: How New Technology Transforms the Way We Create and Communicate.* San Francisco: HarperEdge, 1997.

Lacity, M. and R. Hirchheim. *Information Systems Outsourcing: Myths, Metaphors and Realities.* New York: John Wiley & Sons, Inc., 1995.

Glossary

Added value The additional, tangible benefit derived by an organization through carrying out a business function or process.

Application A software program that supports a specific task, such as word processing.

Application service provider (ASP) A technology that provides access to software through a Web browser, negating the need for the customer to purchase and run the software locally.

Architecture The general technical layout of a computer system.

Artificial intelligence (AI) The branch of computer science concerned with enabling computers to simulate human intelligence. Machine learning, natural language processing, neural networks, and expert systems are all examples of applied artificial intelligence.

Back-end process A process that doesn't represent a company's unique skills, knowledge, or processes. Typical back-end processes include payroll, billing, and accounts payable. A back-end process moved to a shared services unit becomes the core competency of the unit.

Backsourcing The termination of an outsourcing arrangement and the recapture in-house of the outsourced function.

Baseline The starting point for defining needs.

Benchmarking A method of comparing contract services to services delivered.

Best of breed The service provider that is best in its class of services.

Best practice The most effective and desirable method of carrying out a function of process.

Browser A software program that interprets documents on the Web. Netscape Navigator and Microsoft Explorer are the two most popular browsers in use today.

Bylaws Self-imposed rules that constitute a contract between a corporation and its members to conduct business in a particular way.

Capital expenditure An expenditure on tangible and intangible assets which will benefit more than one year of account.

Change management The set of structures, procedures and rules governing the adoption and implementation of changes in the relationship between the customer and the service provider.

Client-server A computer architecture in which the workload is split between desktop PCs or handheld wireless devices (clients) and more powerful or higher-capacity computers (servers) that are connected via a network such as the Internet.

Cluster analysis One of several computationally efficient techniques that can be used to identify patterns and relationships in large amounts of customer data.

Collusion A fraudulent arrangement between two or more parties whereby, for example, prices are manipulated so as to undermine competitive tendering.

Communications protocol A set of standards designed to allow computers to exchange data.

Competitive insourcing A process where internal employees may engage in bidding to compete with competitive, third-party bidders for a defined scope of work.

Contract A binding agreement made between two or more parties which is enforceable at law.

Contractor A firm or person who has entered into a contract to supply goods and/or services.

Cooperative A business model in which individuals, business units, or businesses join together, most commonly to pool their purchasing power and lower their operating costs. Cooperatives are jointly owned and operated, with management elected from members of the cooperative.

Core competency A company's unique skills, knowledge, and processes. Contrast with back-end processes.

Critical path The shortest path to the final product or service in resource scheduling. The critical path represents the minimum length of time in which a project can be completed.

Customer relationship management (CRM) The dynamic process of managing a customer-company relationship such that customers elect to continue mutually beneficial commercial exchanges and are dissuaded from participating in exchanges that are unprofitable to the company.

Customer segment A homogeneous group of similar customers with similar needs, wants, lifestyle, interaction opportunities, profile, and purchase cycle.

Cycle time The time it takes to convert an idea into a new product or service or to improve an existing product or service. Typical cycle times vary from two years for an automobile to six weeks for a software product.

Data mart An organized, searchable database system, organized according to the user's likely needs.

Data mining The process of extracting meaningful relationships from usually very large quantities of seemingly unrelated data.

Data warehouse A central database, frequently very large, that can provide authorized users with access to all of a company's information. A data warehouse is usually provided with data from a variety of non-compatible sources.

Decision support system Software tools that allow managers to make decisions by reviewing and manipulating data in a data warehouse.

Disruptive technology A technology that empowers a different group of users and gets better over time. The PC is a disruptive technology, in that it empowered individuals to perform tasks once relegated to large data centers.

Downsizing Reduction in employee headcount. Downsizing also includes the cancellation of ancillary services, unnecessary software licenses and desktop PC leases, to office furniture, e-mail accounts, and recovery of server space.

Due diligence A thorough effort to intercept potential problems before they occur.

Economic Darwinism Survival of the fittest—the most economically successful—companies in the marketplace.

Economies of scale Reduction in the costs of production due to increasing production capacity.

eLearning The use of the Web, intranets, wireless computing, and other digital means of teaching and learning at home and in the workplace.

Electronic data interchange (EDI) A standard transmission format for business information sent from one computer to another.

Encryption The process of encoding data to prevent someone without the proper key from understanding the data, even though they may have access to the data.

Enforceability The conditions under which the terms, conditions and obligations of the parties under an agreement will be adopted and confirmed by a court of competent jurisdiction.

Enterprise resource planning (ERP) The category of software designed to improve the internal processes of a company.

Expert system A type of computer program that makes decisions or solves problems in a particular field, by using knowledge and analytical rules defined by experts in the field.

Firewall A software and/or hardware security system that allows or denies access to information and the transfer of information from one network to another based on predefined access rules.

Forecasting A mathematical method of extrapolating historical performance data to aid in planning.

Frequently asked question (FAQ) Lists of frequently asked questions and the appropriate answers are often posted on a Web site for users with questions of their own.

Functional specifications The technical document that specifies exactly what a software and/or hardware system will deliver.

Gantt chart A graphical production scheduling method showing various production stages and how long each stage should take.

Governance Activities and policies extended on behalf of senior management of the parent corporation, such as performance standards, purchasing policy, information technology strategy, and investment strategy.

Holding company A corporation organized for the purpose of owning stock in and managing one or more corporations.

Indemnification A method of shifting legal liability from one party to another by contract.

Infrastructure In the context of information technology, the system of servers, cables, and other hardware, together with the software that ties it together, for the purpose of supporting the operation of devices on a network.

Insourcing The transfer of an outsourced function to an internal department of the customer, to be managed entirely by employees.

Internalization The process of matching the content in a Web site to suit the language and culture of specific customers.

Internet *An* internet is a collection of local area networks connected by a wide area network. *The* Internet is the World Wide Web, one of many internets.

Internet service provider (ISP) A commercial organization that provides clients with access to the Internet.

Knowledge management A variety of general and specific technologies for knowledge collection (e.g., data mining, text summarizing, the use of intelligent agents, and a variety of information retrieval methodologies), knowledge storage and retrieval (e.g., knowledge bases and information repositories), and knowledge dissemination and application (e.g., intranets and internets, groupware, decision support tools, and collaborative systems).

Legacy system An existing information system in which a company has already invested considerable time and money. Legacy systems usually present major integration problems when new, potentially incompatible systems are introduced.

Liability Legal responsibility to do, pay, or suffer something.

Linear programming A method of determining optimal solutions regarding materials, labor, and process in conditions of constrained production capacity. Linear programming is most often applied to situations where limited resources must be allocated between competing activities.

Localization The process of adapting a Web site to a particular country or region.

Lost opportunity cost The cost of not applying resources to an alternative investment.

Loyalty A positive inner feeling or emotional bond between a customer and a business or a brand. Loyalty can't be assessed directly, but can be inferred from a customer's actions.

Loyalty effect The quantifiable behavior normally associated with loyalty, such as repeatedly transacting business with a particular retailer or Web site.

Marginal cost The change in cost as the result of one more or less unit of output.

Marketing The process associated with promoting products or services for sale, traditionally involving product, price, place, and promotion.

Mass customization Providing products as per customer specifications using traditional manufacturing techniques. Mass customization is difficult to implement in practice.

Mean time between failures (MTBF) The average time interval, usually expressed in hours, that will elapse before a device fails and requires service.

Mean time before replacement (MTBR) The average time interval, usually expressed in hours, that will elapse before a system is no longer optimal and is replaced by a better system.

Network hardware The cables, routers, bridges, firewalls, and software that enable computers to connect to shared printers, databases, and to each other.

Operations The analysis of problems associated with operating a business, designed to provide a scientific basis for decision making.

Optical character recognition (OCR) A technology that automatically converts text printed on paper into machine readable text that can be incorporated into a computer system.

Outsourcing Entrusting a business process to an external services provider for a significant period of time.

Out-tasking A limited form of outsourcing in which a task is contracted out to a consultant or other service provider.

Overhead The expense of running the business as opposed to the direct costs of personnel and materials used to produce the end result. Typical overhead costs include heat, rent, telephone, computers, and other office equipment.

PERT chart A method for project planning by analyzing the time required for each step. Rarely referred to as Program Evaluation and Review Technique.

Process management An evaluation and restructuring of system functions to make certain processes are carried out in the most efficient and economical way.

Process map A graphic description of a process, showing the sequence of process tasks, that is developed for a specific purpose and from a selected viewpoint.

Process optimization The removal or re-engineering of processes that don't add significant value to product or service, impede time to market, or result in sub-optimal quality.

Profit center A segment of a business for which costs, revenues, and profits are separately calculated.

Quality Those characteristics of an item which make it able to perform its specified function and be fit for its purpose.

Re-engineering The process of analyzing, modeling, and streamlining internal processes so that a company can deliver better quality products and services.

Request for proposal (RFP) A document that requests prospective service providers to propose the term, conditions and other elements of an agreement to deliver specified services.

Requirements specifications The qualitative document that specifies the needs that must be addressed by a particular technology. The requirements specification is written in language such as "the CRM system will allow marketing to sort customers by age."

Residual value The value remaining in a device, as a function of time. The longer the time from the original purchase date, the lower the residual value.

Return on assets (ROA) The ratio of operating earnings to net operating assets. The ROA is a test of whether a business is earning enough to cover its cost of capital.

Return on equity (ROE) The ratio of net income to the owner's equity. The ROE is a measure of the return on investment for an owner's equity capital invested in the shared services unit.

Return on investment (ROI) Profit resulting from investing in a company, process, or activity. The profit could be money, time savings, or other positive result.

Sales force automation (SFA) The use of software and other technologies and processes to facilitate the sales process.

Server A computer that controls access to the network and net-based resources.

Service level agreement (SLA) An agreement between the parent corporation or other customer and the shared services unit in which the unit agrees to provide services to a specified performance level.

Slack In the context of project management, the time in which a minor process or activity can be completed in advance of the next major operation or activity that depends on it.

Sourcing The process of identifying potential suppliers of specified services or goods.

Statistical process control A benchmarking method based on statistical quality control.

Strategic services Processes that directly affect a company's ability to compete.

Structure chart A graphic description of a process that shows the modular structure of a system, the hierarchy into which the modules are arranged, and the data and control interfaces among modules.

Supply chain management An integrated process for managing all levels of the flow of information from an enterprise to its suppliers and customers, including its own internal manufacturing resources.

Synergy The benefit derived from the cooperation between two business entities.

Systems integration The merging of diverse hardware, software, and communications systems into a consolidated operating unit.

Telemedicine Practicing medicine at a distance.

Total cost of ownership (TCO) The cost of owning a device or technology, including operating expenses.

Total quality management (TQM) A customer-centric philosophy based on constant improvement to meet customer demands.

Touch point The point of contact between a customer and a company. Touch points include the wired Web, the wireless Web, telephone, fax, e-mail, and person-to-person conversations.

Value chain The sequence of events in a process that adds value to the final product or service.

Voice recognition The ability of a computer to recognize the spoken word for the purpose of data input and receiving commands. Also called speech recognition.

Warranty A contractual undertaking given by the supplier, to provide a specified level of product or service support.

Web hosting The service of providing server hardware and connectivity to the Internet. Additional hosting services include charge card transaction processing, e-mail, and personalized customer interfaces.

Wireless devices Wireless Personal Digital Assistants (PDAs), wireless laptops, pagers, and cell phones that extend voice and data communications beyond the tethered desktop.

Index

D